T0277394

Magic to Do

MAGIC TO DO

Pippin's Fantastic, Fraught
Journey to Broadway and Beyond

ELYSA GARDNER

APPLAUSE
THEATRE & CINEMA BOOKS
Essex, Connecticut

APPLAUSE
THEATRE & CINEMA BOOKS

An imprint of Globe Pequot, the trade division of
The Rowman & Littlefield Publishing Group, Inc.
4501 Forbes Blvd., Ste. 200
Lanham, MD 20706
www.rowman.com

Distributed by NATIONAL BOOK NETWORK

Library of Congress Cataloging-in-Publication Data

Names: Gardner, Elysa, author.
Title: Magic to do : Pippin's fantastic, fraught journey to Broadway and
    beyond / Elysa Gardner.
Description: Guilford, Connecticut : Applause Theatre & Cinema, 2022. |
    Includes index. | Summary: "Magic to Do documents the creation and
    enduring legacy of Pippin, the musical that brought very different
    talents and personalities together-seldom harmoniously, but with
    thrilling results. Arriving at a time of tension and change in theater,
    culture, and politics, Pippin remains widely loved by theater fans, and
    Elyse Gardner examines its evolution and enduring influence, as well as
    the many vivid characters and storied conflicts that shaped the original
    production" —Provided by publisher.
Identifiers: LCCN 2022006617 (print) | LCCN 2022006618 (ebook) | ISBN
    9781493064359 (cloth) | ISBN 9781493064366 (epub)
Subjects: LCSH: Schwartz, Stephen. Pippin. | Musicals—History and
    criticism.
Classification: LCC ML410.S42 G37 2022 (print) | LCC ML410.S42 (ebook) |
    DDC 782.1/4—dc23
LC record available at https://lccn.loc.gov/2022006617
LC ebook record available at https://lccn.loc.gov/2022006618

For Mom and Dad, who introduced me to Pippin
and to musical theater, and for Tony Walton,
who I'm sure is busy making heaven look even more fabulous.

CONTENTS

Whose Show Was It, Anyway?

MEMORY CAN BE A TRICKY THING, PARTICULARLY AFTER A VEXING OR traumatic experience. Stephen Schwartz, for instance, was all of twenty-three years old when he met one of Broadway's most venerated director/choreographers in the fall of 1971, but the composer and lyricist of beloved musicals ranging from *Godspell* to *Wicked* can recall only a few details of their first encounter. "It's crazy," Schwartz admits. "I mean, that was a momentous meeting. You'd think I would always remember exactly where I was when I met Bob Fosse. But I don't."

The meeting took place somewhere in the Los Angeles area, in a film studio. Schwartz was in town—he thinks—for the local premiere of *Godspell*, by then a smash hit off-Broadway. Fosse was editing footage of his screen adaptation of *Cabaret*, which would help propel his career to new heights after a relatively short but painful dry spell. Pleasantries were exchanged; Schwartz mentioned how much he had enjoyed Fosse's previous movie, *Sweet Charity*, which some critics and audiences had met with less enthusiasm. The younger artist then played a few songs from another musical he was working on, called *Pippin*, and the showbiz veteran offered praise in return. "I just remember it being very pleasant, that Bob was congenial and complimentary," says Schwartz. But *Pippin* producer Stuart Ostrow, who had arranged the meeting in hopes that Fosse would helm the show, remembers precisely how the director summed up its book to him after a first read. And it wasn't with bouquets.

"He thought it was a college jape," says Ostrow. "Actually, he called it a piece of shit. But I paid him a lot of money to do it, and he needed the money."

It was on this unromantic note, according to the producer, that one of the most fractious and fruitful collaborations in musical theater was launched, between two of the most celebrated artists of their respective generations—men who would never work together after completing *Pippin* and would speak again only once, briefly and years later, during a chance encounter. In the interim, mind you, they would have some choice words about each other, several of which were shared with journalists. "I think he's very talented," Fosse conceded to the *New York Times*, discussing Schwartz for an article that ran shortly after *Pippin*'s opening date of October 23, 1972. "But not as talented as *he* thinks he is." About two months earlier, Schwartz had told *Newsday* that working on *Pippin* had been "one of the worst experiences of my life. I don't think I'll ever work on Broadway again." In 1976, by which point the wunderkind actually had three hit musicals running there—*Pippin*, *The Magic Show*, and a new production of *Godspell*—he was still recovering. "Bob Fosse is not interested in writers," he told a reporter.

It can actually be said, without sarcasm, that Fosse's best friends were writers. None were closer than the playwrights and screenwriters Paddy Chayefsky and Herb Gardner, who would pop up in Washington, D.C., just as Fosse was preparing *Pippin* for its out-of-town premiere in September 1972. Their visit wasn't purely social, according to Schwartz and various cast members; they arrived as script doctors, those frequently uncredited scribes who are often enlisted when shows require first aid. Fosse was still on good terms with *Pippin*'s librettist, Roger O. Hirson, but his relationship with Schwartz had so deteriorated that at one point, at least, the director had ordered the composer barred from rehearsals. Where Hirson pretty much accepted whatever changes Fosse was demanding, Ostrow explains, "Stephen kept complaining, and finally Fosse said, 'I can't stand him—please take him out of here.'"

The contrast was ironic, given that Fosse's main issue with *Pippin*, from the start, seems to have been Hirson's book—which was, in fact, based on an undergraduate project. As a junior majoring in drama at the

Carnegie Institute of Technology, soon to become Carnegie Mellon University, Schwartz had collaborated with another student, fellow drama major Ron Strauss, on *Pippin, Pippin*—a medieval musical melodrama inspired by the life of Charlemagne's eldest son, known as Pepin the Hunchback, and his rebellion against his father. The *Pippin* first presented to Fosse had, in addition to a new libretto, an entirely different set of tunes crafted by Schwartz alone, and Fosse seemed genuinely keen on them. "I loved the score of *Godspell*," he said in an *After Dark* magazine interview that ran shortly before rehearsals for *Pippin* began in the summer of 1972. "*Pippin* has been composed by the same boy . . . I like his score very much." Fosse added that he had "wanted to get back to Broadway"—further suggesting that cash had not, in fact, been his sole incentive in taking on the musical.

Hirson, a television veteran whose accomplishments in theater included a Tony Award nomination for the 1966 musical *Walking Happy*, brought more of an absurdist sensibility to Pippin's journey—the prince's name had been anglicized at Carnegie, and his spine corrected—while also placing more emphasis on the character's quest for self-fulfillment. "It had been sort of a family melodrama, but once Roger came in, it became more and more the story of a young man in search of himself," says Schwartz—a man promoted to a prince by a group of traveling performers, then taken on a wild ride that forced him to repeatedly reconsider his place and purpose in the universe.

Fosse was, to put it mildly, skeptical. Not that he wasn't hip to the existential ennui of the Me generation and the cultural revolution its members had forged. The innate, forward-thinking grooviness of Fosse's own work had evolved with the times, reflecting shifting social and sexual dynamics as well as passions shared by baby boomers and older artists, from a love of Fellini films to a vehement opposition to the Vietnam War—two things he and Schwartz could agree on, at least. But Fosse was "frightened by the naïveté of the concept," as he put it to the *Times*, that Hirson—no flower child himself, at a year older than the director—had fashioned with Schwartz, he admitted. The director had "an aversion to sentimentality," as he would put it years later in a *Rolling Stone* interview, that had only been exacerbated by the lackluster reception to the *Charity* film.

At least some sentimentality, as Fosse defined it, had already been drained from *Pippin* by the time rehearsals started in the summer of 1972, after Fosse had spent a few months working with Hirson, who was hardly averse to drying things up a bit. In the latter's 1970 draft of the musical, Pippin's quixotic journey was already riddled with failure and disappointment. Hirson had fractured the fourth wall as well, bookending the account with a character called the Old Man, who appeared with a caravan of performers—a nod to Ingmar Bergman's *The Seventh Seal*, a film beloved by Schwartz.

Under Fosse's guidance, the wall shattered into pieces and was reconstructed as a dance floor. The character of Pippin was introduced to the audience as someone the troupe had selected to play that part, with the troupe members taking on other principal roles: Pippin's father, Charlemagne, or Charles; his stepmother, Fastrada; his paternal grandmother, Berthe; and his lover, a young widow, Catherine. Catherine's son, Theo, and Fastrada's son and Pippin's half brother, Lewis, and other unnamed members of the community, from a beggar to a nobleman, also took part in Pippin's story, which still began with the protagonist's arrival from school in Padua.

For the uninitiated, Pippin returns home certain that a marvelous destiny awaits him, if only he can figure out what it is. The Players then lure him into a string of misadventures ranging from drugged debauchery to patricide, dangling romanticized notions of war, sex, political power, domestic love, and finally—once Pippin has been disillusioned in these pursuits—suicide. To their great dismay, he rejects this last option, choosing instead to settle down with Catherine and Theo. As show people, the Players were embodiments of Fosse's by then deeply ambivalent perception of his profession and himself—seductive and full of tricks, but damaged and potentially dangerous.

What had been the part of the Old Man was reconceived and expanded to become the Leading Player, a constant presence in charge of keeping Pippin on course. The part was designed to accommodate the multiple talents of an extraordinary and decidedly not old performer named Ben Vereen, who had first impressed Fosse singing and dancing in the company of a touring production of *Charity*. Schwartz rewrote or repurposed a few songs accordingly, and would add more as rehearsals progressed and in Washington. The director remained pleased with Schwartz's output. "He thought the songs were over-rhymed, or that they were often too wordy," Schwartz allows. "But he really liked the music, and didn't give me a hard time about it—and in truth, he didn't give me *too* much of a hard time about the lyrics."

Still, by the time *Pippin* opened at New York's Imperial Theatre, it was a substantially different show than the one that Schwartz had envisioned, and the cold war that had festered between Fosse and himself was hardly over. In 1973, Schwartz filed arbitration against Ostrow—Fosse's staunch ally, notwithstanding his appreciation of Schwartz's talents—seeking permission to negotiate the leasing of *Pippin* in Australia and New Zealand and, more broadly and significantly, to establish the authors' rights to make their own revisions to Fosse's revised version of the musical. A panel ruled in Schwartz's favor by a vote of two to one, paving the way for Schwartz and Hirson to amend the musical before publishing it.

Reading the original Broadway iteration of *Pippin* again in 2020 proved revelatory for Schwartz. "I've realized that the show needed to be rescued *by* Bob Fosse to succeed on Broadway," he proposes today, "but it needed to be rescued *from* him to have a long afterlife. I had thought that the thing that really bothered me was the sort of cheap, vulgar humor he brought into it—and that did bother me. But now I see my main issue was his undercutting the characters, especially the title character, and undercutting emotion. And keeping such an aesthetic distance that the audience could enjoy it, but not care about it as much."

At the same time, Schwartz feels that he and Hirson initially "over-corrected" the work post-arbitration; some of Fosse's contributions that were deleted have been restored over the years, either verbatim or in spirit. Schwartz also believes that his youth, relative inexperience, and heady success prior to *Pippin*—on the heels of *Godspell*, he had also written lyrics for Leonard Bernstein's *Mass*—"gave me a sort of obstinacy and arrogance, if you will—a stubbornness about what I wanted the show to be. I didn't know how to collaborate." Seeing various productions of *Pippin* has convinced him "of the brilliance not only of Bob's staging, but also the value of some of the concepts and tonality he brought to it, his really pushing the post-modern aspect."

When the director Diane Paulus approached Schwartz nearly four decades after *Pippin*'s premiere, he pressed her, on granting the rights for what would become the first Broadway revival, to keep all this in mind. "He said that the Fosse element was really important," notes Paulus, who promptly recruited Chet Walker—a replacement cast member in the original staging who later served as Fosse's assistant and helped conceive the posthumous tribute *Fosse*—to choreograph, as the program indicated, "in the style of Bob Fosse." The production wound up collecting four Tony Awards, just one fewer than the original, and Schwartz considers its book and lyrics—with some Fosse touches reinstated, accompanied by other adjustments that had been sanctioned over time, including a new ending in which Catherine's young son, Theo, plays a central role—the "definitive" version of *Pippin*. "I like to say that I've become the guardian of Bob's vision," he muses. "I'm sure somewhere Bob is looking up and laughing."

It's worth noting that *Pippin* first arrived around the time theater observers were noting an increasing popularity in something called the concept musical—a piece in which style and themes are more prominent than the plot, and thus the director's vision can loom at least as large as those of the librettist, lyricist, and composer. The notion of a concept musical has long been controversial; some have applied the label, for instance, to the groundbreaking collaborations between Stephen Sondheim and director/producer Harold Prince in the early 1970s, but the centrality of Sondheim's scores and the sharp narratives crafted with his collaborators for shows such as *Company*, *Follies*, and *A Little Night Music* belie this assessment. Granted, there were few critics who put *Pippin* near this league; a number of reviews gave most or even all of the credit to Fosse, at times dismissing the authors outright. "*Pippin* is the most beautifully gotten-up musical ever to surround a near-vacuum," carped John Simon in *New York*. "*Pippin*, at the Imperial, is simultaneously a great show and a poor musical," *The New Yorker*'s Brendan Gill agreed. In the *Times*, Clive Barnes wrote that Fosse's staging "takes a painfully ordinary little show and launches it into space." Barnes "found most of the music somewhat characterless"—though he added, "Perhaps it needs to be heard more. I enjoyed *Godspell* more with repetition," and allowed that *Pippin*'s score was "consistently tuneful and contains a few rock ballads that could prove memorable."

In fact, for most who would become acquainted with *Pippin* through its original cast recording—or through some of the professional and amateur productions conceptualized by other directors over the years—Schwartz's music and lyrics have proven as or even more key to the show's appeal than any other element. *Pippin*'s score, like *Godspell*'s, touches on influences from classical and medieval music to Gilbert and Sullivan operetta while embracing contemporary pop, with a deep nod to the singer/songwriter movement of the 1960s and 1970s. All of this was accomplished with a canny theatricality that had been evident but not as pronounced in the less character-driven *Godspell*, or in many of the musicals that were starting to pop up on and off-Broadway after the groundbreaking success of 1968's *Hair*, from Melvin van Peebles's incendiary, jazz-and-R&B-infused song cycle *Ain't Supposed to Die a Natural Death* to Andrew Lloyd Webber's bombastic rock opera *Jesus Christ Superstar*.

Pippin's 1972 cast album was, notably, the first Broadway cast recording released on Motown Records, whose exuberant hits broke boundaries between pop and R&B and had been a key source of inspiration for Schwartz. Label stars such as Michael Jackson, with and without the Jackson 5, and the post–Diana Ross Supremes were recruited to cover songs from the show for bonus tracks. If the album didn't rocket to the upper reaches of the pop charts—or produce a hit single, as *Godspell* had with "Day by Day"—it would leave an indelible impression on generations of musical theater fans and composers. Jeanine Tesori, whose acclaimed shows include *Thoroughly Modern Millie*, *Caroline, or Change*, and *Fun Home*, hadn't spent much time listening to show tunes before *Pippin*'s richly melodic, rhythmically savvy music and the cast album's often piano-driven arrangements converted her: "I loved groove piano playing, and I had never equated a Broadway show with that sound. People forget that the piano is a percussive instrument—Stephen uses it that way." Justin Paul, who with creative partner Benj Pasek has won Tony, Grammy, and Academy Awards for works including *Dear Evan Hansen* and the film *La La Land*, says of Schwartz, "The way he channeled the sounds of his day into a narrative structure, and put it all in his own voice and infused it all with a theatricality and a specificity of character—that's the model for how we write."

If Schwartz could make pop and soul textures fly in a theatrical context, Fosse brought a distinct, fluid musicality not only to *Pippin*'s dance numbers but to the overall staging. Like any great choreographer, he was passionate about music, and his tastes were eclectic; Ann Reinking, an original cast member who famously became Fosse's lover and protégée, once noted that some of the dance routines in *Pippin*—among them the iconic "Manson Trio," performed as chorus members representing soldiers leave fake body parts strewn across the stage in a darkly comic testament to the ravages of war—were first arranged to tracks from Harry Nilsson's 1971 album *Nilsson Schmilsson*. The beguilingly moody work of late nineteenth-century French composer Erik Satie would inform Fosse's choreography for a short ballet that followed another number. Bebe Neuwirth, while working with Fosse on a Broadway revival of *Sweet Charity* in 1986, the year before he died, noticed his intense involvement in all aspects of that production during technical rehearsals, including the music. "He might say, 'There's too much light up stage right; can we dim that?' He might say, 'I'm getting too much trumpet on the fourth bar of this.' I remember him picking out the percussion parts at one point. So you'd better believe Bob Fosse had something to do with the orchestrations in *Pippin*."

Schwartz acknowledges this, and is backed up by Tesori, who worked with *Pippin* orchestrator Ralph Burns, Fosse's frequent collaborator, on *Millie*. She cites "Big Spender," *Charity*'s opening number, with its trademark vamp—different from the seductive numbers that introduced *Pippin* and Fosse's next musical, *Chicago*, but with that same "combination of darkness and lightness," as Tesori puts it, "all that dissonance in there. I know as a composer that you develop it, but it's like the writer is the mother and the director is the father, and the show is the baby—it looks like both of them." The sophistication of Fosse's choreography and direction also helped distinguish *Pippin* from other musicals informed by contemporary sounds.

In fact, any debate over how much of *Pippin*'s initial success is owed to its authors and how much can be credited to the auteur who largely called the shots overlooks the transcendent synergy between them. No one would mistake Hirson's episodic, avant-leaning libretto for a text by Oscar Hammerstein II—or Bertolt Brecht, for that matter. "I don't think anybody has said, 'Oh, my God, *Pippin*—that *book!*,'" admits one of the show's ardent fans, Stephen Flaherty, the composer of *Ragtime, Once on This Island* and other notable post-*Pippin* musicals. But Fosse made the book's malleability a virtue, not only changing lines as he pleased—not always to his collaborators' liking—but creating a canvas on which he could impose everything from the vaudeville and burlesque traditions he had soaked up as an adolescent performer to Grand Guignol and, with a big hand from the brilliant designers Patricia Zipprodt and Tony Walton, commedia dell'arte.

Within *Pippin*'s relatively loose structure, Hirson also posed questions that spoke to members of Schwartz's generation and those that would follow on their own terms. Writing in *The Public Medievalist* in 2014, the historian Paul B. Sturvetant described the musical as a morality play for its time, in which "Pippin attempts to learn how to face life rather than death." The "trifecta of war, hedonism, and politics" peddled by the Leading Player and his minions, Sturvetant observed, represent "how the moral options of 1972 presented only a catch-22 to the dissatisfied young people of its day. In war there is no glory, only death. In hedonism there is no escape, only emptiness. And in politics, there is no justice, only tyranny." (Although Schwartz would not entirely endorse this last point, political corruption and hypocrisy are certainly themes in the show.)

Seldom, moreover, had a Broadway musical defined a protagonist not through his relationships with others, but primarily in terms of his search for himself. Even Don Quixote in *Man of La Mancha* had his Dulcinea, whereas it is Catherine who initially pursues Pippin, as Pippin's pursuit of greatness on his own terms takes precedence, through most of the show, over any personal bonds. The Leading Player, however prominent a character, is there chiefly to steer our young hero, albeit not in the direction he expects. It's common, of course, for young people to imagine themselves at the center of the universe, capable of fantastic achievements, but

Schwartz's generation came of age as a new emphasis on sexual liberation and other forms of exploring helped make self-actualization a particularly high priority.

One might assume it was Fosse, given his well-documented fascination with death, who arranged that Pippin's quest would bring him so close to self-destruction. But in fact, the hero is already encouraged to off himself in Hirson's 1970 draft, and by the same means: jumping into a fire. In the pre-Fosse version, in fact, suicide is mentioned in the musical's very first scene, when the Old Man details the story of Peregrinus Proteus, a Greek philosopher who burned himself alive at the Olympic Games in AD 165. "There was always darkness in the path that Pippin was on, and I liked that," Schwartz stresses. "What Bob injected into the show that I responded to negatively was cynicism"—for example, the winking interjections that were inserted into dialogue and songs that, Fosse worried, might otherwise be judged maudlin.

There was also sex, of course: The first glaring signs that Schwartz's partnership with Fosse would not be smooth emerged at auditions, when the latter insisted on casting gorgeous dancers as the unnamed female "Players" despite Schwartz's pleas for a couple of "singers who move," as they have traditionally been called. (The nonprincipal males in *Pippin* were cast chiefly for their dancing ability as well, though as with the women, singing and acting also figured substantially in their responsibilities—another factor that was unusual at a time when separate singing and dancing choruses were generally employed.) Where Fosse's choreography had always been sexy—or "sensual," as some of his dancers prefer to describe it, stressing his underappreciated tastefulness—*Pippin* introduced a more free-flowing, albeit typically controlled, eroticism. In the first love scene between Pippin and Catherine, respectively played in the original production by John Rubinstein and Jill Clayburgh, a pair of dancers—one male, one female—simulated their coital fumbling. "With You," written as a declaration of monogamous love, was eventually staged with Pippin singing to a ménage of women, semiclothed by Zipprodt, as they writhed around and on top of him, segueing into an orgiastic ballet.

Schwartz was appalled—at first. He has since come to approve of the sly humor, the juxtaposition of love and lust. "That was a place where Bob was absolutely right and I was not," he says. "And now that I'm older, I can appreciate Bob's understanding that when you're young, when you're at the age that Pippin is, you think that every relationship is the one that's going to last forever—until you're distracted by another one."

Some have proposed that the differences between Schwartz and Fosse at the time mirrored those between Pippin himself—the naive, idealistic dreamer and yearner—and the Leading Player, the jaded ring-master whispering in his ear, selling hedonism and peril. The analogy is tempting: Schwartz was tender in life experience and, by his own admission, green in terms of professional relationships; Fosse was decades into a career that had begun in burlesque clubs, and had long been juggling too much work with too much play—drugs and womanizing—as he would document several years later in his largely autobiographical film *All That Jazz*. Indeed, the role of the Leading Player grew more prominent as rehearsals for *Pippin* progressed, to the point that Schwartz worried his hero might be overshadowed by a charismatic buddy/antagonist.

But such comparisons are simplistic, failing to take into account, for instance, Fosse's own restlessness and yearning as an artist—in an opening-night note to his director, Rubinstein would liken "little Pippin" to "little Bob"—or the insecurity that hounded him relentlessly, according to colleagues. "Bob constantly had to prove himself," remembers Gene Foote, who performed in the original cast of *Pippin* and in other Fosse productions. "He would say, 'You're only as good as your next show.'" To this day, his dancers and actors—there was no real distinction in his view—recall that he pushed himself harder than he pushed them, which was plenty hard. "We all worked our asses off for him, because he worked his ass off for us," says Candy Brown, another original cast member, who worked with Fosse regularly in the early 1970s. Brown's first project with Fosse, Liza Minnelli's 1972 TV special *Liza with a Z*, had yet to wrap production when *Pippin* started rehearsals; the following year, Fosse would win three Emmy and two Tony Awards and an Oscar for the trifecta of *Liza*, *Pippin*, and *Cabaret*—and land in a psychiatric facility, depleted and depressed.

Yet those who worked most closely with Fosse on *Pippin*, Schwartz included, recall none of the bitterness or gloom some say would emerge later, after the director suffered his first massive heart attack in 1974. Instead, there could be an impish playfulness, particularly with his dancers. "I will always remember the glee in Bob Fosse's eyes," says Chet Walker of his *Pippin* audition. "The little boy in him was always there." Pamela Sousa—like Brown, an original cast member of both *Pippin* and *Chicago*—recalls how, during rehearsals, Fosse would entertain his charges with lively tales of his adventures and foibles in Hollywood. Schwartz, too, developed lasting friendships through his work on *Pippin* and would become well known—during a career that has also encompassed film and earned him three Oscars of his own as well as four Grammy Awards—for his amiability and generosity with colleagues, particularly in mentoring other artists down the line (Pasek and Paul among them).

Many others were integral to *Pippin*'s success, of course: the designers who matched the crisp wit and sinuous carnality of Fosse's vision; the musicians who arranged and orchestrated songs for the production, and helped Schwartz record them for the cast album; Ostrow, who with Fosse steered the production through an early loss of financial support, then conceived a history-making TV commercial that proved a box office boon at a crucial juncture; and of course the performers, who hailed from Brooklyn, Beverly Hills, Tennessee, and Hungary, a few of them barely into their twenties at the time, all of them utterly devoted to the man that surviving cast members refer to, with unyielding affection, as Bob, Bobby, or Mr. Fosse—sometimes shifting from one to another in the course of a few sentences, depending on the memory and the context.

Timing also worked in the musical's favor. Four years after *Hair* signaled the dawning of the Age of Aquarius on Broadway, theater audiences, if not all critics, were learning to embrace contemporary sounds and mores. And more than a decade and a half into the Vietnam War and just a few years after the horrific murders that had inspired the naming of the Manson Trio, *Pippin*'s blend of idealism and disenchantment—a balance achieved precisely because Fosse had found aspects of Schwartz and Hirson's work naive, and Schwartz had determined elements of Fosse's to be cynical—was surely appreciated by many dreamers and yearners who had grown wise to the limits of flower power but were still longing for better things, for themselves as much as the world. When Rubinstein sang, in what would become the show's most famous song, of pining for his "Corner of the Sky"—Schwartz's lyrics declared, "I won't rest until I know I'll have it all"—he might have been raising his voice for legions of Pippins who would, as the 1970s segued into the decade of Reaganomics, more openly juggle righteous concerns about peace and justice with less lofty, more individually tailored ambitions.

Fifty years after its Broadway premiere, with Fosse and Hirson and a number of original cast members and other key contributors gone, *Pippin* continues to inspire fascination and debate. If not as familiar outside theater circles as *West Side Story* or *Hamilton* or, God help us, *Les Misérables*, the child born of Schwartz and Fosse's brief, tumultuous partnership remains a popular title for theaters around the world, to say nothing of schools and camps and other amateur outlets. Many cite the essential universality of Pippin's journey, though Stephen Flaherty also uses another word: "I think a lot of it has to do with the alchemy of the piece, the artists that were brought together at this moment in time. So much of the joy and the DNA of the show is from that first production." For Gene Foote, *Pippin* was simply "the most exciting show I've ever performed in. And the most difficult." The key to magic, after all, lies in making it look easy—and in musical theater, that most collaborative of art forms, that often means making very disparate, even conflicting parts work in sync. And through three months of rehearsals and nearly two thousand performances stretching from October of 1972 into June 1977, in spite of everything, they did.

CHAPTER ONE

The Prince and the Prodigy

It was 1967, in the spring before the Summer of Love, and at Carnegie Mellon University in Pittsburgh, Pennsylvania, the student-run Scotch'n'Soda Club was readying its annual musical production—the third of four to be cowritten by Stephen Schwartz in as many years. Schwartz was a junior at the School of Fine Arts; a drama major, he had elected, for a short spell, to wear a cape around campus, a sartorial choice inspired as much by the times as his field of study. "Pretty much everyone was experimenting," he recalls, "and no one judged how flamboyantly you dressed, what drugs you were trying, or whom you were sleeping with."

Having just turned nineteen in March, Schwartz was a bit younger than his classmates. He had started kindergarten at the age of four, then been promoted in the spring of his fifth grade year, so that he entered the seventh grade the following fall. As precocious musically as he was academically, he had won a scholarship to the Juilliard School of Music Preparatory Division and spent four years studying piano there as well as composition, orchestration, and theory. The teenage Schwartz commuted to Manhattan from the suburb of Roslyn Heights, New York, where he had grown up listening to classical music while accompanying his parents to the original productions of *My Fair Lady*, *West Side Story*, and *Gypsy*. Stan and Sheila Schwartz also exposed their son to "what we would now call world music, plus groups like the Weavers and other folk music—Joan Baez when she was first getting started, very early Judy Collins. That was all very influential on me." Young Stephen was less attracted, he admits, to the rock music popular in the late 1950s, "the kind of stuff they drew on for *Grease*, for instance—everything in three chords and six-eight time. Or even Elvis and Jerry Lee Lewis. I didn't hate it, but what was being played on radio wasn't very interesting to me."

That changed in the early 1960s, with the advent of a Detroit-based record company founded by Berry Gordy Jr., originally as Tamla Records and then, more famously, as Motown, a parent company that included an eponymous label as well as Tamla and eventually other subsidiaries. Arriving at the Carnegie Institute of Technology—it became Carnegie Mellon University after merging with the Mellon Institute of Industrial Research in 1967—Schwartz discovered the Supremes' 1964 album *Where Did Our Love Go* in his roommate's collection, "and I became just obsessed with it, and with the Motown sound," particularly the work of the songwriting and production team known as Holland-Dozier-Holland. Lamont Dozier and brothers Brian and Eddie Holland crafted rhythmically driving, melodically thrilling, masterfully arranged hits for the Supremes and other Motown A-listers, such as the Four Tops, Martha and the Vandellas, and a young Marvin Gaye. Schwartz was also drawn to the densely orchestrated recordings of the Beach Boys and the mid- to late-period Beatles, and to soulful singer/songwriters like James Taylor (with whom Schwartz would eventually collaborate on the 1977 musical *Working*), Joni Mitchell, Laura Nyro, and Paul Simon and master craftsmen like Burt Bacharach, who would venture into Broadway musicals himself with 1968's *Promises, Promises*. "But the first breakthrough for me in terms of what we call pop music was Motown," Schwartz says. "The beat of that sound, the instrumentation, the way chord changes were used—all of that appealed to me."

Just as Leonard Bernstein and George Gershwin had been inspired by jazz, Schwartz, another Jewish kid with classical training and Broadway aspirations, soaked up music that had its origins in Black culture but appealed to multiracial audiences—music that, in this case, not only showcased Black performers, writers, and producers but also established the rise, in Gordy, of a leading Black entrepreneur. Years later, fittingly, Gordy would be a key figure in *Pippin*'s success, investing hundreds of thousands of dollars in the show even as it struggled to secure other backing and releasing the musical's original cast recording on Motown.

As a budding lyricist, Schwartz was developing a sense of structure that was definitely more Broadway-centric. Oscar Hammerstein II's work with Richard Rodgers was hugely influential, of course, as were the musicals of Sheldon Harnick and Jerry Bock (*Fiddler on the Roof, She Loves Me, Fiorello!*) and another Stephen S.—Sondheim—and shows scored by Bernstein and Jule Styne with various lyricists, including Sondheim. The Sondheim/Styne collaboration *Gypsy* and Styne and Bob Merrill's *Funny Girl* would especially inspire *Pippin*: "The way the second song in both those shows was an 'I Want' song"—like *Pippin*'s "Corner of the Sky," which introduces us to the protagonist and illuminates the desires and goals driving him—"and the use of little motifs, like 'I had a dream' in *Gypsy* or the Nicky Arnstein theme in *Funny Girl*—I really admired things like that. And studied how Sondheim built to a finish at the end of 'Comedy Tonight,' in *A Funny Thing Happened on the Way to the Forum*, the way he crafted the endings of his songs to get a big hand. I was noticing how these writers structured songs and told stories, and thinking of ways to incorporate it into what I would do—though once I started being more attracted to contemporary pop music, it was not about imitating their musical styles beyond song structure."

Schwartz's parents had nurtured his creative ambitions. Stan himself had an affinity for the visual arts—"He was one of those people who could look at something and draw it beautifully," his son says—and that interest informed some of the projects he pursued as a businessman, with varying degrees of success. "But he had fought in World War II and had a family to support soon after that, and he was of a generation where instead of going into the arts, you were supposed to get a real job." Both Stan and Sheila were intent that their precocious son would not feel similarly restricted. "There was a role reversal when I went to college, where I was the one saying, 'Well, shouldn't I get a real degree, rather than a BFA?' My dad told me—and I love this about his point of view—that nothing is permanent and you can always change your mind. He said, 'You can always go to another school and study something else after a year, but this is what you want right now.' I really internalized that perspective and retain it to this day."

The younger Schwartz had chosen drama over music as a major "because I knew that I wanted to write musical theater, and I'd already studied music for years." The admissions process involved submitting a play: "I'd written a sort of theater-of-the-absurd piece. It was so sophomoric that it's embarrassing to talk about, but it was called *The Race*, or something like that; there were a bunch of characters running some kind of mysterious race and then you found out in the end that they were dead, and it was about where in the afterlife they would wind up. I remember there was a politician who was a Joseph McCarthy type. It's amazing that I got into college with something like that." By his sophomore year, Schwartz had switched his area of concentration from playwriting to directing "because it was the broadest of fields; you studied every aspect of theater: set design and lighting design and costume design and stage craft—plus four years of acting, which was especially helpful to me in learning how to write actable songs. Basically, I wanted to learn as much as I could about putting on shows."

Alas, the head of Carnegie's drama department at the time, Earle R. Gister, who would later become chair of the acting program at the Yale School of Drama, did not rank musical theater high on his list of priorities or the priorities he laid out for his pupils. Training at the institution, which has since become a breeding ground for Broadway musical stars—among them Tony Award winners Billy Porter, Leslie Odom I Jr., Renée Elise Goldsberry, and Patina Miller, a star of the 2013 Broadway revival of *Pippin*—was "geared towards having us work in repertory theater," remembers original *Godspell* cast member Robin Lamont, with an emphasis on Shakespeare and Chekhov. Drama students hoping to take part in a musical had to turn to Scotch'n'Soda, and, ironically, they could not even perform in the club's productions; they had to choose another discipline in which to participate, such as design or, in Schwartz's case, composition and direction. Schwartz would have to receive special permission from Gister to direct, in his senior year, *The Diary of Adam and Eve*—the first of three segments comprising Bock and Harnick's *The Apple Tree*—for the drama department. Gister had protested that there was no one in the department who could provide musical accompaniment, "and I said, 'I'll play.' I told him that's what I was doing during the summer, working as a musical director in summer stock" (at the New London Barn Playhouse in New Hampshire).

The resulting production helped open the door for drama department stagings of *Guys and Dolls* and, two years after Schwartz graduated, an original musical by drama major John-Michael Tebelak. Conceived as Tebelak's senior thesis and initially titled *The Godspell*, it would eventually reunite Schwartz with Tebelak in New York and in musical theater history. By then, remembers Stephen Nathan, class of 1970 and *Godspell*'s original Jesus, "The students had started to take control of the university in different ways. We'd been trained for classical theater, and any commercial stuff seemed to be looked down upon. But it was the '60s, and we were going, 'No, this is bullshit.'" They developed an ally in directing teacher Charles "Word" Baker, who had helmed the original production of *The Fantasticks* off-Broadway. Nathan recalls, "One day in acting class, Word said to us, 'Everybody's going to sing a song,' and he pointed at me and said, 'You're going to go first.' And I was thrilled."

Schwartz's association with Scotch'n'Soda had begun in his freshman year, when then-junior Iris Ratner—later to become novelist and screenwriter Iris Rainer Dart, author of *Beaches*—needed a composer to collaborate on her musical *Whatserface*, which members of the club had chosen the previous spring, in 1964, for its annual production the following year. The show was a success, so when Ratner and Schwartz submitted a proposal for the 1966 musical, it was heartily approved. It was around the time that *Nouveau*, as that show was titled, premiered that Schwartz made the connection from which *Pippin* was born.

"We had these practice rooms in the Fine Arts building, and I used to go in and play piano in the evening," Schwartz recalls. "One night I heard music coming out of another room, and I really liked what I was hearing." He knocked on the door and found Ron Strauss, another drama student who happened to be a musician. Schwartz asked Strauss, a freshman, what he was working on, and the latter briefly relayed his vision of a musical centered on the Frankish prince who had been Charlemagne's eldest son. David Spangler, a freshman music major at the time who was and remains a close friend to Schwartz, remembers, "Ron was nice-looking, but he was very, very shy. He kind of lurked around the practice rooms. He was the sort of guy who may have had trouble finishing a good idea, because he didn't have a lot of confidence." Schwartz, fortuitously, had enough chutzpah for both of them, and suggested that Strauss's show could be a candidate for Scotch'n'Soda's next production—and that they should work on it together.

The project assumed the title *Pippin, Pippin,* also the name of a song Strauss had been playing that night. The apparently timid young man had found an ideal foil in Schwartz, who by then loomed large on campus, according to Spangler: "Everyone knew that he was smart, and that he was gifted, and that there was a bit of an attitude there. He had a strong personality and strong opinions, and I respected that." Nathan remembers it a bit differently: "Stephen was sort of the quiet center of any group he was in. He was an observer. He never really courted attention, in my recollection; he was just such a magnetic presence that it came his way." In any case, *Pippin, Pippin's* creators became equal partners; as Schwartz remembers it, "Ron had written quite a few songs when we started working together, and I wrote the bulk of the new ones. I'm not sure how much of the libretto he had written, but we worked on a new script together, and there were new characters added." (Schwartz also directed and choreographed the student production under the curiously vanilla stage name "Lawrence Stephens," which he adopted as cowriter as well.)

The plot of *Pippin, Pippin* had the same essential "tent poles," as Spangler puts it, as what would become the first act of *Pippin* in its pre-Fosse iteration. Strauss had been fascinated by the historical Pepin, born around AD 770 to Himiltrud, a noblewoman widely believed to have been one of Charlemagne's many concubines. Professor Helmut Reimitz, director of the medieval studies program in Princeton University's history department, explains that legitimacy was not yet a clear-cut matter among the Carolingians, the Frankish aristocrats who forged an empire under Charlemagne after forming a dynasty under his father. "Before Louis the Pious"—Pepin's half-brother, who would succeed Charles as king of the Franks and emperor of the Romans—"all secular rulers had several wives—mostly in succession of each other, though sometimes there would be one wife and several concubines, which was important, because a king needed successors," says Reimitz. Charles would have three sons by Hildegard, whom he married after Pepin's birth and who bore the king more children than any of his other wives or concubines.

Around 790, apparently, Charles was planning to appoint Hildegard's sons kings of territories formerly governed by powerful dukes or, in Italy's case, another king; Reimitz believes this plan could have given Pippin the idea to claim rule over Bavaria, where Charles had deposed his cousin, Duke Tassilo, in 788.

Reimitz points out that there is reason to approach the written history of this period with skepticism, down to the record of Pepin's hunched back: "The Carolingians had an unprecedented level of control over who wrote their biographies; it's probably never been reached again." What is known is that Charlemagne's son Carloman—who like his older brother, Charles the Younger, died before the elder Charles, leaving the throne to Louis—was taken to Rome as a child and rechristened Pepin, a move that signaled his half brother would not be in the line of succession. Charlemagne's court scholar, the original Pepin later feigned illness to avoid traveling with his father to Bavaria, where a campaign against the Avars had been launched, and conspired with disgruntled Frankish leaders to try to usurp the throne. The plot was discovered, and Pepin was, as his dad's loyal documentarian put it (in philologist Lewis Thorpe's translation), "permitted to take up" a life of pious reclusion, "for which he had previously expressed a vocation." In the less biased and more entertaining account of Notker the Stammerer, a Benedictine monk and renowned scholar of the Early Middle Ages, Pepin "was given a sound whipping and was tonsured. As a punishment he was sent for some time to the monastery of Saint Gall, that being among the poorest and most austere of all places in the far-flung Empire."

Schwartz and Strauss took substantial creative license with characters and events, of course. Their Carloman—played by Spangler, who as a music major was allowed to perform—is the son of Fastrada, whom the historical Charles married after Hildegard's death. (Reimitz notes that sources have attributed a certain "cruelty" to Fastrada, who was "a very tough person and a good, influential politician," but that Charles "clearly trusted her with his sons, even though they were not her sons.") As the show opens, he and Pippin are vying to be heir to their father's throne. As would be the case in the later *Pippin*, Fastrada wants her son—named Lewis in the Broadway version—to be king, but Charles himself is less

7

sure; Carloman/Lewis is more physically imposing, but Pippin is older and more intelligent. In the college version, Fastrada enlists the help of her sorceress, Gisela (the name of Charles's sister, historically), who persuades Pippin to visit his grandmother, Berthe (from Bertrada, Charles's mother's actual name), in Prüm, where he meets and, after some initial friction, falls in love with her servant, Adrienne.

But Berthe, after learning that Fastrada had convinced Charles to christen Carloman in preparation for his ascension to kingship, convinces Pippin to return to the court, where he is pressed by the nobles—and a whore named Simone—to take part in the assassination of both Charles and Carloman and become king himself. Carloman learns of the plot and tells Fastrada, who advises him not to warn Charles but to gather soldiers to save them both and thus earn even more of his father's favor. When Pippin hesitates to kill his father, though, Charles is able to grab his sword and save himself. The nobles and Simone are then sentenced to death, but Berthe convinces her son to spare Pippin, who is instead exiled to a monastery, like the historical Pepin.

In spirit, *Pippin, Pippin* drew more heavily on an account of another king who had ruled centuries after Charlemagne: England's Henry II—or, at least, Henry as he was reimagined in *The Lion in Winter*, James Goldman's dramatic portrait of domestic turmoil and intrigue among that monarch and his brood. Produced on Broadway in 1966, with Robert Preston and Rosemary Harris cast, respectively, as Henry and his wife, Eleanor—Peter O'Toole and Katharine Hepburn would play them in a screen adaptation released two years later—Goldman's play was all the rage with drama students at Carnegie, and Schwartz and Strauss were aiming, essentially, to craft their own version. "*Lion in Winter* was renowned for its crackling, witty dialogue, and we wanted to have that," Schwartz remembers. "But our show also took itself quite seriously, with this romantically tragic ending, where you have Pippin inside the monastery gates and Adrienne, the girl he loves, outside, and they'll never be together. I mean, the word sophomoric was invented for this—and I truly was a sophomore when I wrote it, even though it was put on in my junior year."

Whatever naive pretensions Schwartz and Strauss were guilty of surely owed something to the political atmosphere of the time. The month that *Pippin, Pippin* made its debut, April 1967, saw massive protests against the Vietnam War in Washington, D.C., New York, and San Francisco. "It was a huge issue when I was at school," Schwartz says. "And when we graduated, we were terrified we would be drafted. They had the lottery system, where they drew numbers and whether you were called depended on your birthday. I was talking to my parents about fleeing to Canada. I didn't get drafted, but I was a protestor—candlelight marches in New York, a couple of things in Washington." Peggy Gordon, another drama major who would be recruited by Tebelak for *Godspell*, was three years behind Schwartz at Carnegie and recalls that engagement and outrage only grew on campus during that period. "We had an enormous sense of history, and we were actively involved in demonstrations. All of this was aggressively discouraged by the head of our department, who wanted us to focus exclusively on becoming actors who would go into regional theater. There were implicit and explicit threats; they could put a warning on your report card, and if you didn't heed the warning, it could lead to your being placed on probation."

Channeling battles of another era, *Pippin, Pippin* was less pointed in its parallels to modern life and strife than its successor would be. In terms of its score, the division of labor broke down so that Strauss contributed more of the "main character numbers," as Schwartz calls them. "He had already written many of them before I got involved. His songs were more ballad-y, and told the emotional part of the story. Mine were more of the Musical Theater 101 songs: a big dance number, or a choral number where everyone sings in counterpoint—songs we needed to fill out the score." They included "Begging Milady's Pardon," an exchange between Berthe and Pippin's stepmother, Fastrada, reminiscent in its structure and sass of *The Threepenny Opera*'s "Jealousy Duet," with the shifting time signatures Schwartz would continually employ to help lend emotional range and nuance to his work. Another Schwartz contribution, "Victorious," was an ensemble number led by Charles and Pippin. Schwartz describes it as "a shameless ripoff of *Carmina Burana*," the Carl Orff cantata, based on the medieval poetry collection of the same name. The cantata would inspire a more original number in *Pippin*, called "Glory," though Bob Fosse and orchestrator Ralph Burns would render the original source nearly unrecognizable by the time of the musical's Broadway premiere.

In retrospect, Schwartz considers "Somebody Loves You"—one of the ballads he crafted for *Pippin, Pippin*, for Adrienne—"the closest to my more adult writing, though the lyrics are pretty clichéd in spots." ("For love is a gentle thing, soft as a song/But it can last for a lifetime long," one verse begins.) For the composer, the song prefigured *Pippin*'s caressingly melodic "With You," sung by the prince himself—to various women over barely two minutes, thanks to Fosse's radical reinterpretation of Schwartz's original premise. But an original cast recording of *Pippin, Pippin*—a vanity album distributed to members of the Carnegie cast after the show's premiere on April 28, 1967—reveals that neither Schwartz's nor Strauss's songs suggest anywhere near the pop influence that would so heavily inform their musical's successor. The tracks layer woodwinds and horns over piano to lend medieval flourishes, but there are virtually none of the nods to contemporary folk or, certainly, soul that were already starting to pop up in musical theater by the late 1960s. It's hardly surprising that Schwartz chose to rewrite the score from top to bottom.

Before he did, there was a moment when it seemed as if *Pippin, Pippin* might be staged professionally. Toward the end of Schwartz's senior year, which marked his final Scotch'n'Soda show—a two-part piece called *Twice Upon a Time*, for which he wrote an act inspired by Voltaire to accompany an act inspired by Shakespeare, written by David Spangler—he received a letter, postmarked New York City, from a man identifying himself as a producer. He had heard a copy of the vanity recording, the writer indicated, and was impressed. "He thought the music had commercial possibilities, and he asked if I would be interested, once I graduated, in pursuing it," says Schwartz. "So I went to Ron, very excitedly. Now Ron had a theatrical family; his cousin is Peter Strauss," the actor. "He had a lot more knowledge than I did about how show business works. He said, 'This can't be real; I've never heard of this guy. But if you want to pursue it, knock yourself out.'"

Although *Pippin, Pippin* had been well received—"Everyone I knew who saw the performance felt that something really important was being born," says Spangler—its creators would not collaborate again, or remain on good terms, moreover. When Schwartz decided to continue developing the musical—once he had graduated, moved to New York, and secured an agent to help him find another producer and creative partner—he made a deal with Strauss, ensuring the latter would receive a "small but significant royalty" from whatever became of it. "I never would have had the idea to do anything about Pippin and Charlemagne had it not been for Ron, even though the final show had nothing in common with the show we did at Carnegie," Schwartz says. "For many years, Ron shared in all the royalties from Broadway and tours. It's my understanding that he has some bitterness now; I don't think he ever reckoned with what the show would become, and perhaps he feels like it was a missed opportunity, for which I bear some responsibility. But I did ask him to participate at the beginning, and he said no." Spangler posits, "Though I don't know what was in Ron's mind at the time, he may have just been wise enough to get out of the way and let this dynamic force"—Schwartz—"thrust this project he had started forward."

The summer after Schwartz's graduation, Spangler would embark on another project with that force. The two had formed a band called the Pipe Dream, with another friend and two female singers, and the group landed a contract to record an album for RCA Records, based on a demo sent in by Schwartz, its principal songwriter. Called *Wanderers—Lovers*, the recording features period-influenced pop, with alternately breezy and baroque arrangements and song titles such as "January Girl," "The Softness of July," and "Mrs. Brown's Limousine." "I think everybody feels, at a certain age, like they're going to be in a pop group," Schwartz now muses. "And it was the time when everybody was forming bands and writing their own songs, and we did get the tiniest bit of traction. Fortunately, my life took a different path."

Pippin's success lay not far down that road; first, though, Schwartz would become attached to another musical that had first sprouted at Carnegie, also featuring a youthful, idealistic protagonist lifted from history—one far more famous than Pepin the Hunchback or any of his kin, and mightier, albeit gentler and humbler, than Charlemagne. Schwartz was about to join a long line of nice young Jewish men who would find creative inspiration in the teachings of their most famous predecessor, as Jesus Christ made his off-Broadway debut as a musical role.

CHAPTER TWO

Fresh Takes on Famous Sons

AFTER GRADUATION, SCHWARTZ SPENT ONE LAST SUMMER AT THE NEW London Barn Playhouse, during which he met his future and current wife. Carole Piasecki, stage name Prandis, played the scheming chorus girl Gladys Bumps in a production of *Pal Joey* for which Schwartz served as both musical director and choreographer (after the person contracted for the latter position became unavailable). The couple wed in June 1969, and Schwartz moved into Prandis's apartment on Manhattan's Upper West Side, a short distance from where he had been living with a friend. A settled, secure home life would be more of a priority for the composer than it was for his soon-to-be collaborator, Bob Fosse, who also married young—the first time, at least—but never established the sort of domestic stability in which Schwartz and, seemingly, the protagonist of *Pippin* would find comfort.

On Broadway, a changing of the guard had been taking place. Following the death in 1960 of Oscar Hammerstein II—the most important librettist and lyricist in elevating American musical theater, and longtime partner of the most important composer, Richard Rodgers—new creative voices had emerged, while others had evolved. Stephen Sondheim was finally getting full musical scores produced, beginning with *A Funny Thing Happened on the Way to the Forum* and the sadly short-lived *Anyone Can Whistle*, which combined ravishing songs with a chaotic book (by his *West Side Story* and *Gypsy* collaborator Arthur Laurents). Jerry Herman gave the world *Milk and Honey*, along with *Mame* and *Hello, Dolly!*; Jerry Bock and Sheldon Harnick delivered *She Loves Me* and *Fiddler on the Roof*, and John Kander and Fred Ebb's *Flora, the Red Menace, Cabaret*, and *Zorba* marked the ascent of another dream team. "It was a very inventive period," says Kander, "with all of us writing and Hal Prince and Jerry Robbins producing and directing. Even the things that didn't work were interesting adventures, I think."

It was *Hair*, of course, that would announce rock and roll's arrival on Broadway. Transferring in 1968, the year after its premiere at the Public Theater, the musical proved a mass-culture phenomenon, predating *Pippin* in its condemnation of the Vietnam War and tearing into taboo subjects from interracial sex to the recreational and spiritual merits of hallucinogens. (Hammerstein had addressed mixed-race relationships as far back as 1927's *Show Boat*, but with less of a carnal slant.) But creators Galt MacDermot, Gerome Ragni, and James Rado would not be cited as frequently as the previous names in terms of inspiring future musical theater writers. While MacDermot's score for *Hair* is enduringly irresistible, fusing rock and soul influences to exuberant effect—he would have another, less sensational hit with *Two Gentlemen of Verona*, which won a Tony for best musical the year before *Pippin* was nominated—Ragni and Rado's book suggests a string of vignettes more than *Pippin's* did, and the duo's lyrics embellished these episodes more than driving the story line.

The early 1970s would bring the ascent of a more iconic fusionist of rock and musical theater in Andrew Lloyd Webber, though his impact would be felt most keenly in the spectacle-driven mega-musicals that came to dominate Broadway in the following decades, among them his own *Cats* and *The Phantom of the Opera*. A more established composer was also experimenting with different textures—though Sondheim was obviously not a child of rock and roll, and for all his invention and daring, he never made it his mission to craft musicals that pop fans could love. Character, simply, always drove his work, as much as his genius for weaving dissonant chords into tonal melodies that reinforced the wit and warmth of his lyrics. Jonathan Tunick's swinging, electronically enhanced orchestrations for 1970's *Company*, in which keyboards were sometimes prominent, attach the musical's thirty-something couples and singles to a specific point in time when the generation coming up just behind them—Schwartz's and Lloyd Webber's generation and that of *Hair's* subjects—was starting to face adulthood, something many had sworn to put off as long as possible.

Schwartz, for his part, wasn't wasting any time slacking off. He had landed a high-profile agent through his new bride's connections. A plucky mailroom employee at the prestigious talent agency Ashley-Famous (later to become the International Famous Agency before merging with Creative Management Associates to form International Creative Management) wanted to cultivate his own list of clients, among them Prandis, who would land numerous acting gigs before shifting her focus to family life. The low-level employee convinced an agent to accompany him to a backers' audition at which Schwartz played some of the new music he was developing for *Pippin*. The agent recommended that her colleague, Shirley Bernstein—Leonard's sister—meet with Schwartz. So it was that, before turning twenty-one, Schwartz found himself represented by the sibling of one of his idols.

It was a lucky break, but success would not arrive overnight. Before it did, Schwartz managed to secure a job considerably more glamorous than waiting tables: While making his rounds with Bernstein, shopping selections from *Pippin's* score, he slipped a demo recording of pop songs to executives at RCA Records, who offered him a position in the label's A&R department. "What was hilarious was that I had absolutely no experience in a recording studio at the time," Schwartz muses. But he was a quick study, and further impressed the company suits by writing the song "Butterflies Are Free" for a play produced on Broadway in 1969, the year he was hired. "After that, I became part of the group for whom people looking for a cast album deal auditioned their shows." He was in the studio when Sondheim brought in *Follies* and recommended that RCA record it as a double album. The label passed. "I couldn't believe they said no. They were coming from a commercial point of view, but I just thought, from an artistic standpoint, are you kidding me?"

When not assessing new artists and scores, Schwartz continued to work on *Pippin*. Among the first songs he completed were the title character's romantic ballad "With You" and "No Time at All," a rousing manifesto on living life to its fullest, which would be led by Berthe, with members of the company—the Players, as they would be called—singing along on the choruses, a touch inspired by Schwartz's boyhood exposure to Weavers concerts. The composer had a harder time with the "I Want" song, which would introduce Pippin to the audience. "I had a tune that I liked a lot, and I remember I had the title 'Maybe You'll Show Me.' I was struggling with the song for weeks, and finally thought if it was proving that difficult, there must be something misbegotten about it, so I threw it out."

A solution emerged in the fall of 1970, as Schwartz was brainstorming with his wife while driving back from Washington, D.C., where she was working on a show at the time. "I had this line, 'Why do I feel I don't fit in anywhere I go?' and I wanted to set up a contrast," he remembers. "So I asked her, what are things that fit in places? And she said, 'Well, cats fit on the windowsill.'" Schwartz's juices started flowing, and *Pippin*'s "I Want" song was written quickly, resolving with this declaration: "So many men seem destined/To settle for something small/But I won't rest until I know I have it all."

The lyrics are relevant in Schwartz's decision, in writing a new musical, to cut the title *Pippin, Pippin* in half. "Pippin" is also a common noun, after all, defined in Merriam-Webster's as "a highly admired or very admirable person or thing." Reducing the title to one word emphasized the extent to which Pippin believed it was his fate to be such a person—exceptional, even unique, among men.

The searching, soaring melody that Schwartz crafted for "Corner of the Sky" captured this sense of indomitability. The piano had generally not been a prominent instrument in Broadway orchestras before the advent of rock-influenced musicals in the late 1960s and early 1970s, and "Corner" was one of several songs in *Pippin* that revealed, for anyone who hadn't caught *Godspell* downtown, that it would play a leading role in Schwartz's work. As featured on *Pippin*'s original cast album and in most performances since, the song was propelled by chords as exhilarating as anything Elton John was banging out at the time. *Dear Evan Hansen* composers Benj Pasek and Justin Paul consider the number, in Paul's words, "the gold standard of the 'I Want' song, full stop"; it was, in fact, a template for *Dear Evan Hansen*'s similarly ardent "Waving through a Window." "Literally every musical theater major in the world has his take on 'Corner of the Sky.'" Pasek, who actually played Pippin in a college production at the University of Michigan, notes, "Whenever you're performing an 'I Want' song you look up and start to dream, and Stephen's song is the epitome of that, because you are literally looking for your corner of the sky."

And Schwartz had found the partner he needed to help reshape *Pippin*'s story along those lines. After an early draft by another librettist failed to please the prolific producer David Merrick—who optioned and then dropped rights to the show in 1969—Shirley Bernstein recommended Roger O. Hirson, a veteran television writer who had also done film and theater work. It was with Hirson on board that *Pippin* became a more deeply personal project for its composer. "While the specifics of Pippin's story weren't autobiographical for me, what he was seeking and his journey really did become how I was looking at the world," Schwartz says. "His struggles were struggles that I was going through, and that my friends were going through, and that in a larger sense my generation— the 'Me generation,' as we're unflatteringly called—was experiencing."

A contributor to numerous anthology drama series during TV's Golden Age, among them NBC's *Kraft Television Theatre* and *Armstrong Circle Theatre* and CBS's *Playhouse 90*, Hirson gained attention on Broadway as co-librettist of 1966's *Walking Happy*, a musical adaptation of Harold Brighouse's play from fifty years earlier, with songs by frequent Sinatra collaborators Jimmy Van Heusen and Sammy Cahn. The story focused on a hard-drinking bootmaker and his resourceful eldest daughter, who rocks the boat when she falls for one of her dad's workers. *Happy* earned six Tony Award nominations, including one for best musical and another for Hirson's book, though reviews were mixed. To decide if Hirson was the right collaborator for *Pippin*, Schwartz read two of his plays that had been produced off-Broadway: *Journey to the Day*, a study of group therapy in a state mental hospital, first presented on *Playhouse 90* before being expanded for a 1963 staging, and *World War 2 ½*, a tragicomedy that closed after just one performance in 1969 but that Schwartz found "quirky and funny, with a slightly absurdist tone."

The latter play sealed the deal for Schwartz, and instilled in him a sense of creative kinship with the older writer that would prove mutual.

Hirson's son, David, a dramatist in his own right whose plays include 1991's acclaimed comedy *La Bête*, was a teenager at the time, and recalls that his father, who died in 2019, "was excited to be working with a young man of such energy and determination. It rejuvenated him. Their collaboration was one of the happiest experiences of his writing life."

Schwartz favored his new partner's "idiosyncratic" style: "Roger wasn't a well-made-play writer." While soaking up postmodern theater at Carnegie, Schwartz had admired forerunners such as Brecht and Luigi Pirandello, whose *Six Characters in Search of an Author*, with its meta-theatrical approach, would inform *Pippin*. He had even written music for a production of Richard Brinsley Sheridan's eighteenth-century comedy of manners *The Rivals*, directed by Word Baker, "in which the actors playing the Sheridan characters were also part of a second-rate troupe performing *The Rivals*. My memory of this production, and my enjoyment in being part of it, helped lead me to encourage Roger to pursue this notion." Schwartz was also fascinated by performers he caught in off-off-Broadway productions, "who would come off the stage and assault audiences, make them participate. That was very of the moment in the late sixties and early seventies, and it obviously fed into *Pippin* and *Godspell*."

So did the foreign films that Schwartz had loved since earlier in his youth. In addition to Bergman's *Seventh Seal*, which inspired both the traveling-players motif in *Pippin* and imagery in *Godspell*, Fellini's *Juliet of the Spirits*—which follows a middle-aged woman's journey of psychological and sensual self-exploration in fantastical detail, making it hard to distinguish between reality and her flights of fancy—would be a key source. In *Pippin*'s final scene, as it was first presented on Broadway, the character of the Leading Player would tell the audience, speaking on behalf of all the Players, "Why, we're right inside your heads." Schwartz notes, "I always questioned the line, because I thought it was too literal. But yes, in a Fellini way, all of this is happening in Pippin's head, like what happens to Juliet. How much of it is real and how much is she imagining? We don't really know." The line was retained in the Broadway revival more than forty years later and thus in what Schwartz considers the definitive version of the libretto.

Granted, neither Fellini's heroine nor Pirandello's characters would fully make their presence felt until Fosse agreed to direct and started working with Hirson on revising *Pippin*'s book. While it was Hirson and Schwartz's original conceit that all the characters were Players and Pippin the subject they had chosen for a sinister project, this had not been made as immediately clear, and more dialogue had been assigned to certain characters preserved from the show's collegiate predecessor. In a draft from 1970, Fastrada, Berthe, Lewis, and Charles, who is especially prominent, are engaged in the first scene by the Old Man, precursor to the Leading Player, who narrates the story of the Greek philosopher Peregrenius's glorious life and death as other Players, some represented by actors who will appear in minor roles, reenact the saga—then leave after performing an early, abridged version of "Magic to Do," later to become the show's beloved opening number. They don't return until the final scene, when it is Charles—at last revealed, along with the other principals, as members of the troupe—who brings Pippin close to death by pressing the prince to drink a vial of "highly volatile liquid" and then hold a torch to his mouth. Charles also leads the caravan offstage in the end, wrongly assuming that Pippin will follow.

The emphasis in this draft is already on Pippin's personal journey, which begins, as it would in the final version, with his return from school in Padua. There is no longer a sorceress in the story, or a whore; the name Gisela is given to the young woman Pippin meets while visiting his grandmother in the country, as he met Adrienne in *Pippin, Pippin*. This scene also introduces a Balladeer who wryly comments on Pippin's progress, breaking the fourth wall much as the Old Man does initially and leading the chorus through an early version of "Simple Joys," a mischievous paean to the carefree life that would eventually be assigned to the Leading Player. Other characters include Philip, a peasant friendly with the down-to-earth Berthe, and Disiderus, a nobleman who, after Pippin returns to the court and asks a group of lords for their help in overthrowing Charles, suggests that he and others would be amenable— then promptly informs Fastrada of the budding plot, telling her, "My first thoughts were of you . . . all my thoughts are of you, my lady." Pippin succeeds in stabbing his father to death but, in one of Hirson's distinctly unrealistic comic touches, asks Charles for his knife back after realizing how tough it is to be king and is obliged. (Charles would spring back to life, at Pippin's request, on Broadway as well.)

The most notable post–*Pippin, Pippin*, pre-Fosse addition is that of the widow Catherine and her son Theo, in Act Two of the draft, where Pippin's relationships with the boy and especially his mother—whom he remains with rather than joining the troupe—are already as central as they would be on Broadway. The Player portraying Catherine was to be "the misfit of the group, the one that upsets the apple cart," Schwartz explains, by falling in love with Pippin, thus threatening the Leading Player's scheme and his dominance. The characters were actually developed after Schwartz and Hirson began shopping *Pippin* to producers, among them Harold Prince, who was also a successful director by then. Prince passed, but not before offering two pieces of advice that would be crucial. First, Schwartz says, "I remember Hal saying, 'I don't think you should open with 'Corner of the Sky,'" as the show originally did. "He said, 'Something has to come before that.'" Prince further suggested that the musical, which at that point still ended with Pippin's failed assassination attempt on Charles, add a new second act to explore what lay ahead for the protagonist, who was no longer relegated to a monastery. Thus, the love story that would do so much to illustrate Pippin's central conflict—whether to pursue an extraordinary life or find satisfaction in what he perceived as a more mundane one—evolved.

Pippin would find its producer, Stuart Ostrow, about halfway through 1971, by which time Schwartz's two-year tenure at RCA had ended. "I had not been a stunning success," he readily admits, "in terms of producing things that made them a lot of money." Rather than seek a contract renewal, he left the company in February of that year. "I was thinking, what am I going to do? My wife had been working in theater and was making some money, but I thought, what prospects do I have?" One month later—"It was literally only a month, though it felt like forever"— he received a phone call from a college friend, Charles Haid, inviting him to the final performance of a show that had been conceived at Carnegie

and was now wrapping a run at the storied La MaMa Experimental The-
atre Club in the East Village. Haid was working for the producers Edgar
Lansbury—Angela's brother—and Joe Beruh, who wanted to bring
John-Michael Tebelak's *The Godspell* to an off-Broadway stage.

Lansbury remembers being intrigued by the prospect of a show that
combined a religious tenor with an earthy vibe. "There were a couple of
big, glossy cathedral shows being done around that time—the English
ones," he notes. (*Jesus Christ Superstar* actually wouldn't appear on Broadway until that fall, but it had premiered in London, and a recording of
the rock opera was already popular.) *Godspell*, in contrast, "got down to
basics," as Lansbury put it: The show simply followed Jesus as he led his
flock—ten characters presented as clowns—through a series of lessons,
drawn from scripture but expressed through song and dance. The cruci-
fixion scene at the end was followed by celebration, with the company
singing "Long live God" and "Prepare ye the way of the Lord," a reprise
of the opening song's refrain.

Peggy Gordon, one of several Carnegie students who took a leave
of absence to perform in the La MaMa production, notes, "Millions of
Christian kids were leaving their churches in the early '70s, and John-Michael created this emotional and spiritual and psychological antidote," in
which a clown posse surrounded an accessible, affable Jesus—a Messiah
who could be something of a goofball himself, but whose fundamental
wisdom and transcendent compassion were never in question.

Tebelak's original plan was to craft a trilogy of shows. "At the end, the
clowns were supposed to take their makeup off and go out into the world
to preach the gospel," recalls Gilmer McCormick Reinhardt, another cast
member, who took part after her graduation from Carnegie. "The second
part was going to be the Book of Acts, and the third would be the Book
of Revelations." (Tebelak died in 1985 before completing either.) From
the start, *Godspell* was heavily improvisational in structure, with the actors
encouraged to embellish the text—Bible verse, most of it taken from
the Gospel of Matthew—with pop-culture references and comic shtick.
Gordon remembers getting "standing ovations at every performance" at
the off-off-Broadway landmark, "with people weeping. The show was a
diamond in the rough—but it was still a mess."

The main hitch was that *Godspell* desperately needed a new score. Tebelak had tapped a friend, Duane Bolick, to write music to accompany various hymns and psalms, and the resulting songs could be "heavy and ponderous," according to cast member Robin Lamont. "Act Two was an absolute dirge," Gordon agrees. "Every single song was a ballad—and you know, we didn't even know there was anything wrong with that." At one point, Gordon remembers, "Stephen said to us, 'We need an eleven o'clock number'"—a rousing, climactic song performed near the end of a show. "And we said, 'What's an eleven o'clock number?' We were so ignorant."

If the learning curve was steep for *Godspell*'s company, Schwartz faced an even greater challenge in having to write his score in the ludicrously short span of five weeks, so that the show could begin rehearsals in April. Tebelak provided him with material—psalms, hymns, parables—to adapt into lyrics. "Steve would make jokes about being Jewish and having to spend a month coming up with this Jesus stuff," Reinhardt remembers. "But he really got the message of the show. He admired Jesus as a philosopher-saint kind of person"—and, clearly, recognized the fundamental humanism of Tebelak's vision.

Because the music had to be written so quickly, "I used songs I knew as jumping-off points—or diving boards, if you will," Schwartz says. The exhilarating "Bless the Lord," for example, with its deep-groove verses and revved-up choruses, was inspired by Laura Nyro. The ballad "All Good Gifts" "was sort of like a James Taylor song," its plaintive beauty reminiscent of "Fire and Rain." The bouncier "We Beseech Thee," Schwartz notes, "has sort of the same underlying rhythm as the Supremes' 'You Can't Hurry Love,' in what the drums and the bass are doing—that sort of steady bap-bap-bap-bap." (Schwartz retained one song that had been featured in the La MaMa production, the gently glowing "By My Side," with music by Gordon and lyrics by Jay Hamburger.)

Schwartz's contributions to *Godspell* would extend beyond music and lyrics. Gordon, who was very close to Tebelak, observes, "John-Michael was an extremely brilliant conceptual creator and director. But Stephen had been a directing major, and he could cut things, which John-Michael could not." She adds, "John-Michael was emotionally mercurial, so Stephen had to be the grounded center for all of us." The collaborative nature of the show became even more pronounced with Schwartz in the picture. "The musical rehearsals were incredible. We would sit around and all contribute ideas; Stephen wanted to hear everything that anyone could say." Stephen Nathan, who played Jesus, admits, "I didn't know going in if [Schwartz] would be the right fit for this ragtag group of actors who had come together with John-Michael, who was quite an eccentric person. But not only did he fit in well, he had the instincts and the confidence to help solidify the production into the popular success it became. And he did that in a spirit of collaboration and community that was really the whole purpose of doing *Godspell*."

David Letterman's longtime bandleader Paul Shaffer, who at twenty-two years old would conduct the fondly remembered Toronto premiere of *Godspell*—cast members included future stars Martin Short, Gilda Radner, Eugene Levy, and Victor Garber, who would play Jesus in the 1973 screen adaptation—notes that sense of community extended to the musicians featured in the different productions spawned by *Godspell*'s off-Broadway success. "Stephen cast his bands like rock bands," Shaffer says. "Later, when he got to *Pippin*, it became more traditional, in that there was a contractor, an arranger, an orchestrator, a traditional orchestra. But for *Godspell*, he was hiring bands; there would be a guy who knew a drummer, and another guy who had a guitar player in mind, and that's how it was sort of done in each town. He was putting together a rock & roll show—no musical contract, just four guys playing. That was so legitimate to me; I really appreciated it."

Godspell opened at the Cherry Lane Theatre in Greenwich Village on May 17, 1971, to mostly positive reviews, with a very prominent exception. "It is never irreverent, merely naïve and platitudinous in its mixture of *Jesus Christ Superstar*, lovable circus clowns and Billy Graham," wrote Clive Barnes in the *New York Times*, somehow detecting the influence of America's most entrenched evangelist in a musical that basically portrayed Jesus as a hippie. "Personally I thought the whole premise rather nauseating," he continued, but later allowed, "There may well be those who will find freshness and originality here where I could discover only a naive but fey frivolity." Not missing a beat, the producers took out an ad in the *Times* in spotlighting this concession, alongside clips of raves from other critics. *Godspell* was a smash hit, transferring that August from the ninety-nine-seat Cherry Lane to the larger Promenade Theater, where it played for nearly five more years. A cast album produced by Schwartz won a Grammy Award, and a single, "Day by Day," sung by Lamont and the company, peaked at Number Thirteen on *Billboard's* Hot 100 and Number Nine on the *Cash Box* Top 100; the latter position marked the first time a track from a Broadway cast album had reached the Top Ten since Ezio Pinza's recording of "Some Enchanted Evening" more than twenty years prior.

Those who were charmed by the Schwartz-scored *Godspell* early on included Leonard Bernstein, who accompanied his sister Shirley to a performance at the Cherry Lane. The renowned composer and conductor was grappling with a deadline of his own at the time: Jacqueline Kennedy Onassis had commissioned him to write a piece to be performed at the opening of the John F. Kennedy Center for the Performing Arts of Washington, D.C., scheduled for September 8, 1971. *Mass*, the theater work he was developing for the occasion, wanted a collaborator who could help him complete the English-language portions of the text and lyrics and sharpen the dramatic arc of the piece, which would also feature choreography by Alvin Ailey. Having adapted biblical text to resounding success, Schwartz was an ideal candidate, and he quickly formed a close creative and personal bond with his agent's brother, whom he still considers "the nearest thing to a mentor I've ever had."

Mass opened on time, albeit to mixed notices. For Schwartz, there wasn't time to dwell on the press—or his own meteoric rise. "I think I was too busy to take in what was happening," he says now. "Also, I had so little knowledge and experience of how professional show business works, I didn't understand how unusual this was, nor how lucky I was."

Broadway was up next. While a London production of *Godspell* was preparing for a November opening, Ostrow was busy finding a director for *Pippin*. Formerly vice president and general manager of Frank Loesser's publishing and production companies, with Broadway credits including *1776* and *The Apple Tree*—he would later coproduce *M. Butterfly* with David Geffen—Ostrow had tried and failed to secure a batch of original Bob Dylan songs for *Scratch*, a musical adaptation of Stephen Vincent Benét's short story "The Devil and Daniel Webster" (also the source of a 1941 film), with a book by the poet Archibald MacLeish. (The libretto became a play when Dylan put the original songs on an album, *New Morning*, instead, and the play closed after only four performances, just before *Godspell* opened downtown.) So the notion of a theatrical score informed by the contemporary singer/songwriter movement was obviously appealing to the producer. As Ostrow would write decades later in his memoir *Present at the Creation, Leaping in the Dark, and Going against the Grain*, "From the moment [Schwartz] played 'Corner of the Sky' I knew Stephen was the new voice I was looking for. The rest of the score was just as fresh and when he told me it was Carole King who most influenced his music, I felt the earth move under my feet and agreed to produce it on the spot."

Michael Bennett, hot from choreographing Sondheim's *Follies*, was considered for *Pippin* but passed, opting instead to direct a suite of plays called *Twigs*. Ostrow had known Bob Fosse socially before working with him on Broadway, first on a short-lived revue that Fosse doctored, called *The Girls against the Boys*, and then on Loesser's *How to Succeed in Business without Really Trying*. The meeting between Schwartz and Fosse in California was arranged and apparently went off without a hitch. Schwartz arrived as a fan and after sitting down at the piano readily impressed the director, who, as he would tell the magazine *After Dark* before rehearsals began, had very much enjoyed *Godspell*. "He's only twenty-five years old," Fosse enthused—actually aging Schwartz a year—"and some days he's only twelve." At that point, it was likely still an affectionate remark.

In the same interview, Fosse suggested why despite his misgivings about *Pippin*'s book he had thought he could work with it, and what direction he was taking the show in. "It's very episodic, told in very broad, bold strokes," he said. "A little on the burlesque side. I think it's strong entertainment with satiric overtones. It pricks a lot of balloons."

Fosse agreed to begin work on the musical after he had completed *Cabaret*. Ostrow paid the director an advance of $25,000—"the best investment of my career," he would later write. Schwartz was thrilled at the time and phoned Hirson to let him know the good news. David

Hirson does not recall his dad having worked with Fosse previously. "My father knew Bob socially, though at a distance," he says. The director had been an uncredited general supervisor on *Walking Happy*, though, and as Schwartz remembers it, his new creative partner replied, on hearing Fosse's name, "This is our last happy day on the show." If this was overstating the case, it was fair warning for Schwartz, who would become more patently unhappy as *Pippin*'s growing pains truly began.

Chapter Three

Enter the Showman

Back in the early 1980s, years before he would become one of the most successful choreographers of his generation and an A-list musical theater director, Jerry Mitchell walked into a small room in the since-shuttered Minskoff Rehearsal Studios, where Bob Fosse had just been working. "I was afraid to even go in at first," remembers Mitchell, who was then making his living dancing in musicals. When he did, he spotted an ashtray filled with used Tiparillos, slender cigars favored by some cigarette smokers at the time. "They were gnawed so that the plastic was all stretched out. You could see the focus and frustration and jubilation at the way that plastic had been gnawed. And I literally walked into the office and asked for an envelope, and I put the Tiparillos in that envelope, and I wrote on it: 'Fosse's Tiparillos.' Then I marked the date, and I saved them"—until 1999, when he gifted them to Sergio Trujillo, another dancer who would make good as a choreographer, on the opening night of the Broadway tribute *Fosse*, in which Trujillo appeared.

That Fosse was a relentless smoker—while working on *Pippin*, he would tear through three packs of Camels a day, according to Stuart Ostrow—is only one piece of the iconography that continues to surround him thirty-five years after his death. Other choreographers and directors of theater and film have been as seminal and remain as legendary, but mention Agnes de Mille or Jerome Robbins or Stanley Donen or Michael Bennett, and, for most people, no distinct physical image of the artist springs to mind, at least none as sharply, almost cartoonishly, detailed: the hunched shoulders, the toes pointed inward; the hat, tilted slightly to the side or downward, sometimes pinched between the thumb and index finger; and of course the cigarette butt dangling from Fosse's mouth, which could be so thoroughly devoured that some colleagues were concerned he might burn himself.

The body language continues to extend to our notion of a Fosse dancer. He would attribute his style—to the extent he acknowledged he had one—to his "physical problems," as he identified them in a BBC interview a few years before his death: "I always had a slight hunch in my shoulders . . . so as a dancer I began hunching . . . I was losing my hair very early, so I started wearing a lot of hats. And I never had the ballet turnout, so I said, well, I can't turn out like a Baryshnikov or a Nureyev, so I'm going to do the opposite and turn 'em in. So the whole style has come out of my defects."

If Fosse was famous for such self-effacement, he was also known to possess other, sometimes contradictory traits, as one would expect of such a formidable artist and, according to those who knew him, conflicted human being. Once asked for six adjectives to describe himself, he responded in short order, "Eager, pushy, needy, scared, hungry, confident." Several months before *Pippin* opened, he told *After Dark*, "I think I went into choreography in self-defense. Because I couldn't learn anyone else's work." Granted, in the same conversation, he cited a quite different motive for becoming a director: "I didn't like the way directors had the power to ruin my dances—or throw them out altogether." Choreographer and director Chet Walker, who began his long association with Fosse replacing a dancer in *Pippin*, says, "Bob looked at himself as the B movie star, as the second in line. He knew what that was. But he also knew what it took to get a redhead named Gwen Verdon to do certain things. He did that with so many people—people who were brilliant on their own but somehow, in working with him and trusting him, got to another place. That was his gift. And I think it took a toll on him, because emotionally, that's hard to do."

The most self-deprecating aspect of how Fosse described his style to the BBC was, in any case, how reductive the description is. As any of his colleagues or disciples will tell you, his choreography could never be summed up merely in terms of hats and hunches, back bumps and hip thrusts, or the "jazz hands"—fingers splayed, palms facing the audience—he made a household term. "He had a huge range," says Chita Rivera, who appeared in the film version of *Sweet Charity* and played Charity on tour before costarring with Gwen Verdon in Broadway's original *Chicago*. "People think of these tiny movements, but there were times he had me flying—flips and splits and all sorts of things."

"There are just so many layers to his physical language, to the world he created as a choreographer and director," says Bebe Neuwirth, whom Fosse cast as a replacement in *Dancin'* and in the 1986 revival of *Sweet Charity* and who later appeared in productions of *Damn Yankees* and *Fosse* as well as reintroducing Rivera's role, Velma Kelly, in the 1996 production of *Chicago*. "It's not about putting on some fishnet tights and bumping your hips around and being as sexy as you can. It can be very internal, and quite profound. There's humor and there's eccentricity and there's irony—irony not just intellectually but physically; part of you is down and part of you is up. There is dark and light at all times, and many, many shades in between."

That versatility and capacity for balance were evident during Fosse's years growing up in Chicago, one of six children. Much has been written about the popular, agreeable boy who managed a double life, excelling in school and at sports (despite suffering from asthma) while spending nights working in nightclubs as one-half of the "Riff Brothers," a tap-dancing duo formed by a vaudeville veteran named Frederic March, who paired Fosse with another adorable blond lad named Charles Grass. (As a young man, Fosse's father, Cyril, had actually performed in a vaudeville act with his brother.) It was in these venues, soaking in the athletic, lyrical routines of acts like the Nicholas Brothers and the Four Step Brothers, that Fosse first became, as original *Pippin* and *Chicago* cast member Candy Brown puts it, "enamored of Black dancers—and not just the famous ones. I remember him saying he wanted to do an all-Black show." His final Broadway musical, *Big Deal*, would feature a predominantly Black cast; choreographer and director Wayne Cilento, who performed in it—and also in *Dancin'*, which Cilento is planning to revive on Broadway—confirms that Fosse "was infatuated with Black hoofers," adding, "His tap dancing was different from any other choreographer's."

Under different circumstances, Fosse's and Stephen Schwartz's mutual appreciation for and debt to Black Americans' vital contributions to the arts might have brought them closer, but given the clash of personalities and perspectives, it was not to be.

The young Fosse began his studies at Weaver's Chicago Academy of Theater Arts, where his elder sister also took lessons, initially, with a couple of girlfriends; he had a crush on one, but when they quit, the boy stayed on, delving into tap and ballet. "Like other adolescents hide girly magazines in drawers, that's where I kept my ballet shoes," he told the BBC. On graduating high school in 1945, he entered the navy, but, conveniently, Japan surrendered to the Allies just before he started duty; he was thus recruited for an entertainment troupe whose job it was to provide diversion for soldiers still stationed across the Pacific, with a revue called—wait for it—"Hook, Line, and Sinker."

Fosse's service lasted a little under a year, and shortly after leaving, he secured his first job in theater and his first wife—respectively, the national tour of *Call Me Madam* and fellow dancer Marian Niles, who would change her first name to Mary Ann and form a duo with him. Niles was one of three women Fosse would marry, each a dancer, each a bit older than him. He credited the second, Joan McCracken, with expanding his ambitions by encouraging him to seek out more formal training. Taking advantage of the G.I. Bill, he enrolled in classes at the American Theatre Wing in singing and playwriting and diction as well as dance, and studied acting under the renowned Sanford Meisner, who had also taught McCracken—and many more famous names—at the Neighborhood Playhouse.

Not long after this hiatus, Fosse decided to try his luck in Hollywood. The era of big film musicals was ending, but many of the greats were still around, including Fosse's idol, Fred Astaire; Marge and Gower Champion; and Stanley Donen, who was fresh off the success of *Singin' in the Rain*. Fosse got to work with the latter three, along with Debbie Reynolds, in 1953's *Give a Girl a Break*, playing an assistant to Gower Champion's choreographer character while contributing some uncredited choreography himself. He would play the same behind-the-scenes role in the screen adaptation of *Kiss Me, Kate*, developing a routine for "From This

Moment On," a song lifted from another Cole Porter show; it included three couples, among them Fosse and Carol Haney, who would later dance memorably for Fosse in the stage and screen versions of *The Pajama Game*.

Before working with Kelly, Haney had appeared on film and in clubs under the tutelage of Jack Cole, a dancer and choreographer who, most of his successors agree, ultimately exerted a greater influence on Fosse's work than even his beloved Astaire. Verdon actually became Cole's assistant after Haney left his troupe, likely enhancing this impact. Cole's choreography drew on Afro-Caribbean, East Indian, and Indonesian influences. "Jack was the father of American jazz dance," explains the renowned dancer and choreographer Graciela Daniele, who first worked with Fosse in *Chicago*. "He created techniques based on dances from all over the world. It's like, we think of America as the land of immigrants, where people from different places bring different customs and languages. That's what Jack did, and in doing so he taught people like Fosse, Robbins, Michael Bennett—all the great ones." Exotic, erotic, and meticulous, Cole's work helped lay the foundation for Fosse's bumps and lunges and precise isolations, even if Cole's name has remained largely unknown outside dance circles.

Fosse would have to return to Broadway, disillusioned of any aspirations to leading man status, before he could achieve that kind of fame. But before that happened, he finally got a proper choreography credit—and a vehicle for his skills and presence as a performer—in a screen musical adapted from and named after the Ruth McKinney play *My Sister Eileen*, also the source of the stage musical *Wonderful Town*. The results can be viewed by simply Googling "Bob Fosse Tommy Rall," the latter being Fosse's partner in a duet that builds from finger snaps and delicate, jaunty steps to the sort of exhilarating acrobatic displays that Rivera mentions. There is humor and mischief in the jazz turns and tap combinations and triple pirouettes, the leaps and slides, and the equally arresting poses. Fosse arranges his body at one point into a collection of acute angles— hips and legs leaning in opposite directions, one leg crossed behind the other, elbows bent, one hand raising a bowler hat (yes, both he and Rall wear hats) just over his head as it tilts backward. In roughly four minutes, viewers could witness the spectacular dancer that Fosse was and get a hint of the astonishing choreographer he would become.

Back in New York, Fosse found affirmation, earning the first of nine Tony Awards choreographing *Pajama Game* in 1955. Directed by Robbins, with whom he would later collaborate on dance numbers for *Little Me*—Fosse would describe him as a sort of mentor—the production also earned a Tony for Haney in the featured actress category. Verdon would star in three of Fosse's next four musicals: *Damn Yankees*, during which their romance developed; *New Girl in Town*; and *Redhead*. She won Tonys for all three performances, while Fosse won for *Yankees* and *Redhead*; the latter also marked his debut as a Broadway director. His dance vocabulary was expanding as well, to include showstopping numbers such as *Pajama Game*'s "Steam Heat," featuring a trio of Chaplineque clowns, and *Little Me*'s "Rich Kids' Rag," a parody of social dancing that showcased young couples with their backs arched and their noses in the air.

Those looking for deeper and darker shades in Fosse's work could have referred to *New Girl*'s "Red Light Ballet." Director and librettist George Abbott had based the musical on *Anna Christie*, Eugene O'Neill's Pulitzer Prize–winning play about a former prostitute who falls in love with a sailor and struggles to put her past behind her. Although Abbott's book was lighter, it confronted Fosse with rather less breezy material than he'd had in the past and more of a need for the kind of fluid, stylized movement outside dance numbers and sustained sexual tension that *Pippin* would require. The ballet was placed in the second act, after the sailor discovers Anna's history and temporarily abandons her; the jilted heroine joined her former colleagues back at the whorehouse, where they asserted what they see as their only power, armed with corsets and garter belts and burlesque tricks that would have made the Postcard Girls in *Oklahoma!*'s Dream Ballet blush. Neither Abbott, a theater giant who also produced widely, nor Hal Prince, his protégé and a coproducer of the show, approved. Nor did the police officers who were somehow tipped off and padlocked the New Haven theater where *New Girl* had its tryout, warning the show would not go on if the ballet remained. Fosse managed to appease them all by editing and speeding it up.

The director was not always as accommodating. In between marrying Verdon in 1960 and scoring another success with his musical staging for *How to Succeed in Business without Really Trying* the following year, he was either fired from or quit work on *The Conquering Hero*, an adaptation of *Hail the Conquering Hero*, Preston Sturges's film satire about the son of a World War I military hero who poses as a highly decorated marine during World War II. By numerous accounts, Fosse wanted the musical to make a more high-minded political statement than librettist Larry Gelbart envisioned; part of this process involved installing another controversial ballet, "The Battle," which parodied jingoism by casting female dancers as murderous Japanese soldiers with knives in their teeth, and male dancers as the Americans, their gold costumes reflecting their extreme virtue. (Fosse also clashed with the producers in suggesting that he replace Tom Poston in the leading role.) *Hero* flopped, closing after only eight performances in January 1961; a few years later, Fosse would bail on a musical that proved more successful, *Funny Girl*, due to what he perceived as producer Ray Stark's lack of faith in him. For Fosse, trust mattered nearly as much as talent, and while he enjoyed good relationships with certain producers—Stuart Ostrow among them—he was especially wary of those whose contributions to the arts involved primarily holding the purse strings. "How Bob hated money people," one of Fosse's mistresses, Ilse Schwarzwald, told one of his biographers, Martin Gottfried.

A new outlet emerged for Fosse's more tender leanings when Verdon gave birth to their daughter, Nicole, in 1963. Fosse's wife would return to Broadway for the first time since their marriage three years later in a project that he conceived: *Sweet Charity* was based on a film by one of his favorite directors. *Nights of Cabiria*, Federico Fellini's depiction of a working girl seeking fulfillment in love, whose luck never matches her pluck. In the musical, Cabiria the prostitute became Charity the dance hall hostess—or "taxi dancer," as women paid to partner with men in clubs were called earlier in the twentieth century. Fosse, who had long harbored ambitions to write himself—it wasn't coincidental that his closest buddies were in that profession—originally imagined a pair of one-act musicals, one penned by Elaine May and the other by himself, but he wound up writing a draft on his own, though he suspected that it needed more comic finesse to work as a musical.

Enter Neil Simon, who had written the book for *Little Me*. Enlisted to tweak Fosse's *Charity*, Simon wound up essentially rewriting it—he is credited as the sole librettist—and the result is, by all accounts, less true to the spirit of the original film than Fosse's attempt had been, whatever its flaws. Fellini opened the movie with Cabiria being robbed and pushed into a river by her lover; toward the end, another boyfriend walked her to the edge of a cliff, leaving her unharmed only after she had thrown her purse at him. The blow was softened when a crowd surrounded the heroine, making music and dancing, but it was still a grittier resolution—less sentimental—than Simon's, in which Charity's latest beau, Oscar, weasels out of the relationship without stealing anything from her and she dances, as signs over the stage read, "And so she lived . . . *hopefully* . . . ever after."

Charity was nonetheless a considerable hit, leading to a screen adaptation—one that would mark Fosse's debut as a feature film director. (He had only choreographed adaptations of *Pajama Game* and *Damn Yankees*.) It would not be another vehicle for Verdon, though; by the time production began in 1968, the studio had opted for a younger, more visible star: Shirley MacLaine, who had been Haney's understudy in Broadway's *Pajama Game*. That show business held different standards for men and women was not lost on the third Mrs. Bob Fosse, who gamely helped coach MacLaine for the role she had made famous. Nor was Verdon likely unaware that her husband was in a position to benefit from this distinction. Years later, when Verdon and Fosse were no longer a couple—they separated in the early 1970s but never divorced, continuing to collaborate both as artists and in raising Nicole—Fosse, as famous a seducer of beautiful women as any choreographer on record, seemed to acknowledge this advantage. "I do try not to become involved with people I work with," he told Dick Cavett in 1980, "but it's very difficult. You're thrown into a stressful situation; they are very attractive women, and they have a sort of need for the director and choreographer, so there's all sorts of things going on." In a *Rolling Stone* interview a few years after that, he would add, "I like to think I was a pretty good-looking guy, and I cared about the women and had a good sense of humor, but also I'd be a fool if I didn't recognize that I had a certain degree of power over them. Directors are never in short supply of girlfriends."

There were other temptations. As is widely known, Fosse had developed a fondness for drugs stronger than tobacco. "I got hooked on Seconal for a while," Fosse admitted to Cavett. "I was taking Seconal and Dexedrine at the same time, and I was hallucinating. There was one time where Gwen had to pick me off the wall because I thought I could fly." Scotch and cocaine also entered the picture, and more Dexedrine. "I'd wake up in the morning, pop a pill," he told *Rolling Stone*. After lunch, when I couldn't get going, I'd pop another one, and if I wanted to work all night, still another one. There was a certain romanticism about that stuff. There was Bob drinking and smoking and turning out good work. Still popping and screwing around with the girls. 'Isn't it terrific macho behavior,' they said. I probably thought I was indestructible." What helped steady the serial womanizer, ironically, was male bonding with his writer friends. Spending time with Fosse, Candy Brown says, she was struck by "his love for Paddy Chayefsky and Neil Simon and Herb Gardner. Those guys were as thick as thieves. A man doesn't have that kind of camaraderie if he's worried about chasing women and doing drugs twenty-four/seven."

Predictably, Fosse continued to find less of a rapport with the "money people" of show business. He surely rolled his eyes when the suits at Universal Studios sought to brighten *Charity* further by having Oscar remain with the heroine. Two endings were shot, one in which he didn't, the other in which he did. Fosse prevailed, but it was a Pyrrhic victory: After an advance screening received mixed reviews, it was reedited, eliminating about fifteen minutes without Fosse's input, and opened to the box office that fell below Universal's expectations. Even the ending that Fosse chose seems, in retrospect, like a compromise: After Oscar ditches her at a marriage bureau, Charity is consoled in Central Park by a group of conspicuously wholesome flower children—modernized, banal variations on Fellini's troupe—who hold up peace signs as they proclaim, "Love." Peter Stone's screenplay has her mirror their actions, watch them leave, then walk off herself—clinging to the daisy the hippies have given her, offering salutations to an elderly couple, looking up at birds fluttering in the clear blue sky, and swinging her suitcase. Simon's message reappears on-screen—"And so she lived *hopefully* ever after"—next to a frozen image of MacLaine in close-up. No aversion to sentimentality in evidence here.

Having been a hot commodity when *Charity* seemed destined for success, Fosse was suddenly "pretty cold," as he admitted years later to Cavett. "Hollywood is a very fickle place; if you have a failure, the phone doesn't ring as much . . . I mean, no one really wanted me for a pretty long time." No one at a movie studio, anyway. "I could always get a [Broadway] show if I wanted," Fosse pointed out. "But I was determined that the next thing I would do would be a movie musical. Because I still think *Sweet Charity*'s a pretty good film. It's flawed, as everything I do seems flawed, but . . . there's very good stuff in there. I felt I took a bum rap from some of the magazines, and I wanted to prove that given the right material—I thought it was the material I was taking the blame for—I could make a successful movie musical."

He nearly missed his chance to do so with *Cabaret*: "They offered it to, like, five, six, seven, eight directors who turned it down for one reason or another," Fosse told Cavett. "I know Billy Wilder turned it down; I know Gene Kelly turned it down." So did the legendary director and screenwriter Joseph L. Mankiewicz and Hal Prince, who had directed the musical on Broadway but was busy working with Sondheim on *Company*—all of which cleared the way for Cy Feuer, who had been hired to produce the film, to anoint Fosse, with whom he had codirected *Little Me*. Feuer and his partner Ernest H. Martin had also produced *How to Succeed* and *Walking Happy* as well as *Guys and Dolls*.

From the beginning, Fosse and Feuer were in sync on a key point: The filmed *Cabaret* should include only those songs that, in the stage musical, were performed in the Kit Kat Klub, the seedy establishment in Weimar Berlin where central character Sally Bowles led a troupe of women in providing risqué entertainment. The one exception was "Tomorrow Belongs to Me," an eerily rousing signal of the Third Reich's imminent rise; Fosse set it in a beer garden, where a teenage boy led a growing crowd in the song. Fosse's general strategy was to stick closer to the musical's source material: Christopher Isherwood's *The Berlin Stories*, inspired by the

English-born author's time there during the period, and the John Van Druten play *I Am a Camera*, adapted from Isherwood's work.

"I always felt the stage book was very weak," Fosse told *After Dark* of *Cabaret*'s libretto, by Joe Masteroff, "but the cabaret numbers and that cabaret atmosphere were incredible." The director opted for an orchestra consisting of only eight to ten instruments "to make the music more authentic, more like the real period of Berlin in the thirties." He sought the same authenticity and economy in casting the Kit Kat Girls, who performed with Sally—originally a British character but made American for Liza Minnelli, whom composer John Kander and lyricist Fred Ebb had wanted for the Broadway production. (Prince thought she was too strong a singer for Sally, an aspirational creature of limited talent.) "I never used more than six girls" to accompany Minnelli, Fosse said. The stage they performed on was a mere ten by fourteen feet, and "I tried to make the dances look like the period, not as if they were done by me, Bob Fosse, but by some guy who is down and out."

Fosse hired mostly German dancers, except for Kathryn Doby and Louise Quick, both alumnae of the stage and screen versions of *Charity*; Quick had also been his assistant choreographer on *Liza*, and both women would assist him on *Pippin*, in which Doby performed as well. He also recruited *Charity* orchestrator Ralph Burns to adapt Kander and Ebb's score and contribute a few new songs. But Fosse was reined in somewhat by the studio; Emanuel Wolf, who as president and chairman of Allied Artists had bought rights to the musical—splitting the cost with celebrity agent-turned-ABC Pictures president Martin Baum, *Cabaret*'s uncredited executive producer—had Feuer keep close tabs on the budget. The director did not get his first choice of cinematographer—Robert Surtees, who had also worked on *Charity*—and was less than thrilled with Jay Presson Allen's screenplay, or by Wolf's request for cuts during the editing process. But while accepting his Academy Award for best director on March 27, 1973—just two days after he had collected a pair of Tonys for *Pippin*—Fosse found it in his heart to thank Wolf and to single out Feuer, "with whom I had a lot of, uh, disputes—but on a night like this you start having affection for everybody."

By this point, Fosse had reason to feel generous. Beyond the awards—there were eight Oscars in total for *Cabaret*, including acting trophies for Minnelli and Joel Grey, who reprised his Broadway role as the Master of Ceremonies—he had earned the praise of both his peers and some of his most venerated predecessors. Joseph L. Mankiewicz, who wound up losing to Fosse in the directing category, marveled at how the less experienced film director "brought the stink of truth to *Cabaret*," while Vincente Minnelli, Liza's father, deemed it "the perfect movie." The press was similarly bullish; in *The New Yorker*, Pauline Kael, the dean of her generation of film critics, wrote, "Until now there has never been a diamond-hard big movie musical. If it doesn't make money, it will still make movie history."

And *Cabaret* did just that, as one of a small handful of screen adaptations of great stage musicals—arguably the only one between 1965's *The Sound of Music* and 2002's *Chicago*—that both captured the essence of the original version and transcended it in scope, using cinematic techniques to bring audiences further into the distinct, troubled world of its characters. (Remember, there were Nazis in *Sound of Music* as well.) Fosse's vision for the musical was leaner than Prince's had been on Broadway but also bolder—allowing, for instance, for a frank depiction of bisexuality in Sally's confidante and sometime lover, a character named Brian. Based on Isherwood, who was gay, he was played by English actor Michael York. (In the original Broadway production, the character was named Clifford and was straight, though he would be bisexual in revivals helmed by Prince and Sam Mendes.)

If the changing times and the subject matter Fosse was choosing seemed to invite freer expressions of sexuality in general, his direction and particularly his choreography retained a level of discretion, a point emphasized by those who were entrusted with it. "Mr. Fosse was not a vulgarian," says Gene Foote, a Fosse dancer whose Broadway credits have included *Charity*, *Pippin*, and *Chicago*. "Gwen Verdon only did two front bumps in her career, in *Sweet Charity* and *Chicago*, and both times she apologized for them (in character)—she went, 'Oops,' or, 'Excuse me.'" Pamela Sousa, who appeared in the latter two musicals with Foote and Doby and Brown, notes, "Our back bumps and hip circles were still ladylike. It wasn't as out there as dance on Broadway would become later. It was about enticing an audience."

Fosse's dancers also point to the singularity of his style and his directorial skills, even with performers who had minimal dialogue. "With Jerry Robbins, everything he did would serve the musical," says Daniele. "'Tradition,'" from *Fiddler on the Roof,* "was about tradition. *West Side Story* captured the streets of New York. His choreography always expressed what the piece was about. It was wonderful, but the style changed constantly. With Bobby, the piece was also a defining factor—but you always knew it was Fosse. Just like you always knew the latest art by Picasso. And he was a brilliant director. The step between choreography and direction is a jump, and he became greater and greater. The same was true of Robbins, and Michael Bennett. But especially Fosse." In *Chicago,* Daniele would have a mostly dancing role as a Hungarian woman incarcerated for murder; she spoke just two words of English— "Not guilty," in the song "Cell Block Tango"—and Fosse, cleverly, told the actress that because he could not understand her character, he could not believe her. His intent, she now realizes, was to enhance her sense of frustration and thus her character's. "I'll never forget how he made me feel—in my stomach, in my heart—and I brought that onstage with me during every show."

Cabaret was released on February 13, 1972, three and a half months before Fosse would shoot a vehicle for its breakout star, the TV concert special *Liza with a Z.* Editing and postproduction for that project—yet another smash success, winning Fosse three Emmy Awards, one of which he shared with Minnelli and coproducer Fred Ebb, who earned an additional award for writing—would overlap with preparation of and rehearsals for *Pippin*; the stage musical would head to Washington for its pre-Broadway tryout not long after *Liza* aired on September 10. The strain of all that multitasking was obvious, as Brown, one of the backup dancers featured in *Liza,* remembers: "One day he came in to rehearse *Pippin* and you could almost see the cloud over his head. He's got his ever-present cigarette in his mouth, and he's walking around in a circle, and we're all backing up, trying to disappear against the wall, because we didn't know what the problem was. Finally he stopped, and he said, 'I'm really sorry, but I was in the editing room with another project, and the editor dropped a cigar ash on a piece of film that had one of my favorite shots of Liza.' So I waited a beat, and then I said, 'Well, he didn't ruin any of my stuff, did he?'"

Brown's gamble paid off: "Bob looked at me, and then he came over and gave me the biggest hug. And then I knew my purpose—it was to bring him out of these depressive times. To make him realize, it ain't that deep, you know? I had done a similar thing while we were working on *Liza*, when we were learning the song 'Bye Bye Blackbird.' It had this syncopated jazz rhythm, and we were ten dancers who were mediocre singers, and at one point Bob said, 'No, you're not singing it like Liza.' And I said, 'If I could sing it like Liza, I'd have my own TV special.' And immediately I thought, oh, shit—did I say that out loud? Because he could have fired me right there. It wasn't until that moment in *Pippin* rehearsals, when he hugged me, that I knew I was actually there for that—that Bob liked people who are grounded, who are real, who have a sense of humor."

Brown was repeatedly struck by Fosse's generosity and compassion. During rehearsals for *Chicago*, she recalls, he would have to let an actor go when the role was eliminated, "and I still remember the pain in his voice." Years later, she discovered that Fosse had given the actor an engraved Rolex watch. "That was paid for out of Bob's pocket, because that's the kind of human being he was. I never met another director or choreographer like him, and I worked with Gower Champion, with Lester Wilson, with Ron Field. Michael Bennett was brilliant, but he had a real cruel streak. Bob was a very sensitive man, very giving of himself, always."

But such positive energy could never quite make that cloud that Brown spotted disappear; if anything, it expanded in the wake of Fosse's professional triumphs in the early 1970s. In his Oscar acceptance speech, he had joked of fearing that his fresh string of successes "may turn me into some sort of hopeful optimist and ruin my whole life." He needn't have worried: Not two months later, with that award and his Tonys stored safely at home—the Emmys for *Liza* would arrive in November—Fosse checked himself into the Payne Whitney Psychiatric Clinic on the Upper East Side, suffering from depression. He would check out only days later, presumably bored—he had begun to put on shows with the other inmates, he would report—and unhappy with the side effects of lithium but not unburdened of his doubts or demons.

"Over the years, I realized that Bob was obsessed with death," says Brown. "Maybe obsessed is a strong word, but he thought about it a lot." Three years before Fosse died at sixty, he mused to *Rolling Stone*, "I always thought I'd be dead by twenty-five. I wanted to be. I thought it was romantic. I thought people would mourn me: 'Oh, that young career.'" Mortality and its fragility certainly loomed large in much of Fosse's later work—from *Chicago*, with its merry murderesses, to the films *All That Jazz*, in which he essentially imagined his own passing (as a dazzling production number, naturally), and *Star 80*, which traced the short, tragic life of *Playboy* model Dorothy Stratten, ending with a brutal reenactment of her murder.

John Kander remembers that when he and Fred Ebb began working with Fosse on *Chicago*, "It was a very happy time. It was dark material, but we laughed a lot; it was the kind of creative atmosphere I love, where you sit around together and talk a lot, and somebody comes up with an idea, and then somebody comes up with another idea: 'What if we do this?' 'OK, but what if we do that?' I remember Fred saying, a couple of times, 'Let's do this—Bobby will really like it.'" Then, about a week into rehearsals, Fosse suffered two heart attacks—the first at work, the second while in the hospital. When rehearsals finally resumed months later, Kander says, "It was a different atmosphere. We didn't have fights or things like that, but Bob seemed darker, more bitter. He and Fred, because they co-wrote the book, were having meetings together that were pretty tough. All that joy that we had had at the beginning was absent." Daniele, too, "found him down" at this juncture. "His moods were not happy-go-lucky."

Even before the heart attacks and the meltdown, the keen interest in death that Brown and others have ascribed to Fosse may have played some part in drawing him to *Pippin*. But whatever morbid fascination compelled the director was matched by a drive to live and create fully—a force so relentless that, ironically, it helped fuel some of his self-destructive habits. Nicole Fosse, his only child, notes, "My father's work ethic in the dance studio, on the stage, and on the film set was the same as in his personal life. He impressed that work ethic upon me as well: *There is no such thing as perfect. Keep working. Practice the things you are not good at. You are never finished.* I also remember him saying, 'Don't settle for mediocre. It's okay to fail, but only if you fail on your quest to becoming extraordinary.'" It's something Pippin might have said at the start of his quest had he considered failure an option. If less starry-eyed than his young hero, Fosse was every bit as determined to succeed—perhaps more so, because the director was aware of what success could cost, and apparently willing to pay the price.

CHAPTER FOUR

Song and Dance (But Not in That Order)

AUDITIONS ARE A STRESSFUL PERIOD FOR ANY CREATIVE TEAM, A TIME
when the joy of discovery can be accompanied by the agony of discord.
And so it was while trying to cast *Pippin* that Bob Fosse and Stephen
Schwartz locked horns in earnest. The principal roles were generally
not the source of tension. For the title part, Schwartz told the *New York
Times*, after several months of searching, "We're just looking for a boy
who's young and fresh and charming and has a sense of humor and a
voice to fit the songs. That sounds awfully easy, doesn't it—it's impossible."

Casting director Michael Shurtleff approached or at least thought
about several popular singers for the role, teen idols and troubadours who
had little or, more often, no theater experience. John Denver, Arlo Guth-
rie, Peter Noone, and Livingston Taylor were among the names floated.
Musical theater veteran Florence Henderson, by then widely known for
her role in *The Brady Bunch*, suggested Mac Davis, according to Shurtleff's notes, while Hirson put in a request for David Cassidy, who had
appeared in the extremely short-lived Broadway musical *The Fig Leaves
Are Falling*. Cassidy was "tied up with television and not interested in
doing a Broadway show," Shurtleff indicated, adding that the star of *The
Partridge Family* "might have difficulty singing this score anyhow." David
"Davy" Jones's name did appear on the call sheet for an audition in late
1971; Fosse simply wrote "sweet quality" in the margins, and the Monkee
became unavailable before casting was completed anyhow.

Several young actors who were becoming or would soon be familiar names were also contenders for the role of Charlemagne's son. After Chris Sarandon auditioned, on the same day as Jones, Fosse circled his name, adding, "tall," "dark," and "nice voice." Richard Gere, in contrast—one of Shurtleff's early suggestions, along with Christopher Walken, Keir Dullea, James Naughton, and Michael Crawford—got an "x" through his name, accompanied by "NO" in capital letters; the comments indicate that while Gere "sings OK" and "reads OK," there is "something wrong." Schwartz recalls being impressed by one aspiring performer who would gain a lot of attention dancing and singing in movies: "There was a very young actor called John Travolta. For various reasons it was decided he wasn't exactly right for the role, but I went up to him onstage afterwards and said, 'Look, you're not going to get this part, but you're fantastic—and if you're interested, I'd love to have the casting office for *Godspell* know about you, because I think you're perfect for that show.'" Alas, Travolta wound up instead in the original Broadway productions of *Grease*—not in the leading role he would later play on-screen but as a replacement for a supporting part—and *Over Here!*, with *Pippin* alumna Ann Reinking; the rest, from *Welcome Back, Kotter* and the disco era on, is history.

Fosse, meanwhile, had his eye on a young man who was neither a dancer—interestingly, Pippin was among several principal characters, also including Charles and Catherine and Berthe, for whom Fosse's choreography would not require great skill in that arena—nor an especially polished singer. Twenty-five-year-old John Rubinstein had rounded up some notable stage and television credits, from a touring production of *Camelot* starring Howard Keel to appearances on popular TV series such as *Dragnet*, *Ironside*, and *Room 222* and in the film *Journey to Shiloh*. And Rubinstein had been born into show business, with music in his DNA: His parents were the Polish-born concert pianist Arthur Rubinstein and his wife, Aniela, a former dancer and the daughter of conductor and composer Emil Mlynarski. The couple had abandoned their Paris home in 1939, knowing that the German army's arrival was imminent. (When, after extensive legal maneuvering, they were able to reclaim the house fifteen years later from a dentist who had collaborated with the Nazis during the occupation, all their possessions were gone.) They emigrated to New York in the early 1940s and later moved to the Los Angeles neighborhood of Brentwood, where John was born; when he was two, the Rubinsteins settled in Beverly Hills, where for the next five years they socialized with other luminaries, as John befriended a number of their children, among them a future Fosse muse: the daughter of Judy Garland and director Vincente Minnelli.

"Edgar Bergen's daughter, Candy—Candice—and the Minnellis' daughter, Liza, were my two best friends," Rubinstein recalls. "I honestly don't remember going over to Liza's house, but she came over to ours many times, always on Halloween when my mom would host all those kids. Liza was *always* a fairy princess in a spangly white dress and tiara." Years later, in their forties, Minnelli and Rubinstein would appear together in a weird TV special called *Sam Found Out*, composed of three short films, each pairing Minnelli with a different actor—Louis Gossett Jr. and Ryan O'Neal were the other two—in a story involving someone named Sam. The short with Rubinstein was an original musical piece written by John Kander and Fred Ebb, who had by then worked famously with Minnelli and Fosse on *Cabaret*. "Our characters were supposed to get married, but her dog, Sam, hated me and made my life miserable," Rubinstein explains. "In the end, she picked Sam." The human performers sang solos and shared a duet under Marvin Hamlisch's musical direction.

Before *Pippin* came along, Rubinstein had flirted with *Cabaret* himself on two separate occasions. While still an undergraduate studying music and theater at UCLA (he would later study composition at Juilliard), he learned that a replacement was being sought for Joel Grey—a Tony winner for his indelibly chilling performance as the Master of Ceremonies, which Grey would reprise for Fosse in the movie adaptation. Interested in the part, Rubinstein auditioned for Hal Prince, who directed and produced the original stage production. "I think I was nineteen at the time, and I looked about fifteen." He was called back nonetheless, and though he ultimately wasn't cast, "I got a wonderful letter from Hal, basically saying, you were the best who auditioned but you just look too young."

There was a stab at fame a few years later, in the form of a rock music–fueled western called *Zachariah*. "It was a huge flop, but it's become sort of a cult picture, probably because Don Johnson was in it,"

Rubinstein says of the 1971 film. (Johnson would also be seen by Fosse during *Pippin*'s auditions; he earned a scribbled "maybe" on that day's sheet, along with "handsome" and "has energy.") When contacted by that movie's producer, who asked if he had a proficient English accent, Rubinstein said yes. "So the producer said, 'OK, I want you to meet Bob Fosse. He's having trouble with *Cabaret*; he cast Michael York in it, and Michael has a scheduling problem.'" The meeting took place, and Fosse arranged a screen test for York's character, Brian Roberts. "A young lady who I believed was a German girlfriend of Bob's played Liza's part. I had very long hair that I tied up in a bun, so that you couldn't see it from behind the camera. I believe he would have cast me—that's what he said to me later—but Michael York fixed his schedule."

Whatever Fosse's take on Rubinstein's reading, the actor made a positive enough impression that the director thought to call him not long afterward. Rubinstein and his then wife, actress and dancer Judi West—who had, coincidentally, performed with Fosse in a production of *Pal Joey* at New York's City Center—were at home in the Beverly Glen section of Los Angeles in early February 1972 when the phone rang. "He said, 'Hey, it's Bob Fosse. Can you sing?' Well, I'd sung all my life; I'd done musicals at school, and I had done a road trip of a musical where I sang. But my voice is not a singer's voice; it's a person-who-can-hold-a-tune voice. So I said, 'Yes, I can sing, but I would never call myself a singer—nobody would ever want to buy a record of me singing.' Then he said, 'Well, can I come over for dinner?'"

Hours later, as the heavily pregnant West prepared a meal, her husband entertained their guest by singing two Laura Nyro songs, accompanying himself on piano. After dinner, Fosse joined Rubinstein on the sofa. "He had brought with him the script to *Pippin*, and we sat next to each other and I read Pippin and he read all the other parts, from the beginning to the end of the show. We even read song lyrics out, speaking them. That took us a couple of hours, and then he left"—for a bit. Rubinstein and West were getting into bed that night when they heard a knock on the door. "It was Bob. He handed me a cassette tape—it was Stephen playing and singing the whole score of *Pippin*—and he said,

'Learn the second song, and come to New York in three days, to audition for the other people.'"

The song was, naturally, Pippin's "I Want" number, "Corner of the Sky." Three days later, Rubinstein hopped on a plane, as instructed, and on landing headed to the Majestic Theatre, where an open call had drawn some two hundred aspiring performers, each hoping to win the role that Fosse had already decided was Rubinstein's to lose. "There was a line of about three blocks, of young men of all different ages and sizes and varieties—some professional kids in ties and suits, holding briefcases, and other hippie types with long hair and beads and crazy outfits, holding guitars and ukuleles," Rubinstein says. "It was the wildest assortment of young men I've ever seen."

Having an appointment, Rubinstein did not have to wait with them but rather was ushered into the theater, where Fosse huddled with Ostrow, Schwartz, Shurtleff, and Roger Hirson in the orchestra section. The actor headed down into the pit "because I had no music with me. I sat at the piano and played my same two Laura Nyro songs, and then I got up on stage—they had an accompanist there—and I sang 'Corner of the Sky.'" Fosse was sold, and so were the rest, apparently. "I stood there on the stage for a couple of minutes after singing, not longer, and they talked in the back of the house, where I couldn't hear them. Then Bob ran down the aisle, and from the front of the house he said, 'The part's yours if you want it.' Now, that never happens. There was a line of guys waiting to audition, and I believe they saw them all."

The director had only one request: "He told me, 'Go work out a bit,'" remembers Rubinstein, who was still very thin. "If I had auditioned for Diane Paulus in 2013"—for the Broadway revival, in which Rubinstein would do a stint as Charles—"they would have kicked me out without even listening to me, because the Pippins they picked for that production were buff. They were hunks. I was just a skinny kid." With the promise of a starring role for his Broadway debut, the actor flew back to Los Angeles, where he and West welcomed their first child, a baby girl named Jessica, about a week later. He would return to New York when rehearsals started, right after the July 4 weekend.

Pippin's other leading man—the performer who would earn the most rapturous reviews, as well as a Tony Award—had taken a very different path to Broadway. While Rubinstein was playing with the progeny of Hollywood royalty and later, as a teenager in Manhattan, attending plays and musicals on a regular basis—on college breaks, he would "see ten shows if I was there for a week"—Benjamin Augustus Middleton, who became Ben Vereen after being adopted, was coming of age on the streets of another borough. "My world was literally Brooklyn, where I was going to church and singing in church," says Vereen, who was born the same year as Rubinstein, in 1946, in North Carolina; he would not learn of his adoption until more than twenty years later while applying for a passport. Vereen's talents, which extended to drama and dance, landed him in Manhattan's prestigious High School of Performing Arts. Nonetheless, "I knew nothing about theater, to tell you the truth. The first show I saw was *Sweet Charity*, with Juliet Prowse—because Bob Fosse gave me tickets."

Vereen had come to Fosse's attention when he auditioned for a North American tour of *Charity* in 1967. "I had heard about the audition because I picked up a trade paper. I was broke; I jumped a [subway] turnstile, looked at the paper and went to the Palace Theatre. I went in, and it was just like the opening to *All That Jazz*"—Fosse's 1979 film focusing on a hard-living director and choreographer much like himself, which Vereen would appear in. "All these male dancers from all over were standing on that stage." The dancer and aspiring choreographer Eddie Gasper, then one of Fosse's assistants, "was giving us the combination, and then Bob came walking down the aisle. He was smoking a cigarette and the ashes were hanging out of his mouth. As he gave us the steps, they never fell—I think I was even more impressed by that than by the steps themselves."

After getting through the dance audition, Vereen and the others who remained were asked to sing. When Vereen's time came, the director listened intently, "then he stopped and looked at me, and he asked me to sing it a cappella"—without accompaniment. After a dinner break, Vereen learned he had made the cut. Although he had already danced in an off-off-Broadway show, Vereen says, "I had never thought about really having a career in theater. It was a gift Bob Fosse gave me. On our first day of rehearsal, he asked me to sing for the company, which was sweet. He was impressed by how I sang, I guess."

Indeed, Vereen's fluid, soulful tenor would eventually be the standout voice on the *Pippin* cast recording, and was so admired by Schwartz that it nearly wound up on the soundtrack to the film adaptation of *Godspell*. Paul Shaffer recalls that Schwartz wasn't sure if Merrell Jackson, the actor who would sing the rangy "All Good Gifts," was up to the task. "At the sessions, Stephen said, 'There's a performer in *Pippin* named Ben Vereen—the guy sings like an angel. I may bring him in just to do the last chorus, in a higher key.' We didn't end up using him, because it turned out Merrell could really sing—but what a performer Ben Vereen was."

By the time *Pippin* auditions started, Vereen's gifts were no secret to anyone who had been paying attention. After making his Broadway debut in *Hair*, he had appeared in Fosse's film adaptation of *Charity*, then was cast as Judas in the original New York production of *Jesus Christ Superstar* in 1971, receiving a Tony nomination for his performance. Still, Vereen insists, "When I heard about *Pippin*, I didn't expect to get the show. I didn't know anything about it. But Bob asked me to audition, and wanted to show him how much I'd grown since we had worked together. I had put together a nightclub act; I did a little concert in San Francisco. I wanted to show Bob what I could do." Vereen's agent would advise him against taking part in *Pippin*: "He said there was a ninety per cent chance the show wouldn't make it. I said, 'If Bob's doing the show, I want to do it with him.'"

For the audition, Vereen recalls, laughing, "I wore a blue suit that I'd bought with a little money, and alligator shoes, and a shirt and tie. I sang for Bob, and he said, 'Very good—now I want you to read.' I went down to the basement of the theater and read for him"—the part of the Old Man—"and then he said, 'Your reading's not great, but we'll consider it.' He said, 'We'll stay in touch.' Then I got a call saying I'd made the cut."

Shurtleff and others remember a different scenario, in which Vereen's audition had actually been too great for what was then a minor role. Fosse had tried out a number of seasoned character actors and other veterans for the Old Man; he wanted a dancer, and when he couldn't find an older performer whose work was up to par, Shurtleff suggested—"with grave hesitation"—young Vereen, whom he also knew from having worked on *Superstar*. "I sent the script of *Pippin* to Ben and asked him to prepare an audition," Shurtleff wrote in *Audition*, a noted guide for fledgling actors since its 1978 publication. "He took the scenes from the script for the Old Man, paltry as they were, and around them he wove three singing numbers, ending up in a big dance solo. For the first time, our 'Old Man' came to life in the person of a young, sexy, humorous Black actor who was an irresistible singer and dancer."

Thus the Old Man became the Leading Player, master of ceremonies to the audience, constant companion and sly foil to Pippin—a much bigger role, in short. And its size and pungency would only expand as rehearsals progressed. "Moral of the story," Shurtleff concluded: "If they ask you to audition for an eighty-year-old character man and you're a handsome young leading man, go audition anyhow. You just might change their minds completely. They just might rewrite the show around you."

Schwartz notes that Fosse was, from the get-go, "extremely enthusiastic about trying to get Ben into the show"—and predictably, no one else needed convincing. Schwartz was mostly bullish on Vereen's costars as well. "I was a huge fan of Eric Berry," the British stage and film veteran who got the part of Charles, or King Charlemagne. "I may have even been the one to suggest him, because I had seen him do Shakespeare off-Broadway." Ostrow had also been an admirer of Berry's work, which stretched from London's West End to Broadway—where he first appeared with Julie Andrews in *The Boy Friend*, also her Broadway debut—and films such as *The Red Shoes* and *Escape by Night*.

Schwartz had caught Leland Palmer downtown too, in *Your Own Thing*, a musical based on *Twelfth Night*. As a Viola transported to the late 1960s, Palmer, who now calls herself Linda Posner, got to show her chops as a singer and dancer. Fosse was even better acquainted with that prowess, having previously cast her in a touring production of *Little Me* and in *Pleasures and Palaces*, a Frank Loesser musical that closed during its pre-Broadway run. Born Linda Jo Palmer—she took Leland Palmer as a stage name because Equity already had a Linda Palmer, and later changed her name to Linda Posner after learning that Posner had been her father's original surname—she had grown up riding horses and initially wanted to be a veterinarian; in high school, a lack of affinity for chemistry and a modern dance class taken as a physical education requirement persuaded her to change course, though she didn't begin studying professionally until she was nineteen. "Then I immersed myself—I took seventeen classes a week for three or four years, ballet and modern and jazz and pantomime. After everything, I decided to sell my horse and move to New York," where her teachers included jazz pioneer Eugene Louis "Luigi" Faccuito and renowned ballet dancer Aubrey Hitchens as well as Martha Graham protégé Bertram Ross.

Posner had performed in four Broadway productions prior to *Pippin*, earning a Tony nomination for featured actress in the second, *A Joyful Noise*. But she was aware that Fosse had a very different type in mind for the part of Fastrada, Pippin's seductive, scheming stepmom. "The notice in the trades called for 'a Joan Baez type'—long legs, long black hair, very voluptuous." Fosse apparently also wanted someone who could dance; audition records and notes show that contenders included Mercedes Ellington, Paula Kelly (who had worked with Fosse on the film version of *Sweet Charity* and appeared to acclaim in the London staging of that musical), Donna McKechnie (a young dancer in the original Broadway company of *How to Succeed . . .*), and McKechnie's future *A Chorus Line* costar Priscilla Lopez—Schwartz's suggestion—who was also considered for Gisela before that role was cut. Chita Rivera, Rita Moreno, and Eartha Kitt were on the wish list but were unavailable to play the vamp for various reasons—though Rivera would inherit the role nearly a decade later in a Toronto production captured for television.

As a lesser-known name, though, Posner took that description in the trades to heart. "I was very tiny, five two, about ninety pounds. Nothing like Joan Baez. But I begged for the audition, and because Bob liked my previous work, he said, 'OK, but she's wrong for the part.' So I came in wearing low riders to show off my midriff, and I had on a bra that was stuffed with about seven socks in each cup. My hair was a sort of reddish, blondish brown, and I wore it in little curls"—not unlike Gwen Verdon, whom Posner would resemble even more in the red wig she eventually wore in the role. (Notably, Posner would play the estranged but supportive wife of Joe Gideon, the Fosse-esque protagonist of *All That Jazz*.) "So there I was, boobs out to here, hips and belly showing, and I sang a Janis Joplin song." Prospective cast members had been encouraged to bring in a contemporary pop tune to show their potential affinity for Schwartz's score. "I belted out 'Take Another Little Piece of My Heart.' And I just blew Bob out of the water. I had the part within a day or two."

Irene Ryan had rather less to prove in auditioning for the role of Berthe, Pippin's feisty paternal grandmother. The list of women envisioned in the role was ambitious; casting notes mention Lotte Lenya, Elsa Lancaster, Ethel Waters, Maureen Stapleton, and Sylvia Sidney, who was quoted as having said, "I read the script, it sucks, I will not audition." (Sidney was not the only established or rising actor who passed after reading the book for various reasons, including the sizes of their prospective roles. Others, the notes indicate, included Elizabeth Wilson, Barbara Barrie, Michael Moriarty, and singer Yvonne Elliman, who had sung Mary Magdalene's part on the original recording of *Jesus Christ Superstar* before playing the role onstage and in the film adaptation.)

But Ryan was a vaudeville veteran who had gotten into show business via a talent contest before entering her teens, qualifications that surely earned her both Fosse's empathy and his respect. She was also a TV star, having spent the decade before *Pippin* playing Daisy May "Granny" Moses on the hit series *The Beverly Hillbillies*. When that show's run ended in 1971, there was no shortage of interest in the actress, pushing seventy at the time but considered ripe for similar roles. Schwartz would, in fact, ponder adjusting a lyric in Berthe's single, showstopping number because of Ryan's fame: "In 'No Time at All,' she sings, 'Now I could waylay some aging roué/And persuade him to stay in some cranny/But it's hard to believe I'm being led astray/By a man who calls me Granny.' I thought, oh, no, everybody's going to think I've used 'Granny' to pander to the fact that this woman was on a TV show. But Stuart said, don't worry, no one will make the connection. Everyone did, of course, but not in a critical way."

Gene Foote, who would be cast in the ensemble, remembers spying Ryan on the steps just inside the Imperial's stage door as other candidates for principal roles were being seen. "She was something—it was so cute.

She was sitting there in a fur coat, and finally someone came out, and she said, 'Excuse me, I'm waiting, and I've been waiting for a while.' And he said, 'Well, who are you?' She told him, and he said, 'Just a moment.' And she said, 'Just tell them that for every minute I wait, the price goes up two thousand dollars.'" Fosse would later remember the amount as a slightly more reasonable one hundred dollars per five minutes, and would add that Ryan accepted his apology for running late "ever so graciously."

The one bit of principal casting that caused Schwartz trepidation was for the role of Catherine. As with Pippin, Shurtleff had considered auditioning popular singers, such as Judy Collins and Carly Simon, who both passed. But Fosse knew that, since Pippin's widowed love interest doesn't arrive onstage until more than halfway through the show, a proven actress was needed to establish and sustain the character, who juggles comical and poignant moments. Bette Midler, who had appeared in Broadway and off-Broadway productions before building a following with her much-ballyhooed performances at the Continental Baths, is listed on the same audition call sheet as Christopher Walken, from Christmas Eve 1971. Adrienne Barbeau was scheduled to be seen the same day as Pia Zadora, Stockard Channing on another day. There was interest in Blythe Danner and Bernadette Peters, but neither was available in the end. Madeleine Kahn—who, like Midler, was also considered for Fastrada—was about to make her feature film debut in Peter Bogdanovich's *What's Up, Doc?*; "Expects to become a film star," sneer the notes beside her name, "so isn't much interested in our little girl, Catherine."

Fosse's choice for the role turned out to be Jill Clayburgh, who had played Desdemona to James Earl Jones's Othello at the Mark Taper Forum and had a couple of Broadway credits, including the Sheldon Harnick/Jerry Bock musical *The Rothschilds*. She had also appeared on-screen opposite Robert DeNiro in 1969's *The Wedding Party*—codirected by Brian DePalma, then a graduate student in theater at Sarah Lawrence College—and filmed an adaptation of Philip Roth's *Portnoy's Complaint*. Getting Clayburgh on board may have taken some persuasion: One sheet of notes from 1971 reads, next to her name, "She doesn't like the part and is not interested." But Fosse was, apparently, persistent. "Bob said, 'This girl's going to be a movie star,'" Schwartz recalls. "Once again, he was right. And you needed that quality for a character who makes her entrance so late in the show."

Schwartz fretted, nonetheless, about Clayburgh's proficiency as a singer, or lack thereof. "I remember listening over and over again to the cast recording of *The Rothschilds*, trying to convince myself Jill could sing well enough." Eventually, a romantic duet between Pippin and Catherine would be replaced with the less rangy "Love Song," which Schwartz and Fosse came to prefer. As evidenced by the cast album recordings of Catherine's two other numbers, "Kind of Woman" and "I Guess I'll Miss the Man," Clayburgh's relatively thin voice and precarious technique aren't glaring problems; her reading of the first song, the wry number that introduces the character, benefits especially from what Shurtleff called her "expert, light Carole Lombard-style" comedic acuity. But Schwartz maintains that when Betty Buckley replaced Clayburgh fewer than eight months into the run—so that the latter actress could fulfill another commitment—it was to the production's benefit, and Buckley's subsequent work in musicals and cabaret offers evidence that Catherine's musical numbers certainly gained potency.

A former Miss Fort Worth, Buckley knew Ostrow, having made her Broadway debut as Martha Jefferson in *1776*. She had actually been interested in *Pippin* from the start but was, as she tells it, tricked into not auditioning. "Eric Shepherd, who was my agent, said there was no part for me. I thought, OK, but then I went to see the show when it opened, and there was this wonderful role of Catherine the widow, played by Jill Clayburgh, and I immediately called him and said, what were you talking about? And he said, 'Oh, Betty, I didn't want to tell you, but they didn't want to see you.'" When auditions for a replacement were announced a few months later, a friend in the industry offered to check if the *Pippin* team might reconsider. "A couple of days later, I got a letter from Michael Shurtleff, saying, 'Dear Miss Buckley: From the inception of the show we had hoped you would come in for the role of Catherine, but your agent told us you were out of the business and had moved home to Texas.'" Shurtleff ended the letter, "Stuart Ostrow sends his love, and Bob Fosse looks forward to meeting you."

Buckley's name is, in fact, mentioned several times in the early casting notes for *Pippin*. At one point, it's indicated that she was shooting a TV pilot, at another that she was out of town but might be interested. One call sheet lists her name with "No show" scrawled beside it. But regardless of what Shepherd had initially told the creative team, his client was now perplexed and peeved, and called to tell him so. "I said, 'Is this true? Did you tell them I was out of the business?' He said, 'Show business is complicated, Betty.' I said, 'What are you talking about? They wanted to see me, and they want to see me now.' So he went into all these excuses, and then he finally said, 'Jill [Clayburgh] is also my client, and I didn't want her to have the competition.' Because, basically, he could get $150 more a week with Jill in the part than he would have with me in the part. Here was this very cynical, sarcastic guy, telling me, 'Oh, Betty, grow up—this is show business.' And I said to him, 'Oh, yeah? Well, you grow up—because you're not my agent anymore.'"

For the role of Theo, Catherine's young son, Fosse selected Shane Nickerson, who at eight years old had already appeared in a Hallmark Hall of Fame TV movie, 1971's *All the Way Home*, and on the daytime serial *As the World Turns*. Fastrada's grown but hopelessly dunderheaded son, Lewis, was assigned to rising dancer Christopher Chadman, who would become a favorite of Fosse's and earn acclaim as a choreographer in his own right. Before his career and life were cut short by AIDS in 1995, Chadman appeared in and assisted Fosse on *Dancin'*, starred in a 1976 revival of *Pal Joey*, served as associate choreographer for *Big Deal*, and earned a Fred Astaire Award choreographing the celebrated revival of *Guys and Dolls* that made stars of Nathan Lane and Faith Prince, to list just a few of his Broadway credits.

It was in looking for the nonprincipal Players that *Pippin*'s composer and director came to realize, as did those around them, that their creative partnership might be rocky. Most simply put by Ostrow, "Bobby was very tough about wanting dancers, while Stephen was very tough about wanting singers. I usually went with Fosse." Traditionally, most Broadway ensembles combined "singers who move" with "dancers who sing." (There were exceptions; some musicals didn't call for complex choreography, while in others, such as *West Side Story*, company members, including principals, had to juggle substantial vocal and dance parts.) But Fosse didn't even mention singing when explaining his strategy to *After Dark*. "The cast will be small for a musical. About eighteen, dancers included," he said. "The dancing group will be small, but integrated into the production so they'll all play parts. There won't be any separate dancing chorus. I'm going to use a *lot* of movement. Even the actors we're hiring must be 'movable.' I see the show as very fluid—lots of movement and theatricality."

In choosing his dancers, Fosse took into account their sensitivities as well as his own needs. Explaining his approach years later, he said of prospective cast members, "I allow them to run in groups several times until I have relieved my conscience that I have taught them as well as I possibly can and that I am as fair as I possibly can be." The next step was to break the remaining applicants down into smaller groups, have them sing, and then have them possibly read a portion of the script. Typically, they would be given "private code" rankings of one, two, or three, with pluses and minuses added to distinguish their performances further. Throughout the process, he sought to put everyone at ease. "I think [what] gets in the way of people auditioning is that they're so sure they're going to get turned down that they develop a sort of defense mechanism that keeps them from being open and gets them a little uptight," he told Dick Cavett. "I've tried various ways to get them to relax. I really try very hard at auditions, because I remember auditioning myself and how panicked I was, and how my hands would sweat and how I'd throw up. I know being up there isn't easy."

Chet Walker notes, "Bob always thanked people for coming to auditions. He shook your hand, looked you in the eye, and said, 'Thank you.' That cemented everything; it said, 'You've done everything you can, and you can go on with your life. See you in rehearsal, or see you next time you audition for me.'" (Louise Quick recalled in one interview how the German dancers Fosse had used in *Cabaret* "were not accustomed to being treated so well. . . . They had never been spoken to like that before.")

Hundreds assembled at the Imperial to compete for what would be fewer than a dozen spots in the *Pippin* ensemble, including two alternates. As was his regular practice, Fosse first gave them a ballet combination with jazz flourishes, set to "Tea for Two," through which he evaluated basic technique and rhythmic intuition. "Bob also used to have people do step-clap, step-clap, to see if they could stay in rhythm," says Candy Brown, whom Fosse had asked to audition after working with her on *Liza with a Z*. "Then he would accelerate it faster and faster. It was surprising to me how many dancers actually could not do that." Pamela Sousa, who at twenty would be the baby among *Pippin*'s dancers, thought the same thing: "It's truly from tap dance training."

Women who made the first cut then moved on to a second combination, as Ann Reinking would remember in a 2007 essay for *Dance Magazine*: "It started with an adagio that was like a jazz version of [Jerome] Robbins' *Afternoon of a Faun*. The music was very romantic, in the style of Erik Satie's *Trois Gymnopedies*. I was surprised that Mr. Fosse picked that kind of music, as he was not particularly known for romanticism. But romantic it was. Our feet and legs were in a turned-in fourth position, torso bent over parallel to the floor, arms in fourth position mimicking the legs. He said it should look like hieroglyphics. On the first two chords of music we contracted and released our backs." Isolations, a hallmark of Fosse's work, followed. "Beautiful arms that waved, sometimes behind our backs, sometimes by our sides. A lot of the port de bras was turned-in in various ways, and the upper body would tilt so one side of the torso was hanging while the other side did the movement. We were always working at least two parts of our bodies at once, if not more—kind of like the interior workings of a beautiful clock. There were turned-in passes with hip isolations as you balanced on half-pointe and then fell into the next movement—always with lovely arms, sustained bends, and unique shouldering."

Fosse told the dancers to direct their movements toward an "imaginary young man" representing Pippin, "an innocent youth searching for perfection—in this case a woman." When the choreographer asked for "soft-boiled hands"—the expressivity that Fosse could find in hands and fingers alone boggled the mind—Reinking was perplexed at first. "But he explained, 'It's as if you are holding soft-boiled eggs at the curve of your fingers when they make a loose fist. But the eggs have no shell: they're just fragile, quivering things that must not be broken while you undulate your hands and arms.' Well, with that, the movement took on such care and dangerous grace. Everything was completely unreal now." Reinking went on to recall other phrases and steps—"busted legs," "tea-cup fingers," "false drama," "tacit power," "loud stillness"—that evoked the emotional complexity and specificity of character Fosse would instill even in the ensemble numbers.

For the third combination, male and female dancers were instructed to improvise, pretending they had a large ball or balloon before them. "We had to toss this balloon up into the air, then catch it on our noses," says Sousa. "And we did these hip circles. So it was imaginative and fun, not just double turns and back bumps and layouts." Kathryn Doby, who would both assist Fosse and perform in the show, observed the dancers with him as Quick demonstrated; Doby recalls instructions for this combination being more general: "Bob just said, 'Think of what people do in the circus.' It could be walking on a tightrope; it could be making something disappear, or it could be a ball, which was something obvious."

As always, Fosse was hands-on, walking onstage to give individual pointers. "He came up to me, and talked very softly," says Cheryl Clark, who was twenty-one. "He said, 'You're very talented, but I want you to go to the end of the line and watch how these women are bumping'—and he did a hand gesture, with fingers closed and palm open, to indicate a clean isolation to the back. I had done musical theater and had some excellent training in jazz and tap before I'd even gotten into ballet, but most of my training after that was in ballet, and I wasn't trained in his jazz style. So I went all the way to the back of the line, past hundreds of girls. He gave me that chance." Says Doby, "Bob always made the auditions personal. He always talked to people, to see how they behaved, what potential they had. He was very good with that. Sometimes I would wonder what he saw in someone that I didn't think had much potential, but he saw things in people that others did not."

Clark made it to the callbacks for singing. "They were seeing Equity members and non-Equity, and it took at least seven hours. Someone who became a friend offered me a piece of chicken in the basement of the Imperial Theatre, because we were so hungry." Clark first sang "From This Moment On"—the Cole Porter song that, unbeknownst to Clark, he had choreographed for *Kiss Me, Kate*—then for her upbeat tune sang the Turtles' bouncy 1967 hit "Happy Together." Foote chose "New World Coming," the Barry Mann/Cynthia Weil tune that had been a hit for the Mamas and the Papas' Cass Elliot in 1970. "It ended with a high B flat, and I heard Stephen Schwartz say to Bob, 'That was a high B flat!' And Bob just said, 'I know.' I think he had already decided who he was going to use." (Brown says that, years later, Hirson told her that during her audition, "Bob said, 'She's in the show'—so there was nothing they could do about it.")

Generally, though, Schwartz was less impressed by what he heard. According to Ostrow, the composer was dead-set against Reinking in particular "because he thought she couldn't sing at all. And Fosse said to me, 'Either I get that dancer in the show or I quit.' So I asked Stephen to leave. I said, 'If you upset the director and make trouble, you can't be here.'" Schwartz denies having had any problem with Reinking, though, noting, "Annie was actually one of the better singers in the group. And Candy Brown." Schwartz approved Reinking and Brown, in fact, as understudies for the roles of Catherine and Fastrada, respectively. "I don't think there was any one ensemble member, male or female, that I specifically objected to; it was the cumulative effect of having *no* really strong singers." Clark, too, was charmed by Reinking: "I sat in the wings when Annie sang 'Don't Tell Mama'"—from *Cabaret*—"and I thought she was wonderful. We both had long brown hair; hers was practically down to her waist. She seemed so mature to me; little did I know she was only one year older than I was."

There was another long-haired, leggy beauty who by all accounts—including her own—would have given any composer qualms. "I was a dancer who *couldn't* sing," admits Jennifer Nairn-Smith, the woman who had shared her drumstick with Clark. A native Australian who had danced in the New York City Ballet before making her Broadway debut as a showgirl in *Follies*, Nairn-Smith had no substantial training in jazz dance; since arriving in New York and landing at the School of American Ballet, she had considered George Balanchine as her mentor and guru. "With Balanchine, your knees are pulled up tight; with jazz, they're bent. To this day, my knees won't bend." What Nairn-Smith did have was a killer body, topped by a supermodel-worthy face. "She couldn't carry a tune, but no one cared, because she was so gorgeous," says Brown. "I don't think anybody had ever seen anyone so stunning," Clark concurs. "As stunning as Catherine Deneuve. She came onstage with her long, long hair wound up, so that it looked very phallic."

Nairn-Smith unwound her hair before singing "because I thought, I'm going to be like a Beatle." On the subject of her physical charms at this time, she does not demur: "I had everything you wanted. I'm very high-waisted, which Balanchine loved—he loved a long thigh bone. And I had on this killer green leotard from Amsterdam, which was high cut, for the audition. I know that Stephen Schwartz didn't want me in the show at all, but Fosse wanted the body."

Sousa, whose own considerable prettiness was more of a girl-next-door type, sang Carole King's bouncy "I Feel the Earth Move Under My Feet," which was very popular among dancers at the time. Forty-four-year-old Richard Korthaze, who had worked with Fosse on a few projects and would be the eldest cast member, decided against a contemporary tune, opting instead for "something from *Brigadoon*; I think it was 'Almost Like Being in Love.'" Schwartz still wanted stronger vocalists, though, and appealed one last time to Fosse. "I remember pleading, 'Just give me two of each—two guys who can *really* sing and two women who can *really* sing.' I thought that they could help the ensemble vocals, and maybe they wouldn't have to do the most difficult choreography. With two men and two women who were better singers, I thought, I could get a strong enough choral sound. But the answer was no."

Since understudies were needed for principal roles, Foote and Roger Hamilton were assigned, respectively, the Leading Player and Charles. (Standbys were appointed for Pippin, Berthe, and Catherine's son, Theo, as well as the Leading Player.) Foote remembers reading the same early version of the script first given to Vereen: "It said, 'An old man walks out of the darkness and says, 'Closer. Come closer.' And everyone else was coming out and shouting, 'Closer! Come closer!' Well, when it was my turn, I walked out onstage, and no one was looking at me—they were all talking to each other. So I just looked out into the theater, and said, 'Psst.' And they all turned around. And I went"—Foote lowers his voice to a seductive purr—"No, closer. Come *closer*.' And Bob loved it"—so much, Foote believes, that Fosse incorporated his ploy into the show. "What was the first moment in *Pippin*? You saw all these hands floating in the air, and then you saw Ben's face, and he goes, 'Psst!' I never discussed it with Bob, but I do think he got that from me."

On the final day of ensemble auditions, Fosse had narrowed the men down to ten contenders for five spots. After singing and dancing, Foote, Hamilton, Korthaze, and two other Broadway veterans, John Mineo and Paul Solen, "were told to go home and dress the way we like to dress, because we were coming back to line up for Patricia Zipprodt," the costume designer, Foote recalls. For the women, there were only four spots since dance captain Kathryn Doby had already been cast as a Player. "They lined twenty or twenty-five of us up on stage," Sousa recalls. "And Bob said, 'OK, the first three girls on the left, take a step to the left.' Well, the first girl on the left was the cutest African-American—Candy Brown. Then there was this beautiful girl with very straight hair, who looked like a ballet dancer—Ann Reinking. Then me. Then Jennifer Nairn-Smith joined us. And I'm looking down the line at all these other girls that had done shows, dancers I knew of, who were wonderful. I thought, 'Oh, he doesn't want *us*.' But it was the other dancers he released. He went with the unknowns, in a way—we had experience, but not as much." Nairn-Smith and Doby were in their thirties, but the rest were under twenty-five. (The men were older, ranging from their late twenties to their forties.)

"To be honest, I think we all had something special, and I guess Bob saw that," says Sousa. "We were asked to stay in the dressing room, and then Pat Zipprodt came in and took pictures of us. I think since her design was going to be very open and very free, she wanted to make it more personal, to really get a sense of our bodies, what each person's look was, so that she could develop costumes to fit that."

Fosse would choose Roger A. Bigelow, who at the time was dancing with Sousa in another Broadway musical, *Sugar* (under another powerhouse director-choreographer, Gower Champion) to serve as the male dance alternate, or swing—the performer tasked with learning all the other parts in order to be able to step in for any member at any time.

Cheryl Clark, having not made the final cut, accepted a contract for a new tour of *Promises, Promises* she had been dancing in; she was all the way upstate in Latham, a hamlet near Albany, when the roommate with whom she shared an East 84th Street apartment received a phone call from Fosse and his longtime production stage manager, Phil Friedman. "Tish gave him the name of the motel we were staying in, and Phil Friedman called me and said, 'Mr. Fosse would like to talk to you.' Then Bob got on the phone, and he asked if I was the girl with long, long hair, who had worn a green leotard and sung these three songs. I said yes and yes and yes, and he said, 'I think you're the girl I'm looking for.' I said, 'I certainly hope so, Mr. Fosse.'"

Friedman then got on the phone, "and he said, 'You're going to be hired as the swing girl.' And I said, what's that? And he said, 'Oh, it's real easy. Just make sure you bring a notebook and a pen.'" Alas, the *Promises, Promises* tour producer did not want to release Clark. "So our dance captain, Laurent Giroux—who would actually become a replacement player in *Pippin*—he said to the producer, 'Oh, she's terrible—let her go to Broadway.' That's how I got out of my contract!"

Where casting was concerned, at least, all the parts were in place for *Pippin* to begin rehearsals that summer. The musical itself was another matter. Fosse was still far from satisfied with the book, and if the score pleased him better, the audacity that the young composer had shown during auditions surely concerned him. As lighting designer Jules Fisher puts it, "Bob was an autocrat. That's part what of many directors are, what they have to be." And however humble his demeanor, Fosse would have made Charlemagne proud in marking his territory.

CHAPTER FIVE

From a Medieval Musical Drama to "An Anachronistic, Cynical Burlesque"

JOHN RUBINSTEIN NEEDED A DRINK. OR AT LEAST THE ACTOR, WHO drank sparingly on most occasions, was happy to accept one when Bob Fosse offered it. It was the night before rehearsals for *Pippin* would begin, and Rubinstein, who had just flown back to New York with his wife and their four-and-a-half-month-old daughter, had been invited to Fosse's apartment to chat one-on-one, "just to break the ice," Rubinstein remembers. But it wasn't the prospect of meeting the renowned director on his home turf that made Rubinstein anxious; it was the project they were about to embark on.

"Here I was, about to play the title role in a big Broadway musical, my first time on Broadway, and I couldn't have been more flattered or honored or excited," Rubinstein says. "But I had some trepidation about having to sing all these songs when I'm not a good singer, and being in a Bob Fosse production when I'm not a good dancer. I thought, maybe they'll fire me after five days." But the actor's concerns extended beyond doubts about his own aptitude. "I had read that script, and I thought the story was kind of silly. The music was fun and full of energy, the lyrics were very rhymey and intelligent, but the dialogue was kind of stiff; there was all this talk of falcons and Visigoths and princely stuff, jokes and references that were fusty and not very funny. I thought, if the script isn't good, how do I pretend that I'm on board?"

If Rubinstein was worried about how to express all this to Fosse, he needn't have been. After sitting the actor down, the host delivered a pep talk of a sort while echoing the language he had used when Stuart Ostrow first put *Pippin* on his plate. "Bob said to me—I forget exactly how he put it, but it was something like, 'We just have to figure out how to make this shit fly.' He might have even said 'piece of shit,' which is worse, really. I think that's exactly what he said. But he said that *we* had to figure this out, which was so sweet and inclusive; it immediately made me feel like an equal, even though this was my first Broadway show. That was extraordinary—it made me rise ten feet off the ground and think, I will do anything for this man—because he respects me, with no real reason to do so. He made it seem like he and I were going to roll up our sleeves and work on this show together."

Fosse's sleeves had already been rolled up for a while by then, as he and Roger Hirson started revising the libretto even before auditions were completed. The director had truly made his qualms known during a developmental reading in Texas, where Stephen Schwartz was also present. "I think they just put together a group of actors who were down there, to read it through," says Schwartz. "Stuart and Bob and I met afterwards, and I remember that Bob had a dark look on his face; he was very clear about how much trouble we were in and how much work needed to be done. And I remember feeling very crestfallen. That was the beginning of the tension between us about the material and the tone of the show."

An early draft annotated by the director reveals some of his first reactions and inclinations. The script still begins with the Old Man pulling a caravan onstage, but the words "Lights" and "Hand" are written and underlined on top of the first page, as if Fosse were perhaps already working out the soon-to-be-famous opening image of a flurry of gesticulating hands, belonging to the Players, appearing to gleam against a pitch-black background—a trick that would test the ingenuity of lighting designer Jules Fisher and set designer Tony Walton. A few pages later, where Pippin is set to launch into "Corner of the Sky," the director has scrawled "Bows and flows" above the title—the first words of "Both Sides Now," Joni Mitchell's classic take on innocence lost. Schwartz has cited the song as a favorite and notes that Judy Collins's hit recording of it, arranged by

Joshua Rifkin and included on Collins's 1967 album *Wildflowers*, would inspire the orchestration for *Pippin*'s "Morning Glow"—an ensemble number led by Pippin after he kills his father and assumes the role of king—with its prominent harpsichord suggesting both yearning and whimsy. Fosse may have sensed these qualities in Pippin's "I Want" number as well, or he may have been gently mocking the composer, or both.

There are also signs in Fosse's notes of what Schwartz considers the director's crudeness—where Charles calls Lewis an ass at one point, the suffix "hole" was added—and of his special fondness for a certain principal character who was still in gestation, with "Leading Player" written in several times. The introduction of that character and its evolution into a master of ceremonies as well as Pippin's friend and foil would be the keys to reshaping Schwartz and Hirson's musical into what Ostrow approvingly referred to in his memoir as "an anachronistic, cynical burlesque." Ostrow has since used the term "vaudeville," a fair enough substitution, as Fosse drew on both of these interwoven traditions. Fosse himself would describe his vision for *Pippin* to *After Dark* as "a little burlesque. I think it's strong entertainment with satiric overtones." From Ostrow's perspective, "Fosse didn't trust the show, so he kept sending it up, making fun of it."

In a version of the script dated March 20, 1972, the Old Man and the caravan are already gone, as is Hirson's original reference to Peregrinus, the Greek philosopher who had lit himself on fire—though a Player carrying a lit torch jumps onstage briefly near the beginning as the Leading Player promises the audience "a climax never before seen on a public stage." The latter materializes first as "a pair of hands, beckoning seductively to the audience." He then steers the Players through "Magic to Do," urging onlookers to "Journey, journey to a spot ex-/-citing, mystic and exotic/Journey through our anecdotic revue." The song had by now matured into a rousing production number—its driving piano chords, both warm and piquant, nodding immediately to Carole King—that Fosse would milk for all its soulfulness and sex. Schwartz had also expanded and revised "Glory," originally an exchange between Charles and Pippin, and "Simple Joys," because more suitable vehicles for Vereen's talents were required.

The basic plot elements of *Pippin* would remain in place, but Fosse was able to unmoor the characters from the trappings of medieval life and legend. The setting would be cheekily listed in the program as "780 and thereabouts" in "The Holy Roman Empire and Thereabouts." As Rubinstein explains it, "The kid I was playing was supposed to be somebody plucked from an audience by this troupe of malevolent Players, and they promised him that they would make him become extraordinary enough to be remembered for all time, if he followed their directions. He was to portray the role of Pippin in their show, called *Pippin.* Their secret goal was for him to commit suicide in public by immolating himself at the end, and their method of driving him to that point was this crazy musical show in which he would take part, get immersed, lose his sense of self, and 'become' this Pippin character, who would be in such despair and depression by the final moments that he would see the option of becoming memorable by going up in flames on a public stage as a worthy way to achieve immortality."

In the script that would be used opening night, October 23, scenes are titled to reflect the protagonist's journey. "The Opening" establishes the musical-within-a-musical structure; after performing "Magic to Do," the Players dangle elements of Pippin's early life and rumors, and the Leading Player introduces the young man playing him ("He may be a little nervous. . . . This is first time playing the role"), who sings "Corner of the Sky." "Home" unites the young man playing the prince with the Players portraying his father, Fastrada, and Lewis as they enact welcoming Pippin home from his studies in Padua. (There is a brief number called "Welcome Home," which would be cut from the revised book.) Roles established, the internal drama gets under way: In "War," Pippin is schooled in battle by Charles ("War Is a Science"), tries his hand at it ("Glory"), and finds no thrill even in victory. ("I thought there'd be more plumes," he says.) In "The Flesh," the story takes Pippin to the country, where the Leading Player and the troupe member playing Pippin's grandmother suggest more decadent paths to self-fulfillment ("Simple Joys," "No Time at All").

A bevy of babes conveniently materializes ("With You"), but a subsequent orgy leaves Pippin feeling hollow, and in "Revolution," the story returns to the palace, where Pippin sows the seeds of revolt, then proceeds to a monastery in Arles, where Pippin murders Charles and assumes the crown ("Morning Glow"). When being monarch proves too taxing, Pippin announces, "I'd like to give my father his job back," and the Leading Player grants his wish, as the Old Man had in earlier drafts. Restored to life, Charles accepts his son's apology on one condition: "Only don't let it happen again." Pippin then receives "Encouragement" from the Leading Player by way of a musical pep talk ("On the Right Track"), and the setting shifts to "The Hearth," Catherine's estate, where the Player cast as Catherine tries to catch Pippin's interest ("Kind of Woman"). "The troupe had picked her up while traveling from village to village, and her job is to turn the young man playing Pippin off to married life, to home life," explains Betty Buckley, who began playing the role in the spring of 1973. It's a comically aggressive song; after singing her own praises in "Kind of Woman," Catherine assures Pippin, "I'll understand if I'm not you're kind of woman/ Anyone can make one terrible mistake."

Pippin grows frustrated with simple life, tending to the farm animals on the widow's modest estate ("Extraordinary'), but is drawn to her—and she to him, increasingly, much to the Leading Player's annoyance. Catherine and Pippin make love ("Love Song"), and he even grows fond of her son, Theo, tending to the boy when his beloved duck becomes mortally ill. (There is a short song called "Prayer for a Duck"—omitted, along with "Welcome Home," from the cast album.) Pippin remains convinced that he is destined for greater things, though, and Catherine eventually finds herself abandoned ("I Guess I'll Miss the Man"). Still unfulfilled, Pippin is now ready for "The Finale," in which the Leading Player and his followers finally reveal their true intentions for him, as the Player with the torch reappears and sets a dummy ablaze inside a firebox. When Catherine and Theo arrive and Pippin decides, rationally enough, to return to them instead, the Leading Player berates the three of them and orders the production shut down—demanding the lights be turned off, kicking the musicians out of the pit, and ensuring that the characters now seeking ordinary lives are stripped of their wigs, costumes, and makeup.

Vereen's own concept for the Leading Player and his minions involved time travel. "In my mind, I was leading a band of murderers who were immortal beings," he says. "We would go from century to century and keep finding a Pippin, and keep leading him down that same path." Vereen remembers being taken aback by his scarcity of lines when the cast did its first read-through: "I'm looking at the script, and it says, 'Enter Lewis,' 'Enter Catherine'—enter this character and that character, and there was nothing there for me. And Bob is sitting right there across from me, laughing, cracking up, while I'm thinking, 'Oh, my God—I've taken a dud.' When everybody took lunch, I just stayed in my seat, and Bob said, 'Don't worry—we'll fix it.'"

As Ostrow recalls, some of that fixing took shape with neither Hirson nor Schwartz in the room where it happened, at least initially. From the producer's memoir: "Throughout the next few months Bob came to our home in Pound Ridge, each visit with a gorgeous new babe, to 'fix' (his word) the show. . . . What we discovered worked best for *Pippin* were anachronisms. Anything that could lampoon the earnestness of the book (and deflate Schwartz's ego) would delight Fosse." Schwartz, who had socialized a bit with Ostrow before Fosse came on board—having dinner together with their wives on occasion, for instance—muses, "I think Stuart sort of fell under Bob's spell a bit. He kind of wanted to be Bob, I think. That said, with the experience I now have, realizing who I was at the time and who Bob Fosse was and how Broadway shows are made, I definitely understand better that when there was a dispute, he had to more or less always side with Bob."

Hirson's writing prior to Fosse's involvement was not as self-serious as Ostrow's comments might suggest. There are elements of the absurdist humor that helped attract Schwartz in their 1970 draft, such as the talking head of a Visigoth soldier decapitated by Charles's army (identified simply as "Head"), which Fosse kept in. The comedy is hardly prudish, either; Berthe, catching up with Pippin in the country, wants to know not only if Fastrada's hair is thinning but also "if that handsome stable boy still walks across the front court at dawn every morning with his codpiece bursting." (The Broadway script retains another reference to a "good-looking priest" but nothing about this other hunk, curiously, or his protruding pouch.) And the Pippin in this early version actually shows a sharper wit than he would when the production opened. In his first exchange with Fastrada and Lewis, Pippin's conniving stepmother tries to bond with him, cooing, "I would like to get the benefit of your education." He drily responds, "I'm sure there's nothing I could teach you, Fastrada."

Some of Schwartz's biggest misgivings about the Fosse-ized *Pippin*, in fact, had to do with how the director weakened the protagonist, "making him more passive and less witty, taking lines that were active and engaging away from him by either cutting them or giving them to others." One punch line in Hirson's early draft—where Fastrada boasts about Lewis's posture and Pippin quips, "He's a straight stander. No question about that"—was given to Charles and even drawn out slightly for maximum exposure to, "Oh, yes, Lewis is a straight stander. There's no question about that." One of Pippin's similarly loaded retorts to his brother was cut from another early draft and replaced with Charles asking the audience, in reference to Lewis, "Why do I always get nauseous when he calls me 'Father'?" Fosse also inserted sexual innuendo into Lewis's relationship with Fastrada, who at one point engages her son in what the stage directions describe as a "slightly Oedipal" dance, then sticks a consoling thumb into his mouth after Charles disparages him again.

More often, of course, it was the Leading Player whose role grew in ways that, Schwartz feels, deflected attention from *Pippin*'s intended hero—and reflected Fosse's own increasingly jaded take on show business and fear of seeming in the slightest bit dewy-eyed. In a rehearsal script dated August 7, Vereen's character details preparations for Charles's campaign against the Visigoths in a speech that had originally been Pippin's. By the time the book was finalized, wry interjections had been strategically added at emotionally charged moments, such as when Pippin tells his father, in the second scene, that he wants to be "dedicated to something . . . with all my heart and soul," and the Leading Player brightly quips, "That's a nice thought." A couple of scenes later, after Pippin declares that "peace and justice must be restored" after his father's brutal reign, the Leading Player interrupts him with a twist on a previously written line. Taking off the prince's hat and replacing it with a "Castro type" chapeau—one of those anachronisms that presumably tickled Ostrow—the Leading Player proclaims, "You're a revolutionary . . . and Baby, you're beautiful."

In a more glaring adjustment—one that may surprise *Pippin* fans who didn't see Fosse's production—a substantial portion of the finale, sung by Pippin and included on the album and subsequent stagings under other directors, was cut. The piece begins with the Leading Player and his minions urging Pippin to "think about the sun"—that is, the triumph he'll achieve through fiery self-destruction. The performance swells to a rocking peak before their voices fall silent, the orchestra pulls back, and Pippin steps in, singing, in a sudden epiphany, "I'm not a river or a giant bird/That soars to the sea/And if I'm never tied to anything/I'll never be free." At that point, Fosse had the Leading Player step in, but on the recording and in other productions, Pippin continues:

> I wanted magic shows and miracles/Mirages to touch
> I wanted such a little thing from life/I wanted so much
> I never came close, my love/We nearly came near
> It never was there/I think it was here
> They showed me crimson, gold, and lavender/A shining parade
> But there's no color I can have on earth/That won't finally fade
> When I wanted worlds to paint/And costumes to wear
> I think it was here/'Cause it never was there

While perusing the opening-night script for the first time in years, Schwartz was reminded that Fosse made a revision in Pippin's first appearance as well, moving his defining promise—"not to waste my life in commonplace, ordinary things"—from before he sings "Corner of the Sky" to after he completes the song and "thus not giving the character time to be set up," in Schwartz's view.

Schwartz's belief that Fosse could be inclined toward "overstating concepts and underestimating the audience's intelligence" was also reaffirmed by a fresh read. The composer points to Pippin's scenes with Catherine, "like, where she says, 'Pippin, I really want you to stay. I love you. I love you,'" as he appears to be giving up on domesticity. "That line is so ham-fisted. Ironically, it did the opposite of what Bob wanted; it made the moment sentimental." In contrast, regarding the Leading Player's fraught and sometimes flip exchanges with Catherine, Schwartz says, "I've come to feel those are necessary, because that's where the show starts to turn: There's a conflict between those characters that gets stronger and stronger."

Rubinstein doesn't recall being bothered by specific cuts or edits. "It was more about my feeling that the audience required Pippin to have more of a presence," he says, and that the revisions were chipping away at that presence. "During the first forty-five minutes of the show, there were all these fantastic numbers, beautifully lit and costumed and choreographed and brilliantly performed by Ben and Irene and this ensemble of the best dancers on Broadway. It was all terrific, but I felt Pippin sort of disappearing, and when he came back into focus, I no longer felt that connection with the audience. Pippin was the protagonist, the person with whom the audience should relate."

For all of Fosse's emphasis on emotional expression, moreover, his direction to Rubinstein "had to do mostly with staging, timing, and building the momentum and look and spectacle of the entire piece," the actor says. "His work with the dancers and Ben and Leland was obviously mostly about the movement in their big numbers, and the underlying imagery and subtext for the body language. But his work with me was mostly about orchestrating the character into the scope of the whole panoply of the show, not about the actor-type questions of back-story and motivations. Pippin's agenda and desires, his ambitions and disappointments, were all out in the open, sung about or spoken about in very direct terms. He was not hiding anything. Not a lot to discover. A lot to put forward, and a difficult role to play for that reason. That and the high notes! But in many ways, Pippin's path is as clear as a beacon."

Rubinstein has come to believe it was partly his own "greenness" that reduced Pippin's impact in the original production. "Into six, twelve, fourteen months of the run, there were at least a dozen occurrences—each more humiliating than the previous one—where I'd walk out onto 46th Street after the show, and one of the fans waiting there would say to me, 'I heard the only reason to see the show was Ben Vereen—but I thought you were just as good as he was!' Because I was undercooked, and I'm sure

Bob put me in the role partly because of that. I wasn't a great or slick singer, and I didn't have that confidence as a performer. Then I slowly but surely realized that even in those early scenes, where I'm basically shoved to the side to make room for the big dance numbers, there was more I could do—not by trying to steal scenes but by something more intangible, by just being really present. Then Ben and I came to be on equal terms: He was playing the flashy, devil-like character, and I was playing the young man at the center of the story, to whom the audience related and on whom they pinned their hopes."

Many have also discerned shades of Lucifer in the Leading Player, and Vereen's own description of the character as a mass murderer—an immortal one to boot—does little to discourage the analogy. But for the famously sunny performer, at least, the reference suggests something less sinister—more the little guy perched on your shoulder than the big guy vying for your soul. "I saw the Leading Player as part of Pippin's consciousness," Vereen explains. "You can call it the Devil, or call it the Other, or call it exuberance. I was that voice inside his mind, going, 'Try this.' 'Go here.' 'Go there.'" That line from the final scene that evoked Fellini for Schwartz—"Why, we're right inside your heads"—clearly resonated with the actor as well. "The dark side of it really started to develop as John Rubinstein and I played off each other," Vereen says, but he adds that his Leading Player never bore Pippin any malice: "He was Pippin's best friend, and he wanted what he thought was best for his friend. He thought that if Pippin committed suicide, the whole world would know his name, and admire him."

Fosse referred Vereen to more terrestrial role models, who had or would achieve immortality through different means. "Bob said, 'I want you to look at cats like Bill 'Bojangles' Robinson and Jimmy Slyde and (Charles) 'Honi' Coles"—some of the many Black performers he had idolized, tap dancers renowned for their showmanship as well as their technical prowess. If *Pippin* was to follow a troupe of entertainers so magnetic that young men had literally died for them, and the Leading Player was to be the troupe's star and dominant force, the person cast in that role needed to be the ultimate showman; he also had to embody show business at both its most sinister and its most enthralling. "Is this what you want?" he would ask in the final scene, as Pippin, Catherine, and Theo were stripped down to their underclothes. Then Vereen's character would make his pitch to the audience: "I know there are many of you out there . . . extraordinary people . . . who would gladly trade your ordinary lives for the opportunity to do one perfect act—one grand finale."

Fosse understood this charming and threatening creature intuitively, and as he and Vereen refined the character, it would remind reviewers of celebrated semi-villains from *Porgy and Bess*'s Sportin' Life to the Emcee in *Cabaret*. Virtually all agreed, of course, that Vereen's performance was in a league of its own—so much so that fifty years later, when the Broadway revival was cast, it factored into the decision to place a woman in the role. Schwartz explains, "We came to feel that the memory of Ben was still so strong that it would be impossible for a male actor to compete with it. No matter how terrific he would be, everyone would say, 'Well, he's no Ben Vereen.'"

That Vereen's breakout roles on Broadway were fundamentally antagonists—the ultimate antagonist in the case of Judas, his character in *Jesus Christ Superstar*—has raised some questions in recent years. Will Detlefsen, a Drama League fellowship-winning director who has assisted such acclaimed contemporary artists as Alex Timbers and Rachel Chavkin, considered the role of race in productions of *Pippin* while preparing to cast a 2022 staging at Five Towns College in New York's Dix Hills. "Our choreographer is Black," Detlefsen says, "and we were thinking, 'Why has the Leading Player consistently been Black and Pippin consistently been white?'" (While not true in all stagings, this has been the case in many, including both Broadway productions.) Detlefsen, who is white and in his early thirties, proposes, "The story is a hero's journey in a way, and the hero tends to be a white guy, and to have the character who is essentially the villain be a Black man, coming from the shadows"—appearing out of darkness in the musical's opening scene—"kind of bothers me."

For Vereen, who was born in North Carolina while Jim Crow laws were still in effect and came of age at the height of the civil rights movement in the 1960s, race was less of an issue in the context of the musical. "We were working actors," he says, referring to himself and Candy Brown, *Pippin*'s only other original Black cast member aside from standby Northern J. Calloway. "There was a color line, but we showed up, and by showing up, we made it more likely that the next time there would be more of us." Fosse, he emphasizes, was an ally. "As a matter of fact, after doing *Pippin*, he was shooting *Lenny*, and he called me into a screening; there's a scene where Dustin Hoffman"—playing the controversial comedian Lenny Bruce—"says, 'Nigger, nigger, nigger,' and, 'kike, kike, kike,' and so on. And Bob said, 'I don't even *think* in words like that; will this offend people?' I said, no—you've got to break the offending. Words have power, so break that power. He was very conscious. He didn't want to be a part of the problem; he wanted to be a part of the solution."

The other actors cast as Players saw their roles buffed up, subtly but surely, as rehearsals progressed at Broadway Arts at 1755 Broadway between 56th Street and 57th Street. The space, which had previously housed the June Taylor Studios and has since been replaced by another office building, would become Fosse's stomping grounds of choice from that point on; an exact replica would be created three feet off the ground when *All That Jazz* was filmed at Astoria Studios. "It was tacky, and it smelled a lot," recalls lighting designer Jules Fisher, "but Bob liked it; it was like home to him." (The director had favored Variety Arts on 46th Street until that establishment was destroyed in a fire in 1968.)

The work day stretched from 10 a.m. until 6 p.m., with a one hour lunch break, with principals returning between 7 and 10 p.m. whenever needed, at which point Doby and/or Louise Quick might clean up ensemble choreography while Fosse focused on scene work. By August, Fosse had put a note between the title page of the script and the beginning of Act One, reading, "All members of the company will appear in the Prologue and the Finale." By opening night, they were actively abetting their leader in setting up Pippin's story and trying to lure him into the fire at the end. Ostrow recalls that when the Leading Player introduced Charlemagne as "a giant on the battlefield and in the bedroom," Reinking was appointed to repeat the latter bit of flattery, then make a gesture indicating, "'Well, so-so.' And it got a huge laugh."

Musical numbers also became a forum for the Players to deliver a wink and a nudge, sometimes to Schwartz's chagrin. "In 'War Is a Science,' one of the things that bugged me was having the chorus break it up with

'Yuk, yuk' and 'Doodah'"—little exclamations sprinkled inside verses, disrupting the rhythmic flow to remind us that this was all show biz, folks. (Some of the deliberate tics, like "Ha-cha" and "Skidoo," would be more smoothly inserted in *Chicago*'s "All That Jazz.") "It was meant to be a sort of Gilbert and Sullivan patter song for Eric Berry, but instead there was, again, this pulling the rug out from under things to show the audience that Bob was smarter—or at least more cynical—than they were." Similarly, Schwartz was less than thrilled by Fosse's decision to have a trio of female Players lend conspicuously cheeky backing vocals to "Kind of Woman," the Bacharach-inspired waltz that introduces us to Catherine.

Generally, though, Schwartz did not feel hampered as a composer or lyricist, even if Fosse continued to tease him about his obsessive devotion to rhyme. (Notably, despite once approaching Stephen Sondheim about a project, the director never worked with that most fastidious of rhymers, even though they were just a few years apart in age and similarly prolific between the 1950s and 1980s.) But both Fosse and Ostrow remained happy with the young composer's creative output. "Even when he was furious about the show, he never failed to come up with songs when we asked for them, and I really admired that," says Ostrow.

One of those songs evolved partly out of Rubinstein's concern that Pippin was being overshadowed not only by the Leading Player but also by the dynamic choreography, little of which involved his character. From the start, he was front and center in the "Gisela ballet," the dance number that began during "With You," a rapturous ballad that Schwartz had originally meant for Pippin to sing to one woman during what became the orgy scene. In the sequence, which took its name from the character Pippin had dallied with in an earlier script, "I was singing while being sat on by all these gorgeous women—Jennifer Nairn-Smith and Annie Reinking and Pam Sousa and Candy Brown and Kathy Doby. They were sitting on my back and pulling at me and turning me upside down while I was trying to sing this song with a goddamned high A flat. Which was wonderful—I loved it."

The number, for which props included a giant keyhole for Pippin to leer through and an opium pipe for him to smoke, culminated with male dancers lifting and lowering him above the women—after they had frolicked with each other—in a simulation of intercourse. Veteran theater critic Peter Filichia, who traveled to Washington for the pre-Broadway tryout, will "never forget seeing Rubinstein as Pippin accidentally put his hand on a chorus girl's breast, and said, 'I've found it,'" before the full revelry got under way. "We know he hasn't, that there's more to life than that, pleasant as sex can be. But then four people held him parallel to the stage—one by one leg, one by the other leg, one by one arm, one by the other arm—as one woman rolled under him. They lowered him down and rolled him back up again—almost like a pants presser—and she rolled away, and then a new girl came and they pulled him down again. It was a phenomenal way of showing mindless sex."

Rubinstein's actual movement in the dance routine—which ended with our naive hero struggling to shake off these lascivious strangers, at once overwhelmed and unimpressed ("I feel empty and vacant," he complained to the Leading Player)—was, nonetheless, pretty rudimentary, and the actor, like his character, began to yearn for something more. "All these brilliant, amazing dance numbers were going by, and Pippin was just sitting there, sort of left out in the cold. I told Bob this in rehearsal, and he didn't disagree with me. He said, 'Well, what do you think we should do?' I told him that he had me playing the lead in a Bob Fosse musical, but I never got to dance, and he said, 'But John, you can't dance.' And I said, 'I know—but that's your problem.'"

The solution was "On the Right Track," sung—and danced—by the Leading Player and Pippin during the "Encouragement" scene, just before Catherine enters the story and while Pippin is despairing over his latest brief, unfulfilling venture, in serving as king. "It was originally going to be another number where I sat cross-legged and watched Ben Vereen do yet another amazing dance, click his fingers at me, and then do a split at the end," Rubinstein muses. "But Bob came up with the idea that the Leading Player invites Pippin to dance with him, to show him how excellent things can be. And Pippin desperately tries to be as hip and cool as the Leading Player—he snaps his fingers and does his pirouettes, but at the end he just isn't up to it. As indicated by the opening night script, Pippin then says, "Oh, I'll never find it . . . never . . . never . . . never! Shit!" "I'm sure that was Bob's idea," Rubinstein says of the expletive, but adds, "That lightened it, made it more of a self-aware comment, rather than a cry of melodramatic despair. And that made it *funny*, which was part of Bob's genius." The number was rehearsed at night: "At six, while everyone else went home, Bob and Ben and I would have dinner and then come back and work on it."

Fosse also had substantial input on the music for "Track," a study in Schwartz's affinity for dramatically evocative shifts in tempo. "The melody is in four but it's based on three notes, so as those notes repeat over and over again the emphasis is on different places," the composer explains. "I associate that with Kander and Ebb, though 'Puttin' on the Ritz,'" by Irving Berlin, "does that too." On the cast recording, it begins with a slow, sexy vamp, then segues from a playfully brisk verse to a steady rock feel, then from an anxious, marching climax to a burst of horns—relief in the form of pure showbiz flash. Initially, "Bob thought it was so tightly written that it didn't give him much room for choreography," Schwartz notes. "I remember him saying, 'What I'd like you to do is go through the lyrics and cut every single word you can possibly cut—just don't lose any music. Leave empty spaces, and I'll fill them with moves.' That's why the lyrics wound up having this sort of jaggedy construction, which I now find unusual and imaginative. That's one example of a way Bob had a positive influence on the score."

Then there was "Glory," repurposed for Vereen as a production number in which the Leading Player steers the company in singing the praises of war as Charles leads his soldiers into bloody battle—an obvious nod to the ongoing disaster in Vietnam. Working with orchestrator Ralph Burns, a frequent Fosse collaborator, and dance arranger John Berkman, the director retained the influence of Carl Orff's booming cantata *Carmina Burana* intermittently, but the verses became slinky and jazzy, paving the way for the Manson Trio interlude, for which Schwartz added ironically bright instrumental music—"I believe it was played on an RMI electric piano, which was a very common sound in pop recordings of the early seventies," Schwartz says—to suit Fosse's choreography. "Johnny Berkman was hugely influential with songs like 'Glory,' or the dance section of 'With You'"—another segment that would require Schwartz to depart from his original concept, in that case under protest.

In naming the Manson Trio, Fosse drew a bright line under the ugliest implications of Vereen's character. Rehearsals for *Pippin* started about a month before the third anniversary of the Los Angeles killing spree that took the lives of actress Sharon Tate, her unborn child, and several friends as well as businessman Leno LaBianca and his wife, Rosemary. Charles Manson and his followers had just been sentenced to death in 1971, though that penalty was commuted to life in prison when a ruling in California declared it unconstitutional the following year. In their slavish devotion, the musical's troupe of Players was, the director was plainly suggesting, not unlike the Manson Family, or any cult that seeks to convert or destroy outsiders in order to satisfy a twisted, charismatic leader. Kings and presidents were not the only men capable of heinous abuses of power.

"Simple Joys," another Vereen showcase—opening "The Flesh," the scene in which "With You" and "No Time at All" are also performed—retained the textures that Schwartz had envisioned for it. "I didn't write 'Simple Joys' on guitar, but I always meant it to be a guitar song," Schwartz says of the calypso-laced number, sung after Pippin flees his father's kingdom and battlefield. As it turned out, John Mineo, one of the dancers, could play the instrument a bit; thus his Player became a musician, as other male Players would portray, within the musical, a nobleman (Gene Foote), a beggar (Richard Korthaze), a peasant (Paul Solen), and a field marshall (Roger Hamilton, who did double duty as "Head"). "The idea was that Johnny could come out and play while Ben was singing. With a guitar, you can hold a chord a long time, and it's much more about the rhythm than changing chords and harmonic structure. Johnny also had his guitar during 'No Time at All,' but that was more for show."

The other guitar-driven number in *Pippin*, the wry ballad "I Guess I'll Miss the Man"—sung by Catherine after Pippin leaves her—was inspired in part by Pete Seeger and the Weavers' arrangement of the traditional ballad "I Know Where I'm Going," but also modeled after "What Makes Me Love Him" from *The Diary of Adam of Eve*, the portion of Bock and Harnick's *The Apple Tree* that Schwartz had directed in college. "'What Makes Me Love Him' is simple and folky and sort of stays on one level," says Schwartz, noting that Harnick's lyrics were equally influential: "The character of Eve sings, 'What makes me love him/ It's not his singing/I've heard his singing/It sours the milk/And yet, it's gotten to the point/Where I prefer that kind of milk.' Or, 'And though he knows a multitude of things/They're mostly wrong.' Catherine sings, about Pippin, 'Some men are heroes/Some men outshine the sun/Some men are simple, good men/This man wasn't one.' That kind of humor and that folky, understated approach to a love song were definitely influenced by Bock and Harnick, and by that song in particular."

Another tune that would not have felt out of place on AM radio in the early 1970s, the gently sparkling "Love Song," was actually informed by the subtly shifting time signatures of "Oh, Happy We," the comedic duet between the titular hero of Bernstein's *Candide*—a precursor to *Pippin*'s title character, given their shared idealism and how both were systematically stripped of it—and his frivolous bride. It was one of the last two numbers Schwartz crafted for the show, the other being "Extraordinary," Pippin's jaunty lament about doing everyday chores on Catherine's estate ("Patching the roof and pitching the hay/Is not my idea of a perfect day"). The latter song nodded to Fanny Brice via Jule Styne: "In its structure, 'Extraordinary' basically follows that of 'I'm the Greatest Star,' the 'I Want' song from *Funny Girl*. It's laid-back at first, and then when Pippin gets to the bridge it kind of ramps up, and after the bridge it's much more driving."

Again, inspired by his predecessors, Schwartz used changes in tempo and meter to theatrical effect. He would do it once more for *Pippin*'s finale, using what he calls "the 'Day by Day' trick"—segueing, as that hit song from *Godspell* did, from a breezy waltz to a 4/4 time signature, then adding muscle to a simple but catchy refrain by layering in different vocal parts and percussive elements until the number acquired a gospel-like intensity. "Morning Glow," the Act One finale before *Pippin* became a one-act show, was similarly majestic, with the orchestra and chorus gradually swelling behind Pippin to reach a booming urgency reminiscent of *Candide*'s glorious "Make Our Garden Grow."

Whatever cynicism Ostrow and Schwartz observed in Fosse's approach—for better, from the producer's perspective; for worse, from the composer's—it would not detract from the emotional punch of such moments. As always, the director was passionate about his work—despite his ambivalence, in this case, about *the* work—and that ardor carried over into his relationships with cast members, dancers in particular. And since *Pippin* was a relatively small company, those relationships became especially tight, both among the performers and between them and Fosse. "All of us were close, and we're still close," notes Candy Brown. "When Ann [Reinking] passed away," in December 2020, "everybody got on the phone with everybody else. Usually that sort of thing, that loyalty, starts at the top." And over just a few months of rehearsals, it forged a family—less scary than the one its members would play onstage, happily—that was as eclectic as it would be enduring.

CHAPTER SIX

Twelve Players in Search of an Auteur

GROWING UP IN THE 1950S IN JOHNSON CITY, TENNESSEE, GENE FOOTE was not permitted to take dance lessons. "My mother was a nurse, and there were two professions that men did *not* go into," he explains. "One was being a nurse, and the other was dancing. I was the best dancer in school, always; at school dances girls would want to partner with me. But I never had any training." After a year at East Tennessee State, Foote grew restless; his mom insisted that if he wasn't studying, he needed to get a job and start paying her rent. He figured that leaving home was a better option. "So the next day she just packed me a lunch, and I got out on the highway and stuck out my thumb and got a ride to Washington D.C. Then two girls picked me up on their way to the roller derby in Elizabeth, New Jersey, and dropped me off at the Elizabeth Street Ferry, which took me to New York. I arrived on April 1, 1956. It was Easter Sunday, and it was snowing."

So began one of the disparate journeys that led ten dancers, accompanied by two alternates, to be cast as Players in *Pippin*—chorus members in a sense, but with distinct presences that they crafted largely by themselves, with their director's encouragement. Several of the men and women, including Foote, had worked with Fosse before; most would work with him again, on projects ranging from his next original Broadway musical, *Chicago*, to his final one, 1986's *Big Deal*. To be a "Fosse dancer" was a mark of artistic and personal merit, as he valued hard work and loyalty—not in the sycophantic sense, but the quality of inspiring and affirming trust—almost as much as talent. And that talent had to extend beyond impeccable technique. "Our direction for the opening number of *Pippin* was, 'Make love to the audience,'" Foote recalls. "For the opening of *Chicago*, it was, 'Confront the audience with murder in your eyes, and dare them to look at you.' For one movement he gave us in *Chicago*, it was, 'You're wiping the blood off your hands, on the mirror.' All dancing was acting, telling a story or communicating a feeling to the audience."

Foote's original intention when he left Tennessee, in fact, had been to pursue an acting career. But after settling on the Lower East Side, he started dating a young man who was studying at the American Ballet Theatre. While they were dancing one night at a "cha-cha palace," as precursors to discos were called, Foote caught the attention of the ballerina Nora Kaye, who knew his companion. Kaye introduced Foote to her husband, the dancer and director Herbert Ross, and their friends: Jerome Robbins and Stephen Sondheim. "I said, 'What are y'all doin' here?' Because I still had my accent," Foote explains, wincing slightly. "And Jerome Robbins said he was doing research for a new musical called *East Side Story*—that's what the title was then. He said to me, 'Are you a dancer?' And I said, 'I love to dance, but I've never had any lessons.' And he said to me, 'You should dance.' Jerome Robbins said that. To me."

And so at the advanced age of nineteen, Foote started classes at the American Ballet Theatre, where he progressed quickly. Within a year, he was doing eight shows a week in summer stock; he then met up with Robbins again, this time at an audition for the London company of *West Side Story*. "He said to me, 'Gene, I'd like to have you in this show so much, but you can't talk it'—I still had that accent." Robbins suggested he make contact with another renowned choreographer who was trying his hand at directing, Michael Kidd, and Foote landed in the company of a touring production of *Lil Abner*. Spots on Broadway followed in the companies of *The Unsinkable Molly Brown* and *Bajour* (with Leland Palmer—and Michael Bennett—also dancing in the latter), and in 1963, Foote was cast in the first touring company for *How to Succeed in Business without Really Trying*, with Fosse overseeing the "musical staging." In truth, he had been tapped to oversee the choreographer, Hugh Lambert, a dancer who had assisted Fosse favorite Carol Haney on *Flower Drum Song* but had not yet choreographed a Broadway show himself (and wouldn't in the future).

"We were really Bob's first company on *How to Succeed*," Foote says, "because he had been called in on the Broadway production. It was an amazing experience. I learned that when Bob was doing a show, you had to audition for him constantly, because he needed to decide who was going to do each dance section." After a year, Foote was inspired by Fosse to take time off to study drama at the Neighborhood Playhouse; he was then hired for the original Broadway cast of *Sweet Charity*. Five years later, in 1971, Gwen Verdon called Foote about *Liza with a Z.* "I said, 'Unfortunately, Gwen, I am doing *Once Upon a Mattress* with Carol Burnett on television, and there's a three-day overlap.' And Bob said if I couldn't go to the first day of rehearsal, he couldn't use me." When *Pippin* auditions were announced, Foote was reluctant, fearing he had alienated the director. Hours after the Equity dance audition, though, he got a call from Louise Quick. "She said, 'Where were you today? Bob was looking for you.' And I said that I thought if he were interested in me I might hear from him. And she said, 'Well, you're hearing.'"

Candy Brown had never heard of Fosse before he hired her for *Liza with a Z.* "I was impressed with him only because he was married to Gwen Verdon," Brown admits. "I had seen her on *The Ed Sullivan Show*. I wasn't one of those kids who grew up with a burning desire to be in this business. I knew I liked music, liked musicals, loved to dance. But I wanted to be a schoolteacher." Brown had studied dance as a young child in Jamaica, Queens, at a studio run by Bernice Johnson, who years earlier, as Brown tells it, "broken the color line" at Harlem's storied Cotton Club "by being browner, not light-skinned like the other ladies. We did ballet, tap, acrobatics, modern, everything. For a period, if there was a Black person in a Broadway musical, nine out of ten times that person had come out of Bernice Johnson's school." (Ben Vereen had also been a student.) Verdon's husband would in fact pique Brown's interest by casting two Black women in *Liza*: "Back in those days, they would pick one Black girl and one Black boy, just to say, 'Hey, we're cool.' We called it the token era. Bob only needed five girls, so when he chose Loretta Abbott, who had been an Alvin Ailey dancer, I figured that was the end of my chances. Then the next day, I got a call, which I thought was pretty terrific."

As a military kid, Brown had been forced to take a sabbatical in her dance studies: "I spent middle school in Okinawa, and I was more advanced than the other kids my age who were taking dance." Her family then relocated to Minnesota, where she dabbled in choreography during high school. "But it wasn't until my first year of college, when I took a modern dance class to fulfill a phys ed requirement, that I realized how much I really love it. That's when I decided to go back to New York, to pursue a career." Lessons with Ailey associate Thelma Hill, Jack Cole protégé Matt Mattox, and disco visionary JoJo Smith followed—along with Colombia-born modern dance choreographer Eleo Pomare, "who really gave me strong [Martha] Graham technique—then chorus parts in *Hello, Dolly!* and *Purlie*. Philip Rose, the latter show's producer and co-librettist, "wanted me to take over for Melba Moore" in the female lead, Brown recalls. "I was like, 'I can't sing like that.' So he paid for me to take singing lessons, until I finally told him, 'Look, you can't make Aretha Franklin out of Phyllis Diller.'" But she has continued to study voice "on and off—though I would never do a concert." Fosse provided an early vote of confidence: 'I was the only one out of the ten dancers from *Liza with a Z* that he called in for *Pippin*," Brown says.

No one in *Pippin*'s cast had worked more closely with Fosse prior to the show than Kathryn Doby, who did not even have to audition for the production. The Hungarian-born dancer, who had arrived in Canada during her native country's revolution in 1956, then moved to New York, was first hired by the choreographer for an exclusive six-month, four-city tour of *Little Me* featuring original Broadway star Sid Caesar as well as Leland Palmer. Both Doby and Palmer next worked with Fosse on *Pleasures and Palaces* before its Broadway run was aborted; prior to that, Doby had put in time as a June Taylor Dancer, one of sixteen women who performed on *The Jackie Gleason Show*. "It was very prestigious, but I was miserable. I hated being one of sixteen little machines, in sync with everyone else, week after week."

Doby had studied ballet since early childhood. "I had Russian training," in the Vaganova method favored in Hungary, a Communist nation at the time. "But once I got to New York, I realized that wouldn't help me, because I was not built for classical dancing; I wasn't limber enough, and I didn't have the extensions." She studied with Luigi and, like Brown, found a particularly valuable teacher in Mattox: "Since his training was in the Jack Cole school, in isolations, that made it easier for me to pick up Bob's style. Also, as an assistant, I was able to break down his movements, to really show what part of the body was supposed to move. Because Bob moved differently than anyone else."

After performing in the stage and film versions of *Sweet Charity*, Doby began work on the screen adaptation of *Cabaret* as both a Kit Kat dancer and Fosse's chief assistant; her dual service obviously proved to his satisfaction since she was asked to repeat it for *Pippin*. (*Cabaret* proved a personal boon to Doby as well: She met her future husband Wolfgang Glattes, an assistant director on the film; the couple has been together for more than fifty years.) She would later be Fosse's assistant for *Chicago* and *Dancin'*, though Doby performed in neither show. She did turn up in *All That Jazz*, for which she and Foote were assistant choreographers, playing a character named after her—an assistant choreographer to Fosse avatar Joe Gideon, played by Roy Scheider.

The cast member who went back the furthest with Fosse was Richard Korthaze, whose Broadway credits included both *How to Succeed* and the ill-fated *The Conquering Hero* as well as the *Sweet Charity* film. Korthaze recalls first working with Fosse back in the 1950s, "very briefly in Chicago"—the city, not the musical, which wasn't yet a sparkle in Verdon's eye at the time. "I think it was just some television show, but he recognized me when I auditioned for him again." Like Foote, Korthaze had begun his dance studies late, "though I was always a good social dancer in school." He had actually been a voice major at Chicago Musical College (since renamed the Chicago College of Performing Arts) when a fellow student, on returning from a round of auditions in New York, alerted him that vocalists trying out for shows were also assigned dance combinations. Korthaze became a student of Edna L. McRae, a leading force in the Chicago ballet community. "She gave me wonderful basic training in ballet and character dancing, and that gave me the background I needed to audition in New York."

Where his colleagues emphasize how much Fosse's style departed from classic ballet, Korthaze notes, "Bob liked people who had a basic ballet background, because it meant that they were able to isolate parts of their bodies and their legs and feet very well," even if they were not accustomed to incorporating the kinds of isolations that Fosse favored into performance. "He wanted to see how you could move in different styles, so that when he came up with something that wasn't strictly Broadway you could adapt. He wanted dancers who weren't limited to any certain type of movement, whether that was ballet or anything else."

This was certainly true for at least three of the four female dancers whose professional and personal relationships with Fosse began with *Pippin*. Reinking would become the most visible, not only as Fosse's lover and muse but also as an artist who segued from starring roles in high-profile stage and screen projects to an acclaimed career as choreographer in her own right. A Seattle native, Reinking "had a wonderful mix of Russian and English ballet training" in her hometown, according to her teenage beau and lifelong friend William Whitener, including lessons with Ballet Russe de Monte Carlo alumna and local legend Gwenn Barker. She was a Ford Foundation scholarship student at the San Francisco Ballet School before landing a summer residency with the Joffrey Ballet. In an interview shortly before her death in 2020, Reinking recalled how cofounder Robert Joffrey suggested an alternative course. "He'd heard me singing, and I was always a cutup in class," she said in one of her last interviews, for *Broadway World*. "He said, 'You have great personality, you're a good singer, and you pick things up pretty well. I just think you would have a lot more fun if you went on Broadway.'"

Whitener, also a Joffrey student and eventual company member who collaborated with Reinking as artistic director of the Kansas City Ballet and in other works, including Fosse's *Dancin'*, had noticed the same gifts. "We would sing and dance in empty underground parking lots, creating our vision of what a Broadway show must be like. I told her, 'Ann, you should go directly to Broadway.' She dismissed that comment at the time; we were about sixteen—I'm one year younger—and I wasn't Robert Joffrey." Reinking did take part in her high school's musical productions, though, and even landed a spot in a 1965 staging of *Bye Bye Birdie* at the

Seattle Opera House, starring Tom Poston. During the Joffrey residency, Whitener remembers, "We had our own little talent shows after classes, where we would gather in the dormitories and some people would show their additional talents. In Ann's case, that meant singing and dancing *Hello, Dolly* while walking down a staircase. And I vaguely recall Robert Joffrey having heard these talent shows were going on, so he probably witnessed this."

When Reinking first arrived in New York, after graduating high school and saving up enough money to purchase a round-trip ticket, she promptly landed a job in the ballet corps of Radio City Music Hall, where Barker had previously danced. (Reinking also studied ballet in New York with Nenette Charisse, Barker's fellow Ballet Russe alumna and Cyd Charisse's sister-in-law.) But it wasn't long before the other assets Joffrey and Whitener had noticed—not to mention the legendarily fabulous legs, enormous blue eyes, and dazzling smile that would have no doubt made Reinking a standout Rockette had she chosen that route—drew the attention of casting directors for musical theater. Spots on the national tour of *Fiddler on the Roof* and the original Broadway productions of *Cabaret* (as a replacement) and *Coco* found her dancing the choreography of Jerome Robbins, Ronald Field, and Michael Bennett before she met the man who would forever be known as her principal mentor. Granted, Reinking realized Fosse was different from day one: "He had a way of taking the fear out of auditioning, which is big— because auditioning is almost like another craft; you have twenty minutes to show somebody everything you own, and hopefully then some," she told *Broadway World*. "So when he made it more like actual working, I did a lot better than I normally do auditioning, and I was grateful for that. And I was having so much fun." Taking the bus home, "I said, 'Gee, even if I don't get the show, this was the best day I ever had.'"

That evening, famously, Fosse called Reinking to ask her to dinner. "I said, 'Don't you think it's not a good idea? Aren't you being unfair to ask me out and we're still auditioning?'" she recalled in a 2019 interview with *The New Yorker*. "He goes, 'Yeah, but do you want to go out?'" Although the move would have been judged wildly inappropriate by modern-day professional standards, Reinking wasn't put off. "At first, I thought, 'Oh, my gosh, this is a little intense.' But he was so funny during the conversation. I realized I could say no to him." Any romantic entanglement would have to wait, she insisted, so that it could exist apart from the show. The tacit agreement seemed to only pique Fosse's interest, and Reinking's, as rehearsals progressed: "I knew I was falling in love, and it just got to be more and more. So by the time we did start going out I was pretty sunk."

Reinking was apparently not the only woman who got a dinner invitation after auditioning. Although Jennifer Nairn-Smith would become romantically involved with Fosse during rehearsals—before his relationship with Reinking blossomed, though there was likely some overlap—the former New York City Ballet dancer did not receive preferential treatment. Quite the contrary, in fact: "Bob was a little cruel to Jennifer, in front of everybody," John Rubinstein remembers. "She had some difficulty executing the shoulder shimmies and the weird little trademark Fosse hand and hip and turned-in-foot stuff to Bob's perfectionist satisfaction, and he would get on her case." While Nairn-Smith insists that the taskmaster was "never, ever rude with dancers," other cast members noted his frustration. Pamela Sousa refers tactfully to "a woman Bob hired who was so beautiful, but she couldn't do some of the stuff, and he had to get on her. I never remember him yelling, but we felt bad for her, because things didn't come easy. We would try to help her, to work with her on the side."

Nairn-Smith's backstory, as she relays it, was as colorful as that of any character in *Pippin*. Born in Sydney and raised in various parts of Australia, from Tasmania to Queensland, she began ballet lessons at six or seven and immediately thrived. "Both my mother and father were national athletes, so it was in my DNA." She received a scholarship to London's Royal Ballet School at seventeen, "but they kicked me out when I grew two inches. I was five-foot-ten, and six-two *en pointe*." Arriving in New York at twenty, she discovered that George Balanchine didn't consider height a liability, but his School of American Ballet posed a steep learning curve nonetheless. "The British considered it vulgar to lift your leg higher than your hip in my day. But Balanchine? The Russians? They were like skyscrapers—their legs went up to their ears." The St. Petersburg–born choreographer had also "devised a system whereby you had to move exceedingly fast, because he hated when the tempi of the music would change so that dancers could do their tricks."

Although Nairn-Smith was eventually accepted into the City Ballet, her tenure there would not prove long. As she tells it, "I was killed off by vicious girls. Short, mean girls. Short girls are nasty, I can tell you. I've seen a lot of nostrils. They were like Chihuahuas, looking up at me, and they lied about me, lied through their goddamn teeth. They said that I dealt drugs and did drugs, when they were really the ones doing drugs. It came to pass that Balanchine recognized that, but it was too late—I was never able to get back into the company after I was fired." Instead, the statuesque beauty was scooped up by Michael Bennett, who cast her as a replacement showgirl in *Follies*. "I was with these six-foot-tall model types who looked wonderful onstage. But since I really was a dancer, and I could do all these eccentric moves, I could make a real impression visually."

Indeed, for all her struggles with *Pippin*'s choreography, Nairn-Smith clearly brought a particular physical dynamism that went beyond her high waist and endless thighbone—however central those assets may have been in auditions or performance. Cheryl Clark, the swing, notes, "I wasn't petrified about going on for any of the other four women, because I could do what they did—good jazz dancing. I could sing the alto and soprano parts. But there was this quality that Jenny had, even when Bob put her in the back, or if he stuck her with holding a flag as the rest of us were bumping around in 'Glory,'" one of several intricate ensemble numbers led by Vereen, with each dancer assuming a unique purpose and presence. As Sousa puts it, "There were things she could do where she just soared, and Bob needed her for that."

While Sousa was, at twenty, the youngest cast member aside from eight-year-old Shane Nickerson (and Nickerson's ten-year-old standby, Will McMillan), she already had Broadway experience, having been hired by Gower Champion for the company of *Sugar*. Prior to that, fresh out of high school, she had danced in a touring production of *Promises, Promises*. Sousa had begun studies in ballet, tap, and jazz at the age of four, but growing up in San Francisco, she never envisioned a career in musical theater. "I was watching television dancers on my parents' black and white TV," among them June Taylor's group, possibly around the same time Doby (who would be maid of honor at Sousa's 1979 wedding) was suffering through that gig. "That's what I thought I wanted to do, because it looked so cool."

Clark, in contrast, had been a child actor in musical productions at the Starlight Theatre in Kansas City, Missouri. A student of tap and jazz from the age of three, she started ballet lessons at eleven and became "obsessed"; by fifteen, she had earned a scholarship to study with the short-lived but prestigious Harkness Ballet in New York, where she had also earned an academic scholarship to the Professional Children's School. While there, she studied with Mattox and with Cole collaborator Beatrice Kraft, who was teaching East Indian dance. By seventeen, Clark was performing with Harkness's company in France; within two years, she had landed another tour of *Promises, Promises*, joining the ranks of dancers who would do notable work for both Bennett and Fosse, entrenched rivals by the time *A Chorus Line* and *Chicago* competed for Tony Awards in the 1975–1976 season. (Reinking, Sousa, and Clark would each have star turns as *Chorus Line*'s Cassie, the role originated and inspired by Donna McKechnie.)

The male alternate, Roger A. Bigelow, had danced with Sousa in *Sugar* after making his Broadway bow in *Maggie Flynn*. Among the three other men cast as players—all, like Bigelow, now deceased—Roger Hamilton was the oldest; at forty-four, he had been born just months after Korthaze and had also been working on Broadway since the 1950s, most recently with Jill Clayburgh in *The Rothschilds*. John Mineo had appeared in the ensemble of that show—as had Christopher Chadman—and in *Sugar* and was already emerging as one of Broadway's most prolific dancers; he would later turn up in *A Chorus Line*, with Reinking in *Over Here!* and *Dancin'*, and in the 1996 revival of *Chicago* that Reinking starred in and choreographed in Fosse's style. Paul Solen, who two years after *Pippin* performed in the original cast of *Chicago*—along with Clark, Brown, Sousa, and Foote, with Doby assisting Fosse—would have a shorter career and life; like Chadman, he succumbed to AIDS in the 1990s.

Although they had a few lines, it was through movement that the dancers suggested what the Players might be thinking and revealed their own imaginations. Little of the choreography was worked out in prepro-duction, Doby points out, "because there weren't that many numbers that were strictly dance numbers. And for those numbers, Bob really just had the framework of what he wanted to do." Movement—languid or stac-cato, erotic or militaristic—was integrated into every aspect of the story line, and improvisation was heartily encouraged, from "Magic to Do" on. In creating the iconic opening image of hands lit against a pitch-black stage, Doby says, "There were basic movements we had to do, but you could do it with one hand up and one down, or both in one direction or one in another direction, or both right next to each other, like a fire-cracker going off." Another section returned to the circus theme Fosse had drawn on during auditions: "You could walk a tightrope or juggle three balls or throw something up in the air and catch it. You picked what you wanted to do, in slow motion." In rehearsal, says Foote, Fosse's strategy was to observe and absorb. "He would always say, 'Do good work today, because tomorrow it's mine.'"

As in Fosse's work generally, empty flash was discouraged. "Bob would always say, 'Make sure you ask the audience to come to *you*,'" Sousa says. "You're always trying to get them to lean forward in their seats, as opposed to throwing things out at them. That's different from so much dance in theater now, where it's so in your face—like, 'Look at me, aren't I great?'" Korthaze notes, "Bob didn't like numbers that just danced to the audience. He didn't like the typical Broadway, high-kick numbers. They all had to have some kind of dramatic content, which gave us all the chance to create feeling rather than just doing steps."

Doby believes it was with *Pippin* that Fosse's aim to establish danc-ers as actors came to full fruition. "I remember how a few years later, when *A Chorus Line* came around"—premiering on Broadway in July 1975, a few months after creating a singular sensation at the Public The-ater—"everyone was praising Michael Bennett for making people out of the chorus. But Bob had already done that with *Pippin*." Granted, most of the dancers in *Pippin* did not get to play fleshed-out characters or sing individually, as Bennett's musical—developed with dancers and devoted to their stories—allowed them to do. But as Doby points out, "So many of the songs and so much of the staging in *Pippin* involved the dancers.

Because it was such a small cast, and we made up such a big part of it, we got to be involved with anything and everything."

While the principals obviously had lines and musical numbers to define their characters, those cast as the other troupe members "were given a lot of latitude," Brown recalls. "We were a group of commedia dell'arte players, and Bob would tell us the feeling of the scene or what he wanted accomplished in the scene." The dancers were told to "make up our own stories for our characters—why you are in this group and why you are doing what you're doing," says Doby. Then, Sousa explains, "Bob gave us a purpose for a number, and a broad stroke—'You're trying to get Pippin to understand this,' or, 'You're trying to get one over on him'—and within that, he'd allow us to be free. That was frightening for some of us, who at that point had always been told what to do." Pressed for details about the characters and motives they created, the women demur. "That's personal," says Doby politely, and Sousa says, "It's kind of like asking a magician to reveal how he did the trick."

Fosse ultimately had the final say in what their bodies did, of course, down to the precise movements of finger joints and eyeballs. ("In 'War Is a Science,' we had to look left and right, left and right, all at the same time," Foote reports.) But those who danced for Fosse tend to refute, vehemently, the notion that he was more of a pure stylist than a consummate storyteller in the Robbins vein. By the time *Pippin* came along, the choreographer was increasingly integrating dance into the overall movement in his productions and movement into the narrative. Reinking's old friend and colleague William Whitener says, "My major memory of *Pippin* is this beautiful, seamless integration of movement into the storyline. Bob established the ensemble as a key player, but they were also like a Greek chorus, commenting on the action and describing the plot as they moved it forward." Linda Haberman, who in between performing in *Dancin'* and serving as Fosse's assistant for *Big Deal* would appear in a 1981 production of *Pippin* that was captured not quite in its entirety for television (more on that later) remembers, "Whenever you were onstage, you were always moving. Everyone was one hundred fifty per cent invested in the story, and there was this physicality he gave you that you carried as an individual. There was a lot of individuality, within a group."

Brown recalls, "When I started working on *Liza with a Z*, I did not like the choreography at all," she admits. "It was like nothing I had done before, and I remember thinking, 'This is the dumbest shit I have ever had to do.' But as we kept rehearsing, I came to understand it. With Fosse, each move meant something. It wasn't just, 'Five, six, seven, eight—go.' He would say, 'This is what you're trying to do in this scene; this is the feeling you're trying to elicit.' To me, that was the most important thing about Bob's style—that everything was connected to telling a story."

Foote adds, "In every moment, we had a problem to solve, and it was all for the audience." In the scene where Pippin killed Charles at a cathedral in Arles, Foote's Player had to stand on a small ledge that flipped out from the side of the proscenium, eighteen feet above the stage—a hidden ladder provided access—smoking a cigar. "I was playing the nobleman, and I had on a beautiful grey vest and a homburg hat, and that clown face on—we did everything in that clown face. And Bob said to me, 'Gene, could you blow smoke rings up there?' I tried, but they would blow away, and I realized it was because I was above the stage and the air conditioning was blowing." When Foote and John Mineo were asked to perform a cakewalk before "War Is a Science," entering from opposite sides of the stage to lead the audience into Charles's war room, they improvised while Fosse was staging the movement of scenery by actors. "I think Bob was just watching us, and then he choreographed the dance in fifteen minutes. Because John was such a brilliant dancer, and Bob had given us tambourines, so how could you go wrong?" If that instrument and the dance itself had roots in minstrelsy—the cakewalk's history is especially egregious, as slaves performed it for plantation owners before the Civil War—Fosse was no doubt influenced by its presence in vaudeville, which had largely not been subject to the retrospective criticism that later decades would bring.

Foote also had a key role in the "Bolero" scene, in which Pippin and Catherine first make love—or try to—and Pippin initially fails to rise to the occasion. Fosse decided that he wanted a pair of dancers to reflect their awkward struggle and eventual victory. "One day Bob came up to me and said, 'Gene, do you think you could catch Kathryn?' And I said, 'I don't know—how fast can she run?' He said, 'No, I mean, could you catch her in your arms, then drop her?' I didn't know. So he pulled out the mattress they use for the bed scene and had me stand on it, and then he had Kathryn run and jump into my arms, and had me drop her on the mattress, so she wouldn't get hurt." As the number was staged, Doby repeated the jump, and Foote caught her the second time, reinforcing Pippin's success as Rubinstein and Clayburgh sat up and smiled. In between leaps, Foote says, "All we did was lie on the floor and rub against each other's bodies. We were having ourselves, in front of 1500 people. I wore nothing but a little gold G-string, and after one performance I actually got offered a porn film! Someone had seen the show and looked me up in the telephone directory."

For the finale, Fosse then upped the ante, according to Foote: "We all had to masturbate"—or at least pretend that their characters were doing so. "We were asked to choose a sexual preference, to decide what we wanted to do with Pippin. I used to chew on the end of my cape." Doby, like others, remembers the direction being more subtle: "There was a sensual thing about it; you had to think about the thing that gave you the ultimate fulfillment. It all depended on how the actor interpreted that." Fosse did have the Players join their leader in his appeal to theatergoers, after Pippin had rejected a glorious death in favor of domestic contentment with Catherine and Theo. "In the original design, the front of the stage was on an angle jutting out over the orchestra, and I was about two feet from the third person sitting in the first row," Doby remembers. "We all came down to the edge of the stage to try to get someone to do what Pippin didn't."

Doby cites a letter that Fosse would write to his cast in which he directed them to "make self-immolation or suicide seem attractive, exciting and extremely sexual." "Bob said that about six out of every ten people consider suicide at some point," Doby notes, quoting another part of the letter. "He said, 'Get me those six.' It did happen—not once, but four or five times—that somebody came up from the audience, totally mesmerized. Young people. The first time, it was a boy in his early twenties, and we didn't know what to do, so we just kind of led him offstage! It was exactly the kind of thing that had been going on through the whole show: We were trying to mesmerize Pippin into doing things that he maybe he didn't want to do."

Seduction of a less malevolent kind figured into Fosse's interaction with the dancers. "Bob, like all great directors, was a great manipulator," says Brown. But he was not a predator—a point on which the women who performed in *Pippin* are adamant, particularly after watching (or hearing about) the 2019 docudrama miniseries *Fosse/Verdon*, in which the director is seen moodily sleeping his way through the female chorus. "It saddened us to see Bobby portrayed that way," says Sousa. "You didn't see his sense of humor, his joy, his love." At one point in the series, based on Sam Wasson's 2013 biography *Fosse*, the director, played by Sam Rockwell, is kicked in the groin by a cast member; the scene was inspired by an incident documented by Wasson—and by Martin Gottfried in his 1990 biography *All His Jazz: The Life and Death of Bob Fosse*—in which, as Gottfried relays it, in quotes attributed to Nairn-Smith, Fosse "picked me up and shoved me against the wall" when she resisted an advance in his apartment. Nairn-Smith now denies having made that accusation, and the incident itself, which poses a sharp contrast to others' depiction of Fosse as a gentle man who, however ethically shady his propensity for hitting on women he hired, did not assume that his interest would always be reciprocated. Reinking "didn't feel there was any casting couch or anything," she told *The New Yorker*. "I have felt more uncomfortable with other people on a more sinister level, but there was nothing sinister with Bob." Clark says simply, "He was never that type of hideous person who violated people."

There were late-night calls during rehearsals, but like Fosse's first pitch to Reinking, they were generally perceived as nonthreatening. "We would talk, and at the end he might say, 'Do you want to come down and have a drink? We can finish this conversation here,'" Sousa recalls. "And I'd say, 'No, I can't, I've got a commercial call tomorrow,' and he'd just say, 'Oh, OK.' I never felt that it would cost me my job." Brown muses, "Oh, I got those calls—I know several people did. He knew I would wake up, talk, and then go right back to sleep. I think he just wanted someone to listen to him. He would really pour his heart out, or ask deep philosophical questions." Brown admits she was naive, recalling that during *Liza with a Z*, Fosse once asked her if she lived alone. "A friend of mine, an older dancer, asked if he was hitting on me, and I said, 'Oh, no, he's very nice; he's concerned about me.' Look, I was about twenty, he was about forty-five—the same age as my father. An old white man. It never occurred to me that he could have been flirting."

Clark would encounter that flirtatiousness while working on *Chicago*, but says that during *Pippin*, "I was more like a daughter to him. I was a twenty-one-year-old kid, very innocent even for that age. I was not sexually active. I actually learned about my sexuality through his movement—and there's nothing tacky or crass about it; it only becomes that way when people get it wrong. But the other women were more mature than I was then. Louise Quick and Kathy Doby had to explain some things to me in rehearsal—like, when we were humping spears at one point, I honestly didn't know what that was supposed to mean. And Bob would just say to Kathy, 'Please go over to Cheryl, and explain what that means to her.' He pronounced the 'ch' in my name like you would in 'church.' I didn't know we were insinuating a sexual move."

Sousa remembers showing up on the first day of rehearsal with a cold sore. "I wanted to be this good-looking, sexy girl, of course, and I tried to cover it up. Then at one of the first breaks, Bob came up to me and said, 'Pam, I just love that you're here. Oh, you got a cold sore—I get them all the time.' That really broke the ice, and made me feel better." As their work progressed, Fosse continued to monitor each individual as he had in auditions, mindful of their different artistic and personal sensibilities. "I was basically this big doofus kid," muses Brown, "and he would take me aside sometimes, when he wasn't needed, and teach me a hat trick or something. I feel like he raised me, in a lot of ways."

Such nurturing was accompanied by an insistence on mutual respect and a certain measure of decorum. "Attitude was very important to Mr. Fosse," Foote says. "He wouldn't fire you for not being able to do a step, but he would fire you in a minute for bad attitude." (Vereen tells the story of a dancer who learned this the hard way while working on another show: "We had had to do this one step all morning, and then after lunch we were asked to do it again, and this guy behind me was saying, 'We've got to do that step again, man?' And Bob heard him from across the room, and he had the stage manager walk over and tell the guy, 'Thank you very much—your plane ticket will be waiting for you.'") Food was verboten in the rehearsal room, though coffee and cola and, naturally, cigarettes were allowed. "I gather we were allowed to smoke because Bob smoked all the time," says Korthaze.

"Equity rules were that you had to rehearse for an hour, then take a five-minute break, or take a ten-minute break after an hour and a half," Sousa remembers. "But we loved creating with Bob so much that they would have to remind us to take breaks after every couple of hours. We would all light up—we all used to smoke—and Bobby would tell us fascinating, funny stories about working in film, about Gower Champion and Tommy Rall. And then Phil Friedman would have to say, 'Bobby, it's been 20 minutes.'"

Cast members socialized with their director outside rehearsals as well. About once a month, several of the women would gather at Kathryn Doby's place to play poker, "and inevitably, Fosse and Stanley Lebowsky"—*Pippin*'s musical director, with whom Fosse would also forge a close and lasting bond—"would crash," says Sousa. Fosse adored the game, Doby notes—they had played into the wee hours while shooting *Cabaret*—"though his way of playing was totally different. He made up his own rules. It was the director trying to see how much he could get away with." There were gatherings at Fosse's apartment as well, and at the summer home he still shared with Verdon in the Hamptons. "He just liked us, so he would have us over," says Brown. "I would sometimes hang out with Nicole," Fosse's daughter, "who was around nine, because I was like a big, goofy kid."

There were also occasional lunches and, more frequently, given Fosse's poor sleeping habits, dinners. "He would usually take a nap during lunch, and someone would just bring him a sandwich and coffee," Doby says, noting the director kept a cot in the smaller of the two rehearsal rooms. As Foote remembers it, "He would take us out quite often, but he wouldn't eat in front of us. He was a very shy man, and he didn't like to eat in front of people." Fosse could nonetheless, not surprisingly, take delight in directing a conversation. "We could all be sitting around a table—fifteen or twenty or thirty people—and he would say, 'What's your favorite song?'" Linda Posner recalls. "So we would all be searching through the histories of our lives, going through the hit parade, while he just sat there. Finally, someone would say, 'What's your favorite song, Bob?' And he'd say, 'In this moment . . .'—and just name whatever song came into his head. 'That's my favorite song today.' The idea was, be here now. Be in the present."

Fosse could be as ardent an observer as he was a director in social situations. Korthaze, who would join Brown, Clark, Foote, Solen, and Sousa in the original cast of *Chicago*, remembers him being present when the cast hung out after performances in Philadelphia during that show's pre-Broadway run. "We would gather together at what were called variety clubs, a group of clubs at various hotels around the country where we would go to relax and have a beer and socialize with each other. Bob was always a part of that. He would spend a little time, have a drink, and watch how we reacted to each other socially, so that he could get a better idea of what we were like personally."

The next morning at rehearsal, Fosse would be just as sharp-eyed about business. "His favorite expression was 'Uno mas,'" Korthaze muses—Spanish for "one more" or, in this context, "Do it again." "He was always experimenting with a number; he'd come in with an idea, but if it didn't work he would redo it, change it, come up with variations. Then you did it over and over until he liked it, and saw that everybody could do it." Much the same process applied to Fosse's work with other artists; holding firm to his belief that—as he was teaching Nicole—there was no such thing as perfection, he kept all his collaborators on their toes as *Pippin* continued to evolve.

"Lawrence Stephens" (Stephen Schwartz) with Rebecca Smith, his Fastrada in *Pippin, Pippin*, rehearsing at Carnegie Tech in 1966
COURTESY OF STEPHEN SCHWARTZ

A good day: from left, Stephen Schwartz, Roger Hirson, Bob Fosse (leaning back) and Stuart Ostrow, all still smiling at a reading.
PHOTO BY VAN WILLIAMS

Bob Fosse, foreground, rehearses, from left in back, Ben Vereen (in white hat, taking a break), Paul Solen, Kathryn Doby, John Mineo, Ann Reinking, Richard Korthaze, and Jennifer Nairn-Smith in *Glory*

Lighting designer Jules Fisher, does some offstage magic for Fosse, center, Jennifer Nairn-Smith, Christopher Chadman, and Gene Foote, while John Mineo plays guitar in the back

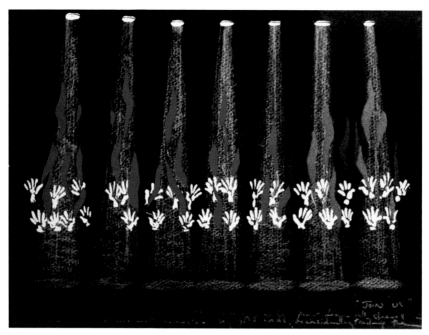

An early design for Tony Walton's set, with Players's hands indicated
DESIGN BY TONY WALTON / COURTESY TONY WALTON

The Leading Player wields his magic, in Tony Walton's design . . .
DESIGN BY TONY WALTON / COURTESY TONY WALTON

. . . and live, via Ben Vereen
DESIGN BY TONY WALTON / COURTESY TONY WALTON

MOVING EYE MURAL — (ROPE LOOPS IN ARCHES)

Tony Walton's "moving-eye mural," as sketched . . .
DESIGN BY TONY WALTON / COURTESY TONY WALTON

. . . and onstage, in a scene with, from left, Christopher Chadman, Leland Palmer, and John Rubinstein

Pippin (John Rubinstein) greets father Charles (Eric Berry) in the monastery . . .

. . . and, after offing the old man, is crowned king
DESIGN BY TONY WALTON / COURTESY TONY WALTON

John Rubinstein, surrounded by the Players, as the "Gisela ballet" segues into a full orgy
PHOTO BY MARTHA SWOPE © THE NEW YORK PUBLIC LIBRARY FOR THE PERFORMING ARTS

Ben Vereen, in black, surrounded by the cast
PHOTO BY MARTHA SWOPE © THE NEW YORK PUBLIC LIBRARY FOR THE PERFORMING ARTS

The Players pose:

Paul Solen

Richard Korthaze

Pamela Sousa

Ann Reinking

Candy Brown

Laurent Giroux
(replacement)

Mineo and Foote

Eric Berry

John Rubinstein

Kathryn Doby

Betty Buckley
(replacement)

Shane Nickerson

Costumer Patricia Zipprodt designs an angelic guise for Pippin . . .

. . . and a buffoonish one for his half-brother, Lewis

Something naughty for Pamela Sousa's Player . . .

. . . and naughtier for Kathryn Doby's Player

The female Players, as envisioned by Zipprodt . . .

. . . and caught in the flesh: Clockwise from top left, Pamela Sousa, Candy Brown, Kathryn Doby, swing Cheryl Clark (on floor), Ann Reinking, Jennifer Nairn-Smith (center)

A swing's notes: A heavily annotated page from Cheryl Clark's script

Sheet music for "Marking Time," a number eventually cut from *Pippin*

Sheet music for the opening
number, "Magic to Do"
COURTESY OF JOHN RUBINSTEIN

Stephen Schwartz's
opening night gift
to John Rubinstein,
embellished by Bob
Fosse ("How sweet!")
and Stuart Ostrow
COURTESY OF JOHN
RUBINSTEIN

Blood lust: from left, Candy Brown, Ben Vereen and Pamela Sousa as the Manson Trio

PHOTO BY MARTHA SWOPE © THE NEW YORK PUBLIC LIBRARY FOR THE PERFORMING ARTS

Promotional poster featuring the Manson Trio

COURTESY OF KATHRYN DOBY

John Rubinstein, left, and Jill Clayburgh as Pippin and Catherine, on the bed

PHOTO BY MARTHA SWOPE © THE NEW YORK PUBLIC LIBRARY FOR THE PERFORMING ARTS

From left, Christopher Chadman—in Kathryn Doby's wig and garment—a dresser, and Candy Brown
COURTESY OF PAMELA SOUSA

Clockwise from left, stage manager Paul Phillps; cast members Christopher Chadman, Candy Brown, Paul Solen, Pamela Sousa, and producer Stuart Ostrow at dinner
COURTESY OF PAMELA SOUSA

From left, John Rubinstein (with flugelhorn), Ben Vereen, Candy Brown, Shane Nickerson and Will McMillan (respectively, the child actor playing Theo and his understudy), Christopher Chadman, and Bob Fosse waiting to be allowed back into Kennedy Center following a bomb scare
COURTESY OF CHERYL CLARK

From left, Ann Reinking, Pamela Sousa, and Cheryl Clark (filling in for Candy Brown) don blonde wigs to back up Jill Clayburgh in "Kind of Woman"
COURTESY CHERYL CLARK

Three of Pippin's principals, out of costume, reflect for a promotional photo: From left, Jill Clayburgh, John Rubinstein, Irene Ryan
PHOTO BY MARTHA SWOPE
© THE NEW YORK PUBLIC LIBRARY FOR THE PERFORMING ARTS

The company of Bridewell Theatre's 1998 London production, which introduced "the Theo ending"
COURTESY OF MITCH SEBASTIAN

The deaf actor Tyrone Girodano, left, and the hearing actor Michael Arden share the role of Pippin in Deaf West's 2009 production
COURTESY OF JEFF CALHOUN

Life is a circus: The cast of Diane Paulus's 2013 Broadway revival
JOAN MARCUS PHOTOGRAPHY

On the right track: Professional Performing Arts School students Diego Lucano, left,
and Leonay Shepherd as Pippin and the Leading Player in 2020
COURTESY OF GARY R. VORWALD, GV PHOTOGRAPHY

CHAPTER SEVEN

Order, Design, Composition, Tension, and All That Jazz

It's a measure of Bob Fosse's creative and personal rapport with the members of *Pippin*'s design team that while the director had worked with just one of them, hair designer Romaine Green, on a previous Broadway production, he would work with all of them on his next one. Scenic designer Tony Walton, then Julie Andrews's husband, had been a friend, and lighting designer Jules Fisher was a mutual admirer, having lit and produced the play *Lenny*, which Fosse would bring to the screen in 1974, with Dustin Hoffman playing the iconoclastic comedian Lenny Bruce. Costumer Patricia Zipprodt had collaborated with Fosse on another film adaptation, *Sweet Charity*. Each of the three earned a Tony Award nomination for their work on *Pippin*—Fisher and Walton were winners—and another for *Chicago*, on which they again teamed with *Pippin*'s sound designer, Abe Jacob, and Green, who had assisted Ernest Adler for *Pippin* and done Gwen Verdon's hair for *Sweet Charity*.

The chemistry these artists enjoyed with Fosse was not without friction. "He could be very friendly, very much your pal for a while, and then all of a sudden things would change," recalls Jacob, who was only twenty-seven when rehearsals for *Pippin* began but had already replaced the sound designer on *Jesus Christ, Superstar* and served as a consultant on *Hair*. "There was a side of him that wasn't pleasant, where he could say demeaning things," says Fisher, another *Hair* and *Superstar* alum who at thirty-four had accumulated more than forty-five Broadway credits prior

99

to *Pippin*. Fisher recalls that while he was working on a later Fosse musical, *Dancin'*, the director told set designer Peter Larkin, "one of the great American designers of the century," not to take up any space that the dancers would use; Larkin wound up placing vertical panels of stretched cloth all the way upstage, flat against the back wall, "which was quite brilliant, and beautiful, and solved every problem. And Bob looked at it and said, 'My tailor could have done that.' It was like saying to Picasso, 'My child could take some crayons and do that.'"

Fisher allows, "That was just Bob's way sometimes. I think he saw it half as humor, and maybe half as defending his reputation for doing that kind of thing. I won't say it was to get us to work harder, because we all wanted to work harder; none of the people that worked with Bob were slackers." His own working relationship with Fosse, Fisher says, was "excellent, artistically. If it had some contention, that came out in the form of, 'Hurry up,' and 'How long is this going to take?' That's not uncommon—everyone wants the lighting to be faster. Lighting rehearsals are done with the actors onstage, and it's expensive for the producer. Once we were in previews, I might have been working on lighting for the second act while the scenery on stage was for Act One, and he would come onstage and say, 'That looks ridiculous,' and I'd have to explain it wasn't for the scene. That's the kind of thing he was impatient about. But I was able in almost all instances to just say, 'Don't worry, Bob, we'll get there.'"

As he did with dancers, Fosse pushed designers to serve his imagination while drawing on their own. Repetition was to be avoided at all costs. "He had no qualms about asking for things that no one had ever done before, or things he had just dreamed up," says Fisher. "He once asked me to do something unusual, and I told him I could do it. He said, 'Will it work?' I said it would, and he asked how I knew, and I told him it was because I'd done it before. And he said, 'Well, then, I don't want it. I want something different.'"

Fosse got his wish in *Pippin*'s opening moments. "That was the first challenge, to start in total blackness," Fisher says. "Bob said, 'I just want to see hands—nothing else.' That's a very complicated thing to do, to have hands appear and disappear choreographically." "I had read about some really astonishing lighting techniques that Abe Feder developed with Orson Welles in their Mercury Theatre days, that seemed perfect for a way to reveal the Fosse dancer, legs first," says Walton, who had designed both scenery and costumes for New York and London productions before signing on. (His first Tony nod was for the 1966 Schwartz favorite *The Apple Tree*, where he had worked with Stuart Ostrow.) "Feder and Welles had done a production of *Julius Caesar* where these people popped out of the dark, feet first; then their legs were revealed, then midriffs. I did a painting of that, where the lighting mostly came from above, and Jules said, 'Maybe we could actually light it from the floor.' I said we would need to build a special ramped deck to do that, and Bob said he would like that, because his dancers loved to work on a raked stage—they got to run upstage and then down, and got a tremendous surge of energy as they turned. So we built an angled stage where you could burrow in and make big slots, and Jules had these tractor lamps—topped by grill work—lighting up through the surface of the deck, which I don't think had been done before, and it was a very striking effect."

As Fisher explains it, "There was basically a very narrow band of light built into the floor of the stage, that went straight up, like the headlight of a car." The dancers stood just upstage of it, their heads and bodies covered by a drape of the pitch-black fabric used by magicians; thus, they couldn't be seen until they took off their gloves and dropped them on the long black runners they stood on, placing their hands into the upward-angled light beams. (Several pages of typed notes marked "Setting Elements" indicate that the masking wings, borders, and backdrop were made of the same velour and that Walton used the material in other scenes requiring magic effects.) Once the runners had been whisked into the wings, Ben Vereen came onstage, and the follow spot hit him. The effect was enhanced by the use of dry ice, which caught the light and further camouflaged the dancers' bodies. When Fosse first saw his designers' work in action, Fisher remembers, "He turned to Tony and said. 'Now *that's* what I call a set.' It was pure black! The show got off to a very powerful start because of Bob asking for the impossible. He made sure the audience would expect magic throughout the performance."

Walton further whetted those expectations by then revealing a palace portal, made almost entirely of gold rope, that rose up out of a second slim trough in the deck to form the framework of Charlemagne's castle. Vereen's Leading Player first engaged the audience with sleight of hand, making a red scarf disappear and then pulling a piece of the same material out of the stage until it became clear that the fabric was decorating the portal—which, lifted upward, eventually filled the width of the stage. "I had never seen anything like it, and I haven't since," Fisher marvels—though Walton says that Fosse had suggested the gold rope after noticing his set designer had used it to create graphic lines in his designs, inspired by medieval artwork. (Robert Randolph, Fosse's scenic and lighting designer on *Charity*, recruited design students to do the necessary macramé for the portal with the rope and red silk.) An aficionado of magic himself, Fisher was approached during previews by a teenager who shared his passion. "He said, 'I'm David Kotkin, and I live in New Jersey, and I'm a magician. I could teach Ben Vereen how to do that trick better.' I talked to Bob, and he said, sure, let him try; it can't hurt." The young man would eventually adopt the stage name David Copperfield; he and Fisher still keep in touch.

The rest of *Pippin*'s scenery, Fisher notes, was similarly delicate and imaginative. "This was a Broadway spectacle that looked hand-made, like a child could do it. Of course, a child couldn't do it—it was aesthetically beautiful, and more than that, there was the pure inventiveness of it." "War" and the country scene used silk drops dyed in alternating red and green, with silhouettes of mannequins with jerking legs filling out Charlemagne's army; "Revolution" featured a mural on which eight faces were painted with eyes that appeared to move, attached to a pair of staircase units so that the eyes could swivel from Fastrada to Lewis as they conspired against Pippin. Walton says, "*Pippin* was so exciting because it was the first time I worked with Jules. By a piece of luck, when he brought his lighting plots over for me to see, Richard Pilbrow happened to be staying overnight." A fellow Brit whose Broadway credits stretch from Arthur Penn's 1964 staging of *Golden Boy* to a musical adaptation of *A Tale of Two Cities* produced in 2008, Pilbrow spent a couple of hours conferring with Fisher. "I think Jules—who was at that time noted for his focus on white light—would be the first to say he learned an astonishing amount about working in color," Walton posits, "and you couldn't work with Bob Fosse without getting involved with great swatches of color."

It was Walton who designed *Pippin*'s promotional poster—and cast album cover, consequently—with its strip of white against a deep magenta background, the strip festooned with commedia dell'arte clowns (a few of them conspicuously female upon close observation) spelling out the musical's title with the assistance of a drum, a headstand, and other circus props and antics. "Bob had said to me that one of the disappointments he had about Broadway is that when he studied the poster for a show, it didn't give him a hint of what the show would look like, what its visual alphabet would be," Walton explains. "At that time, I was signed out to costume design as well as set design. But once I started showing him possible poster images, he would zero in on something like the shoelaces characters were wearing; I realized that this would be a pretty intense collaboration, so I retired from the role of costume designer—and Pat Zipprodt came on board."

Fisher recalls, "Almost all of Bob's shows were dark, in terms of the floor, the walls, the scenery. He loved black, because the dancer could stand out. As opposed to giving the audience a set that was glistening, that had richness, he was always taking things away. It was, how can we do less with more? Which got you to the essence of what the scene was about." Where *Pippin* was concerned, Fosse's minimalism may also have served a practical purpose: Although the production was originally budgeted at $700,000, according to *Variety*—some recall it being $750,000, though either figure would have been lavish at the time—Ostrow had to reduce the budget to half a million when at least one substantial investor pulled out early on. As the show's co–general manager Ira Bernstein recalls, "Bob had to sit down and put his pencil to the grindstone, and we were all able to help him figure it out. We cut the size of the show physically and the size of the cast—and in the long run, we all felt that maybe we got a better show as a result." (It has been widely reported that Ostrow mortgaged his house to raise funds, but the producer says he didn't take that route until years later for another production, the Broadway premiere of *M. Butterfly*.)

Walton notes that in their first design meetings for *Pippin*, Fosse proposed a rural and rustic palette: "He said, 'You'll have this troupe of players who are really farmers and farmhands, taking their wagons through the fields.' So I thought I had to forego my usual passion for color and just work with greens and browns and so on." But when a power failure at Zipprodt's Martha's Vineyard residence led her to take some unfinished costume sketches to Walton—who had, after all, been a successful costumer himself—he studied the drawings, which at that point had just flecks of color and detail, and encouraged her to push the envelope. "I said, 'Take this as you choose, Pat, but I just did a production, of *The Love of Three Oranges* at Sadler Wells Opera in London, where almost all the costumes were white and off-white except for the principals, who all had their own colors.' She said, 'Ooh, that's scary'—and it was, but it turned out really well. So at the next meeting we all had, she said, 'Bob, something has happened that has made me think about this differently, and I'd like to show you what the result was.'"

Zipprodt, who had been hired by Ostrow after working on several of his Broadway productions, knew that Fosse wanted something "magical" and "anachronistic," as he had told her in one of their first conversations about *Pippin*. In a follow-up exchange, he used the phrase "Jesus Christ in tennis shorts," as the costume designer remembered fondly in one interview: "That was a wonderfully rich image. It gave me a whole slant. He was after the unexpected." Although likely a bit too surprised by the bursts of color Zipprodt showed him after conferring with Walton—"Bob took a look and said, 'Are you crazy?'" Walton recalls—Fosse eventually approved of the purplish blue robe she fashioned for Charlemagne, the bright crimson getup designed for Pippin, and similarly bold choices for other principals.

Such indulgences were made with discretion. In an article published shortly after *Pippin* opened, in the magazine *Theatre Crafts*, Zipprodt pointed out that she wasn't especially drawn to primary colors, musing, "Everyone thinks that theater is bright—and red. But theater is really about holding red back so that you can use it with a *whallop*." The article noted that from the darkness of *Pippin*'s opening number, "the players emerge dressed in ghostly off-whites, bisques, and tans. Designer Zipprodt sees these colors and menacing and bordering on evil. Marvelous, celastic masks, *Clockwork Orange*-type noses, and eerie latex body armor create even more uneasiness about the players. White garbed, they wander through the action, moving props, handing in canes and hats, or whatever is required to propel the action. As they move into their play about Pippin, they put costumes on over their whites. Here, in the story world, colors begin to appear." The makeup also called for a clown's white base. "After the 'War' sequence the girls had to change to 'beauty' makeup, and do it fast," Kathryn Doby remembers. "Then after the Gisela ballet, it was back to white again. The abuse took a toll on our skin; we all had problems, until our skin toughened up and kind of got used to it."

The masks, prosthetics, and props, with their character-defining and satirical properties, clearly drew from the commedia dell'arte traditions that began flourishing in Europe in the sixteenth century; their influences traced to medieval times and further back to ancient Rome. "I believe the commedia dell'arte flavoring of the costumes may have stemmed from my original poster designs," Walton says, but as Zipprodt told *Theatre Crafts*, she had done plenty of additional homework: "I have gone to the Byzantines, to the Carolingians, to Chartres' stained glass windows, and manuscript illuminations." Her richly detailed sketches indicate this depth of research but also, in keeping with the production's other anachronistic flourishes, mix and transcend period touches; the women's costumes in particular reveal an elegant, empowered sensuality that seems distinctly modern. There is a drawing of female Players in skimpy vests and painted-on legwear in various animated poses, suggesting sexy action figures. Fastrada suggests a flapper with flower power, one hand dangling a feather from her headband, sheer fabric dipping below a short dress of rich, warm hues. Suits of armor are drawn with red dots placed strategically on the breastplates—they would be grazed with silver paint to match the shimmering elastic covering the dancers elsewhere—offering a preview of how graphically the female anatomy would be represented in the "Glory" scene.

If essentially wearing rubber body parts didn't make the dancers uncomfortable, other designs did, initially. Pamela Sousa recalls the first time they ran through the Gisela ballet in costume: "We had been rehearsing in leotards and tights and crop tops. What we had to wear now was pretty revealing, especially the tops; mine had two straps over my nipples and one in the middle, and I was afraid to move, because I thought one of my breasts would pop out. So we were all dancing kind of stiffly, and Bob was like, 'Where are my sexy girls?' We were all just afraid something would show. Luckily, Patty Zipprodt was sweet enough to show us how double-faced tape works, and we were able to make the right adjustments, make things tighter, so that we were fine after a couple of rehearsals."

It was while working on the Gisela ballet one day that cast members witnessed a particularly heated exchange between Fosse and Stephen Schwartz. John Rubinstein recalls, "I was standing next to John Berkman," who served as rehearsal pianist as well as dance arranger, "and Bob said, 'John, give me sixteen or twenty bars of something; I want to try something with the dancers.' And Stephen, who was in the room, got up and said, 'No, I don't want any more music at this point.' And they argued in front of us. It was relatively contained at first, no swearing, but you could see the tension growing between them. And finally, Stephen said to Bob, 'Don't forget—I'm the one with the Top Ten hit.' Because of his song from *Godspell*, 'Day by Day.' There was a moment of silence, and then Bob said—very quietly, without throwing a tantrum—'Get out.' And Stephen walked out of the room, and wasn't at rehearsal again."

Schwartz does not remember how long or to what extent he was barred from the rehearsal process. He worked out several additional songs with Fosse later, including two in Washington, where Schwartz saw them practiced by cast members, "so it's not as if I wasn't involved in ongoing work." Several performers, including Rubinstein, recall him watching rehearsals in Washington but not being an active participant. (Schwartz notes that he doesn't regularly participate in rehearsals for current productions of his shows.) "I knew that the cast was extremely devoted to Bob and loyal to him, so while I didn't have the feeling they were being turned against me, I did feel isolated," Schwartz says. "Remember, I had just come from doing *Godspell*, which was such a collaborative process, with everybody in the room all the time, almost making it up together. It was, I would come to learn, more of an amateur situation, like the way you do shows in college, or in summer stock." Or at least, the sense of fellowship enjoyed by Fosse's dancers was not extended to everyone.

One of Schwartz's first wake-up calls had come during vocal rehearsals and did not involve Fosse. "For *Godspell*, we created the vocal arrangements in the room: Whoever was going to sing the lead vocal would sing the song, and the rest of the cast would just start singing along, and I would hear a vocal line and be like, 'That's great—why don't all the boys sing what Jeffrey's singing?' I was so inexperienced. The very first day I was with the *Pippin* ensemble—I'll never forget this—John Rubinstein came in and sang his part on 'Morning Glow,' and I said, 'Now everyone sing along and see what you can come up with.' And they all just looked at me as if I was from Mars. They were dancers, not singers, and most of them had done Broadway shows where a musical director or vocal arranger would hand them their vocal parts. So I just went home and wrote the vocal arrangement. I still wonder what some of the vocal parts for the show would have wound up being if I'd had singers who liked being part of creating the back-up vocals."

Surviving cast members offer differing accounts of the discord between Fosse and Schwartz and its impact. "When we were in Washington, I would sit with Stephen in the back of the house sometimes, when other stuff was going on," says Rubinstein, still a friend. "I would complain to him that I felt the audience wasn't following me, that it was always with Ben. I didn't realize my own undercooked work was part of the problem. And Steve also felt that Pippin was underrepresented." But the actor would also bend an ear to his director, he admits, "when Bob would complain about Steve, because he was right about stuff too. It wasn't a political manipulation; I was just honest with both of them, because I genuinely felt both were right from different angles."

Vereen "didn't see a rift between Bob and Steve," he insists. "I was just focused on doing the best job I could do, so it wasn't until later that I found out they were like oil and water." His dedication to Fosse notwithstanding, Vereen—who did a stint as the Wonderful Wizard of Oz in Schwartz's *Wicked* back in 2005 and 2006—formed a bond with *Pippin*'s composer as well: "When I first met Stephen, he was like a little boy. He wasn't quite a kid, but he seemed like one. A genius of a man. I love that man." Sousa also "adored Stephen," she says. "I remember talking to him in D.C., while waiting in the wings," during technical rehearsals. "In those days it took forever to tech a show, so we had a lot of down time, and we would just chitchat. He was fun to be with, and very sweet. Whatever tension there was between Bobby and him, it didn't affect the company."

Gene Foote perceived more "negativity" from Schwartz. During a photo shoot for the cover of the *New York Daily News* teaming the composer and cast, as Foote remembers it, "Stephen was speaking badly about Mr. Fosse, and at one point I said I would not take any more pictures with him, and I walked offstage. The next day we had a rehearsal, and Mr. Fosse came up to me and embraced me in front of the entire company—I think Phil Friedman had told him what happened." Richard Korthaze simply says, "It was clear that Stephen didn't really like what Bobby was doing; he wanted the show to go in a different direction. But Bob wouldn't have argued with him in front of the company."

Candy Brown agrees that didn't happen often, but recalls Schwartz being ordered out of rehearsal at least temporarily—and, on another occasion, the cast being asked to leave. "Usually Stephen would just say, 'I'm not crazy about that,' and Bob would just say, 'Don't worry, it's going to be fine.' Then one day they were having words, and this time they told the rest of us to leave the room. And we heard a whole lot of hootin' and hollerin'. That's how I found out, that this was bigger than we knew." Brown or any of her colleagues might have also read the interview Schwartz eventually gave to *Newsday*, which ran on September 10, roughly a month and a half before *Pippin* opened. The production, he told reporter Jerry Parker, was by then "no longer a collaboration. It's just a job. You're told what to do and you do it or they fire you and get someone else. I might as well have no mind at all."

In contrast, *Pippin's* librettist, with whom Brown grew close, "was quite amenable," she says. "Roger was just thrilled to be there, I think. He'd had a modicum of success as a television writer, and while he was a friend and loyal to Stephen, he knew the business, and he knew where his bread was buttered, so he didn't want to make waves with Bob." Schwartz was and remains sympathetic to this dilemma, though he admits, "I wished at the time that Roger would have been willing to stand up to

Bob more. Maybe he was humoring me when he said, 'I agree with you, that's a bad choice, but Bob really wants it.' Whatever the case was, Roger was a very good writer and he'd had success, particularly on television, but he had worked on a couple of musicals that weren't as successful, and here he had this show that increasingly held the promise of being a hit. And I think he really wanted that—who wouldn't? So he adopted a go-along-to-get-along attitude."

David Hirson doesn't contradict this. His father, he says, "was certainly aware that when Bob came on board the world that he and Stephen had created was going to change. He knew it was in the nature of production, especially in the commercial theater, and especially with a director as formidable as Fosse. That's why, when friction developed, he made it his business to keep the peace as much as possible. He was experienced enough to know how easily everything can fall apart—that it doesn't take much for a show to derail in rehearsals or out of town. His heart had been broken by that a few times. So when it came to Fosse's production of *Pippin*, his instinct was to resist the swelling tide of conflict. He wanted to get the show on!"

Doby felt that Schwartz's resistance to Fosse's revisions was "understandable, because Stephen was very young, and he had become a big star with *Godspell*. *Pippin* was something he had started years ago, so it was kind of his baby, and he didn't want to let go of it, and that created problems. Bob was an entertainer first, and he wanted the show to be entertaining—that was the important thing. So Stephen was not welcome at rehearsals. At one point, Bob asked our production stage manager to do whatever he could so that Stephen wouldn't be there."

Like Doby—and Schwartz himself—Walton emphasizes the role that Schwartz's youth and inexperience played in the conflict. "And something I would have found incredibly difficult, if I were Stephen," Walton adds, "was that while Bob was drawn to Stephen's score, he had so many scores already in his head that it was not hard for him to switch something—like the Manson Trio, for instance—to a different melody and rhythm while he was choreographing and rehearsing it." As Ann Reinking noted, that celebrated routine, which set up the climax of "Glory," was initially developed as *Nilsson Schmilsson* played on repeat; Reinking identified the specific track as Harry Nilsson's cover of the rhythm-and-blues standard "Let the Good Times Roll"—which, as Schwartz notes, featured a similar vamp to the one that would later introduce "All That Jazz" in Fosse's production of *Chicago*. "If I were Stephen and I had walked in and seen that going on," Walton says, "I would have been seriously upset."

Fosse nonetheless sustained his faith in *Pippin*'s score, even when the director and his collaborators had different ideas than Schwartz about how to present it. Abe Jacob recalls having "very few conversations" with the composer: "I think after his dealings with Fosse, Stephen didn't want any comments getting back to Bobby that would make things more difficult." It was orchestrator Ralph Burns who most frequently sat at the console with Jacob, "telling us how Bobby wanted the music to sound." Schwartz says that while he liked Burns and enjoyed working with him, "I didn't feel that he entirely got the feel of what I was trying to do with the score in some areas. I felt that he didn't rely enough on the rhythm section—piano, guitar, bass, drums. I was trying to write a pop score, somewhat like *Godspell*, which used only those four instruments, and then have it be filled out. With Ralph, it sounded too 'Broadway' to my ears in spots—particularly his use of brass, which is a very Broadway sound." Schwartz's preferences would be reflected in changes made for the cast album, and for the Broadway revival four decades later.

As Broadway musicals were evolving to incorporate contemporary sounds, they were also embracing, gradually, advances in technology. "The most important thing in a musical is to hear the lyrics," Jacob stresses, echoing countless voice coaches who have had to teach young singers weaned on pop music to enunciate. "I didn't know much about wireless microphones, and neither did anyone else at the time. In the past, stars could be given mics—Yul Brynner, Carol Channing, people like that—but they weren't easily used or hidden, so they weren't popular. In *Hair* and *Superstar*, we were able to use microphones on cords, which made this easier. For *Pippin*, Bobby obviously didn't want anything to interfere with his choreography, so we put shotgun microphones across the front of the stage." An exception was made for Ryan when she sang 'No Time at All." In lieu of an elaborate dance routine, Fosse used a piece of parchment that Walton had fashioned into a scroll, hung behind Ryan and the Players, on which the song's lyrics were printed. As Ryan and the company sang, a bouncing ball physically punctuated the words so that the audience got to read and, eventually, sing along with the chorus.

Schwartz had not been thrilled with the number, initially. In the *Newsday* interview, he explained, "It's supposed to be a rock number for an old lady. That's the humor of it; that's what it's got going for it. Naturally, since it's being done by an old lady there's a touch of vaudeville in it. I walked in today to see a run-through and they were doing straight vaudeville. Not a hint of rock. Not a hint!" So, he admitted, "I had a fight about it. They said, 'If she does it this way, we think it will stop the show.' I said, 'I don't care of it stops the show. I don't like it.'" But Schwartz concluded, "Maybe if it stops the show, it doesn't matter whether I like it."

"No Time" would indeed stop the show cold, Pamela Sousa recalls, with Ryan expertly milking the song's combination of ribald comedy and tender wisdom ("I believe if I refuse to grow old/I can stay young till I die"). "In those days we were still limited in what we could do with electronics, so the head spot man would have to move the bouncing ball manually," Sousa says. "And when it was over, the audience just went crazy—and Irene would stay in the wings the entire time they applauded. Phil Friedman used to say to her, 'Irene, you can go back to your room now,' but she would just say, 'No, I'm stayin' here—I want to hear all my applause!' She wouldn't leave until it was finished."

The polar opposite of "No Time," in terms of the work it demanded of the dancers, was "War Is a Science," one of those numbers that found Fosse repeating "Uno mas" again and again—and that was only after he was able to calm Rubinstein down. "It's the king's number, but Pippin is supposed to keep jumping up and interrupting," the actor notes. "So one day I was doing all kinds of funny stuff far on stage left—hand-slapping and knee-slapping so that it looked like Pippin was trying to do the choreography but couldn't do it, just like I couldn't. Bob came up to me at the end of rehearsal, and said, 'Uh, John?' 'Yeah?' 'It's Eric's number.' And I thought, what? I was just doing what I thought I was supposed to do, being Pippin trying to fit in, then being reprimanded by Charles. "And

Bob said, 'It's. Eric's. Number.' That was Bob the old vaudevillian—Pippin was supposed to be unable to grasp the choreography and to interrupt, but he knew it was Eric Berry's scene, and I was being too funny. I wasn't scene-stealing on purpose, but I had to learn not to steal the focus."

Brown still sounds exhausted when "War" is mentioned. "Wooh, we spent a *lot* of time working on that. We had three or four different versions at one point, and Bob would say, 'OK, for the first sixteen bars, do the A version, and then do the B version—no, do the C version, and then go back to the B.' Oh, we were a mess, trying to figure that one out." In spite of Fosse's unflagging work ethic, the process may have been complicated, at least occasionally, by the various substances he was pumping into his brain. "I was naïve at that time; I didn't know when people were buzzed or high or whatever," Brown says. "But there was one afternoon where Bob literally had us move one finger back and forth for—God, maybe three hours? I thought he was being persnickety, but looking back, I can't help but think he must have been on something."

Ostrow doesn't bother with speculation. "Bob was totally high; he would use drugs every day. I didn't know which ones—I didn't want to know. He would say to me, 'I can't sleep; I don't know what to do.' And I would tell him—I hated myself for having said this, but I told him, 'Bobby, whatever you're doing, just keep doing it, because you're doing a great job, and we're going to be a smash hit.'" Fosse's fellow artists, as one would expect, were at least a little less coldly pragmatic. "Bob was struggling with pills and drinking—that wasn't a secret," says Linda Posner, but adds, "He always gave his all, and so we gave our all."

As this was 1972, recreational intoxicants were no doubt readily accessible to everyone else. In *Fosse*, Sam Wasson quotes an unnamed dancer reporting an abundance of "poppers"—as inhalants such as amyl nitrite, quite trendy at the time, were called—backstage, along with stage hands "handing out PCP." But if the performers were indulging in anything stronger than cigarettes and Coke—the kind that comes in a can—with any regularity, no one is saying so. "I was never into drugs—that just wasn't me," Brown says, while Jennifer Nairn-Smith and Cheryl Clark weren't party people in any respect, they insist. Neither was Posner, who says, "I was very dedicated to my body, so I didn't even drink or smoke. I usually didn't even go out with the gang after the show."

That Fosse was still overseeing work on *Liza with a Z*—he would head from *Pippin* rehearsals to the cutting room at 1600 Broadway—surely contributed to the restlessness and exhaustion that kept both uppers and downers attractive. So did continuing financial concerns. In August, *Variety* reported that *Pippin* would have its four-week-long pre-Broadway run at the Kennedy Center's Opera House rather than the National Theatre, a commercial venue in Washington, as had been initially planned. As a government-sponsored entity, the Center was able to invest $100,000 that Ostrow apparently still needed—in exchange for, according to the article, 20 percent of the show, in addition to a $50,000 weekly gross for the engagement at the Opera House. The Nederlander family, which operated the National, issued a statement suggesting that this arrangement set a concerning precedent: "The regular Broadway producers are told that if they book the Kennedy Center they can increase their profits at the expense of the American taxpayer—taking advantage of tax-free buildings and grounds, building maintenance at the taxpayers' expense, and Congressional appropriations." A subsequent dispute between the Kennedy Center and the local musicians' union nearly forced the show to move its tryout to Boston before a new contract was agreed on, enabling the Opera House to keep the engagement.

To the extent that Fosse allowed himself downtime, it appears that he took some of the stress home with him. Daughter Nicole, who was only nine years old when *Pippin* opened, "wasn't really integrated in all the processes of this particular production," she allows, "though I do remember my father saying, 'I need Sam Cohn'"—the superstar talent agent he shared with film and theater luminaries—"often."

As the cast and crew were about to leave for Washington, Fosse was still worried enough about the show's overall prospects that he cut the intermission, along with what would have been the first scene of Act Two—set in a monastery, where Pippin lands of his own free will after resolving, briefly, to pursue a spiritual life. "We were all wearing monk robes and hoods, singing and dancing, twirling the rope belts we wore," Rubinstein says. The decision to turn *Pippin* into a one-act musical came, the actor remembers, shortly after the cast had done a run-through for a small audience including some of Fosse's friends—among them the playwrights Paddy Chayefsky, Herb Gardner, and Neil Simon. Fosse would later concede that it was Chayefsky's suggestion, but when Fisher learned of the adjustment, "I asked Bob why he was cutting the intermission, and he said it was because he didn't think the audience would come back." Thus Washington and Broadway attendees never got to see what Brown describes as "this kind of vaudeville-jazz routine, in monks' robes."

These audiences were the first to witness the seductive, creepy majesty of the Manson Trio during "Glory." Performed while Players dressed as soldiers simulate a killing spree, the dance was preceded by the arrival of three microphones onstage, with the letters "W," "A," and "R" visible on them, along with an "On the Air" sign, to suggest a recording studio. The sign's message changed to "Applause" as a tape of the Leading Player's voice boomed over the loudspeaker; parodying a disc jockey, he brightly recounted the number of casualties and wounded parties produced by various historical conflicts, from the Holy Wars to "that all-time favorite: World War II." Vietnam was even more conspicuous in its omission, given that its final toll could not yet be measured.

Two of the soldiers—Brown and Sousa, their body-hugging armor accessorized with boots and bowler hats and canes—then sandwiched Vereen, and, after bowing deeply, the three began moving in unison to Schwartz's perversely jaunty music, summoning a deliberately mechanical eroticism that seemed to mock both life and death. No dance has more famously reflected Fosse's precision or his dual preoccupation with sex and mortality than this one, with its swiveling hips and shoulders, its bent knees flicking out in straight kicks, suggesting puppets trying to will themselves into human form—or perhaps eager to please a puppet master like Vereen's character, or the real-life cult leader who gave the trio its name.

"I just remember being told to think of the joy of performing—but then to consider that maybe it's your sixteenth show, so you're not loving it as much," says Sousa. "It's not fresh anymore. And at the end of the dance, you had these two worlds colliding, this slow crossover into the reality of war, which is why our smiles went away, and there was this just this vacancy. And Ben said, 'Ta-daa'—very flatly, as if to say, 'Just look at this world.'" Linda Haberman, who accompanied Vereen in the Trio in the televised 1981 staging, also remembers getting specific directions from Fosse: "He told us that war was like a big turn-on, so that every time we thought of blood and killing people it's like a sex act."

The character of Pippin appeared briefly during the dance, crossing the stage with a bloodied hand, as a soldier went past him with a head on a pike-staff. "The stage is littered with limbs and bodies and heads, etc.," read directions immediately following the dance. Nicole Fosse notes that during his navy service in World War II, her father had "tap danced in hospitals for soldiers and sailors his own age, missing their body parts and in dire pain. He never again saw our human desire to be entertained—to escape—through innocent eyes."

If Fosse referenced Manson for obvious reasons, Brown has come to believe the title also signified something larger and more pervasive. "In retrospect, it seems Bob was always very concerned with justice, and with how easy it was in this country to purchase it, spin it, manipulate it—and the ease with which we look the other way. I think I remember him referencing Nero fiddling while Rome burned."

There were other parallels to be found much closer to home, and they extended beyond the atrocities being committed and lies being told about Vietnam. Few people knew it yet, but that past June, the month before *Pippin* rehearsals began, a break-in had occurred at the offices of the Democratic National Committee; that incident and the cover-up that followed would lead to a historic investigation and, eventually, the resignation of President Nixon. And *Pippin*'s next destination was a theater located right next to the scene of the crime: the Watergate Hotel.

CHAPTER EIGHT

Bomb Scares, Death Threats, and More Fun in Washington

SUMMER WAS WINDING DOWN BY THE TIME THE *PIPPIN* CAST AND CREW rolled into the nation's capital, and there was still work to be done before the show's September 20 pre-Broadway opening at the Kennedy Center Opera House. Most of the company members were put up at a Holiday Inn across the street, though John Rubinstein was among a few who got to stay—along with Bob Fosse, Stuart Ostrow, Stephen Schwartz, and Roger Hirson—at the swanky Watergate Hotel, not yet known as the site of a national scandal. Rubinstein brought his wife and baby daughter, Jessica, who learned to crawl there. "We had a beautiful view of the Potomac River and would watch the rowers practice their team sculling," he says.

Everyone had been following the ongoing debacle in Vietnam. The three television networks all had news teams stationed in the field, Rubinstein recalls, documenting "the explosions, the saturation bombings, the jungle ambushes, the helicopter raids, the assassinations of Vietnamese civilians, the burning of villages, the napalming of children, and, importantly, the dead and wounded American servicemen and women as they were loaded onto Hueys and Air Force cargo planes and sent to hospitals, and as they arrived back home." The Pentagon Papers had been released just over a year before *Pippin* started rehearsals, revealing how the American people and even members of Congress had been deceived by government leaders over several administrations. Now the *Pippin* team was in the belly of the beast at which the show took aim—if not directly or consistently, then with graphic detail.

Like Schwartz, Rubinstein had demonstrated against the war and been haunted by the prospect of getting drafted. He got a medical deferment after graduating from UCLA in 1968, but by the time a lottery was instituted toward the end of the following year, he was assigned a number "in the lower middle," making him more likely to be called than those with higher numbers. But he never was. "I lived in trepidation for years, but I was lucky." Ben Vereen, who had a wife and young children, was excused from service, though he had joined Jane Fonda on a tour of U.S. army bases the previous fall—"to protest the war, not the soldiers," he stresses. Richard Korthaze and Gene Foote had aged out of eligibility. "I was drafted for Korea," Foote says, "but they asked me if I was a homosexual, and I said yes. Then they asked if I was passive or aggressive, and I said, 'Whatever turns you on.' And they told me to go home. By the time Vietnam came along, I was already an old lady."

Candy Brown recalls, "There was this program where you could get a bracelet with a soldier's name on it, and I got one. And even though we weren't supposed to wear jewelry onstage, I wore that bracelet, and nobody said anything. So yeah, the war was very much at the forefront of everybody's mind, though we had no idea that Watergate was going down." Foote, however, is certain he saw a woman in a nightgown outside the hotel one evening, "running around like a crazy lady" and bearing an uncanny resemblance to Martha Mitchell, the soon-to-be former wife of Nixon's attorney general, John N. Mitchell, who would be convicted and imprisoned for his role in the Watergate scandal. (Mrs. Mitchell had been known to speak openly and critically about the Nixon administration, and she would claim that shortly after the break-in, she was held against her will in a California hotel room to keep her quiet.)

A more bracing sign of the times was the bomb scare that interrupted a rehearsal of, wouldn't you know it, "War Is a Science." Foote recounts it most vividly: "We were working on one of the four variations we had already learned; Bob still wasn't happy yet so we were doing a new version almost nightly. Leland Palmer had done nothing all day and was asleep in a box in the corner of the rehearsal room when someone burst in to tell us there was a bomb in the building. We all started to run when Bob said, 'Wait, before we go, could we just try this one more time?' Of course, the answer was no; Phil [Friedman] said we had to go. So we left the building and went out onto the lawn—and as soon as we were there Bob wanted to try one more thing. He didn't want to stop working!"

It was a false alarm, happily, and far from the most anxiety-producing development during *Pippin*'s four-week run at the Opera House. A man that Jennifer Nairn-Smith had been dating had apparently learned of her involvement with Fosse, and was not pleased. There were threats of violence, according to cast members. "We had all heard and shared rumors about it," Rubinstein says of the affair between the stunning dancer and her director, "but I personally never saw any evidence of it"—not until just before the trip to Washington, when the cast and crew moved rehearsals from Variety Arts to the Ethel Barrymore Theatre for a few rehearsals. When Rubinstein showed up for work, "Bob had bodyguards on both sides of him as he sat in the house, watching rehearsals"—Ostrow had hired a pair of off-duty police officers after learning of the boyfriend—"and we were frisked as we came in." The backstage drama followed Fosse out of town. "They had to get a limousine to get Bob out of the Kennedy Center safely, because there were actual threats to his life," says Cheryl Clark. In his memoir, Ostrow recalled, "I had to ask my connection at the White House to have the Secret Service escort us to the D.C. city limits."

If Schwartz encountered no such dangers while in Washington, he was "not a happy camper," according to Dean Pitchford, an actor and songwriter who met Schwartz when he successfully auditioned for a replacement spot in *Godspell*'s off-Broadway cast, then served as standby for and eventually played Pippin on Broadway. Pitchford, who would become an Oscar-winning songwriter and screenwriter—his many credits include *Fame* and *Footloose*, as well as a musical theater adaptation of *Carrie*—had been promoted to the role of Jesus on a national tour of *Godspell* that wound up spending two and half years in Washington, during which *Pippin* came to town. With Fosse firmly in charge of the latter show, Schwartz began spending some of his ample downtime with the *Godspell* cast at the Ford's Theatre. "They were all my age, and friends," he says. "It was sort of like, when you have a difficult family life, you go off with friends."

Pitchford, who has remained close to Schwartz, recalls that the composer even began taking notes and calling rehearsals, perhaps trying to unleash his pent-up creative energy in a more welcoming environment. "We were all very happy to see him, but it got exhausting," Pitchford says, laughing. "We were already doing a lot of extra stuff, making special appearances at schools and meeting people on Capitol Hill as part of publicity. So I had dinner with Stephen after the show one night, and I told him, 'We love you madly, but you can't keep rehearsing us. Just come and hang out with us.' So he got in the habit of coming towards the end of the show, and then four or five of us would go to Georgetown and get Italian food. Then he'd call and ask me to have lunch, and I'd hear about what was going on at *Pippin*. He was feeling like the show had gotten away from him. Bobby, as I would eventually witness myself, endeared himself to the cast so much that he could do no wrong. Whenever there was a dust-up, everyone would line up behind Bobby—and Stephen was left feeling very alone. He had a strong relationship with John Rubinstein, but that's because when Bobby was working with his dancers, John was sidelined; he would sit with Stephen while Bobby was working with Ben Vereen and Leland Palmer, who spoke the language he spoke."

While Schwartz, again, didn't feel that the dancers regarded him with any hostility—"Everybody was pretty nice to me, as I remember it," he says—his strained relationship with Fosse complicated this late and crucial phase of the production. The composer doesn't recall even discussing politics with the director, however much their mutual opposition to the war in Vietnam—and war generally—informed *Pippin*. Schwartz would be invited to visit the White House by Frank Gannon, an aide to President Nixon and a fan of both *Godspell* and *Pippin*. He accepted the offer but arrived wearing a button endorsing George McGovern, Nixon's Democratic opponent in that year's upcoming election. "It didn't occur to me that was rude," Schwartz insists. "Then someone told me that either H. R. Haldeman or John Ehrlichmann"—Nixon's White House chief of staff and domestic affairs adviser, respectively—"was also a fan. That was both intriguing and horrifying to me—because I was so rabidly anti-Nixon, and I was learning that his henchmen were fans."

Schwartz's idealism was still fervent enough to make him chafe at an exchange during the scene in which Pippin, having killed Charles, briefly replaces him as king. "Pippin is trying to do all these good things that people are demanding of him, but they don't work, and he winds up going back to basically ruling like his father." Schwartz points to a line that he thinks Hirson wrote while working with Fosse—"Take that man away and hang him!"—echoing Charlemagne in an early encounter with one of his lowly subjects. "I know the scene works as shorthand, but it was very troubling to me politically—because it said, well, there's no such thing as an enlightened ruler; you can't change things. That was not a message I wanted to put out there at the time, and to tell you the truth, it still bothers me a bit politically. However, I have to admit that, as I have with several of the lines Bob added, I've come to like the line, because Charles says it in his first scene—and then when Pippin as king repeats it, Roger added a response from the unfortunate man: 'Not again,' which is funny and has the quirky quality I like about Roger's work."

Schwartz had greatly enjoyed crafting what may be *Pippin*'s most unabashedly sardonic song: "Spread a Little Sunshine"—a saccharine-soaked waltz sung by Fastrada in the scene where she learns of Pippin's plan to kill his father and deceives both men in the hopes that she and Lewis will benefit. The song was crafted during rehearsals and became one of the composer's happier collaborations with Fosse. Another was "Love Song," which Schwartz wrote in Washington to replace "Just between the Two of Us," a duet for Pippin and Catherine that, according to Rubinstein, "was a perfectly nice song, but somehow didn't grab the audience." It also tested Jill Clayburgh's limited vocal range. The romantic leads were called into a hotel room to read and learn the new song and immediately loved it. "We were delirious," Rubinstein remembers.

Alas, their delirium would be too obvious that evening when they had to perform "Two of Us" once more for a live audience. "We ran onstage for the scene"—in which Pippin and Catherine first make love—"and she sat on her little square box that came out of the floor, and I sat next to her, leaning my arm in her lap, and I sang my first line and she sang her first line. But having just heard this new song, and knowing that it was being orchestrated and would go into the show in a night or two, we looked up at each other for the third line—and broke into hysterical laughter. Because we knew this old song was going away—it was halfway in the garbage—and we no longer had to give it respect or decorum, and our discipline just disappeared. And seeing each other laugh made us laugh harder. I remember looking at Stanley Lebowsky, the conductor, who was conducting nothing, just soft accompaniment to this song we weren't singing. We sang about four per cent of it, maybe. And at the end, oh, were we sweating. That was one of the most shameful moments I have ever had onstage."

A second song written in Washington, "Extraordinary," replaced "Marking Time," a deceptively buoyant tune in which Pippin warned Catherine that he wouldn't be around for the long haul. "This was Pippin's eleven o'clock number," says Rubinstein, "his insistence that he would never be tied down to a married life. I really liked the song—it had a good, catchy melody; smart words, and a Laura Nyro–style piano beat." The song is periodically performed in cabaret, notes Schwartz, who remains fond of it as well. But Rubinstein also found "Time" too contemplative for the moment: "I couldn't find a way to give it the strength it needed to show Pippin's frustration and desperate desire to do something 'better.' Clearly, Bob and Roger and Stephen agreed, and they came up with 'Extraordinary,' which was much more appropriate to illustrate Pippin's dilemma."

But Rubinstein admits that he never really enjoyed performing "Extraordinary," which starts as a bouncy mid-tempo number, segues to a frantic bridge, and then builds to a pounding conclusion, with Pippin belting out and holding the penultimate note for several beats. "It might have been because I was simply not a strong enough vocalist to sell it sufficiently," Rubinstein admits. "It has sort of a rock feel, and could have used a more rock & roll-type voice to put it over better." Schwartz notes, "There were other songs that I wrote along the way and really liked that we couldn't use. There was this medieval-style ballad, called 'The Rose, the Thorn, and the Wildwood' that I was particularly fond of musically, though that was before we really got going with the show. As we went along, it became clear what fit the show. I certainly didn't mind losing the song I'd written for the monastery scene"—a Gregorian chant, complete with Latin lyrics.

Schwartz was concerned, however, when the prospect of losing "Kind of Woman" briefly came about. "It's kind of Catherine's 'I Want' song, because she's trying to entice Pippin into being interested in her. When we were in Washington, Bob threatened to take it out for a couple of days, and this time I just said, 'No, I'm sorry, this number has to be in the show.' Because we were introducing a brand new character late in the show, and she needs to establish herself. I told him that I could try to write a different number, but that we had to have something." Schwartz doesn't remember if he invoked his rights under the Dramatists Guild, "but I think my agent, Shirley Bernstein, had a conversation with Stuart Ostrow and told him that they couldn't, contractually, cut a number without the composer's approval, and he's not approving it." Fosse finally proved willing to compromise, keeping the song but adding the campy backing vocals that Schwartz has since lamented.

Behind the scenes, other changes were taking shape. Fosse had grown closer to Ann Reinking, and not just in the carnal sense. After Clark and male swing Roger Bigelow had started spending some time doing shoulder lifts rather than focusing on the others at Kennedy Center rehearsals, Clark recalls, "Annie took me aside, and she said, 'Cheryl, Bobby'—I think she was calling him Bobby by that point—'Bobby wanted me to talk to you. He thinks you're really talented, but he doesn't understand the way you're behaving. I told her that it was hard, as alternates, to have to just be sitting around taking notes all the time. Bob didn't want to lose me, and he chose her to tell me. She saved my job, in a way."

While Nairn-Smith was likely still in the picture, Reinking was fast emerging as a more principal figure in Fosse's life. "Later, as the run of the show continued, Bob's liaison with Jennifer stopped being a 'thing,' at least in my limited awareness," says Rubinstein, "and his liaison with Annie Reinking became a visible, ongoing, much more serious relationship, known about by everyone." (Nairn-Smith would remain in *Pippin* for only about a year, in fact; she says the early departure wasn't her choice any more than leaving Balanchine had been but won't elaborate. "It's too dark," she explains. "When you're as visible as I am, you attract the good and the bad.") "It was clear that Annie really loved Bob," says Clark. "As stunning as Jennifer was, and she became my big sister, Annie was an American beauty rose. That's what I called her." Fosse was plainly more than smitten with Reinking as well—though as a lover, at least, he would prove no more faithful to her than he had to other women he'd really loved before her.

Clark and Nairn-Smith remained friends, and both women say they didn't attend the parties the director threw for colleagues in his room at the Watergate. "I was never one of the girls there," Clark insists. "I was still shy. I would be at our hotel, reading a book on psychology, *Psycho-Cybernetics*—I still have it. And I had my first real boyfriend, who was in the Toronto Symphony." Other cast members, male and female, assembled at Fosse's gatherings both to unwind and to affirm their camaraderie, as one does at any family get-together. "I never stayed too long, because I wasn't a party person," says Richard Korthaze. "I would just make an appearance so I could socialize with other cast members, and Bob would see I was involved." Schwartz, meanwhile, played bridge in his own room with Hirson, Shirley Bernstein, and Arthur Laurents— another Bernstein client who had come to lend support and possibly, given his well-documented appetite for backstage dish, search for signs of dissonance between Fosse and Schwartz.

Performances continued, meanwhile, with more of the tweaks and occasional twists that can accompany out-of-town engagements. The firebox featured in the finale was incorporated for the first time. "There was a more spectacular set planned for the fire trick, but ultimately we couldn't afford it," Schwartz notes; Mineo, as the Player assigned to hold the torch, was tasked with igniting a mannequin covered in flash paper. At another point, Clark got her moment in the spotlight when Kathryn Doby injured her Achilles tendon. "It was a stupid accident, just stepping off a curb," Doby says, but it kept her out of performances for a week and out of the "Bolero" number—where she and Foote appeared opposite Clayburgh and Rubinstein in a choreographic representation of Catherine and Pippin's connubial progress—for longer than that. During several performances at the Kennedy Center and several more on Broadway, including opening night, Clark got to wear that gold, G-string bikini and do a grand jeté into Foote's arms, be gently dropped, and then leap again and be caught. "Gene still brings it up to me," Clark says proudly. "He says, 'Cheryl, you flew so high that I almost didn't catch you!'"

Once the reviews began arriving, the *Pippin* team had cause to feel rewarded for all the work and the agita they'd endured. "Let's hear it loud and clear—as surely you will—for a rare, welcome original, *Pippin*," raved Richard L. Coe, the influential critic of the *Washington Post*. "Last night's premiere at the Kennedy Center Opera House proves that the innovative spirit yet lives in the American musical theater." While Coe conceded that the show still needed some editing, as other critics also would, he had praise for both Fosse—whose choreography, he wrote, "is fourfold more sensuous than anything on display in *Oh! Calcutta!*," an erotic revue that had by then featured naked performers off-Broadway and in London's West End—and Hirson and Schwartz, whom he deemed "immensely resourceful." William Glover, writing for the Associated Press and the *Los Angeles Times*, called the musical "a highly imaginative enterprise," adding that its score indicated that Schwartz's work on *Godspell* "was no creative flash in the pan." The *Boston Globe*'s Kevin Kelly described the music as "a loving embrace that draws the audience to the warm heart of its rhythm and lyrics" and declared the performances "marvelous" and Fosse's choreography and direction "brilliant." And David Richards of the *Washington Star-Tribune* hailed *Pippin* as "breathlessly theatrical and endlessly inventive."

Schwartz's old friend David Spangler, who had come to Washington for the opening, remembers walking back to the Watergate with him that night. "That's when Stephen really unloaded, and told me everything— that he resented what Fosse had done with the show and with the part of Pippin." At the same time, Spangler notes, "He was elated, because he knew then that the show was going to be a hit. That's why he picked up the phone when we got back to the hotel, and called Ron Strauss"—their fellow Carnegie alumnus, who had first conceived *Pippin, Pippin* and thus been assured that he would benefit to at least some extent from its successor. "Stephen said to Ron, 'I just wanted to tell you, you're going to be a very wealthy man.' I'll never forget that."

But Fosse, at least, wasn't satisfied yet. Pleasing the press in a city where squares like Haldeman and Ehrlichmann and Nixon's other cronies held court was one thing; winning over more sophisticated and discerning New York scribes would be another matter. Having dinner at the Watergate one night, Schwartz met Paddy Chayevsky and Herb Gardner, who were clearly not in town by chance or to just pay their director buddy a social visit. "There weren't substantial structural changes made to the show in Washington," Schwartz points out. "There were just some things added, and I'm not sure where they all came from—if Bob wrote some of them, or Herb or Paddy suggested them, or if Bob asked Roger to write them." Two weeks of previews at Broadway's Imperial Theatre would bring about more revisions, one of which went too far for Schwartz—and, since Fosse wouldn't budge this time, helped precipitate a legal dispute that would forever alter the musical's legacy, specifically how it would be performed in key future productions.

CHAPTER NINE

Glory, Glory . . . and Grievances

THE COVER OF *LIFE* MAGAZINE'S NOVEMBER 17, 1972 ISSUE SHOWED A close-up of Richard Nixon's seemingly grimacing face, accompanied by the headline, "The Big Win: What will Nixon do with it?" The president had just handily earned a second term, scoring five hundred and twenty electoral votes to George McGovern's seventeen, but in this photo, at least, he didn't look like the cat who got the cream. The inside story, an analysis of the victory, referred only fleetingly to "the Watergate bugging case and the related charges of political espionage," by then prominent news stories that would bring some of Nixon's closest associates to trial before a Senate committee early the following year. But Vietnam got more notice from the article's author, Hugh Sidey, who asserted that the war "must be ended"—a blunt statement coming from an establishment publication, but hardly a shocking one more than four years after Walter Cronkite had declared the war "mired in stalemate."

That issue of *Life*, incidentally, also included a feature on Broadway's latest hit show, perkily titled "Holy Roman Razzmatazz: A Happy Reign for 'Pippin.'" A lavish photo spread reveling in Patricia Zipprodt's eclectic, provocative costumes—and the equally ogle-worthy dancers who wore them—was accompanied at one point by the caption, "A boo for war, a boost for sex." The short article itself was practically an ad for the show, though it did contain this caveat: "*Pippin*'s songs and book are seldom more than routine crackerjack. But the whole box is so packed with eye-popping theatrical prizes, including several fine performances, that *Pippin* is assured of a long, happy reign."

It's doubtful that Stephen Schwartz or even Roger Hirson, despite his readiness to make concessions to Bob Fosse, found gratification in how the piece promoted their show: as a superior but glib entertainment—a triumph of "razzmatazz" over substance for an audience in need of distraction from the sobering events addressed in the magazine's cover story. Perception had been moving in this direction, of course, since Stuart Ostrow first handed Fosse a copy of the libretto, and as *Pippin* moved into the Imperial Theatre for its final rehearsals and first Broadway previews, there was no indication that the pattern would reverse course. The Leading Player and his minions continued to disrupt the music and the drama with jazzy little interjections and mocking commentary. Charles acquired a grandiloquent speech defending his tyranny to his son, delivered shortly before Pippin kills him but deflated by this exchange:

LEADING PLAYER: God, that was beautiful, Charles.

CHARLES: Oh, did you like it?

LEADING PLAYER: I loved it.

CHARLES: Oh, thank you so much.

Later, while directing Catherine, the misfit Player, to read a line differently, the Leading Player got to snort, "Jesus. Actresses." And in the final scene, where Pippin's foil urged him not to let the crowd down by chickening out of self-destruction, the line got extended to, "Hey you're not going to disappoint all these people at . . . dollars a seat?" (The amount isn't listed in the opening-night script, though presumably it would look like pocket change compared to the current price of a Broadway ticket.)

Like Schwartz, Rubinstein didn't know or doesn't recall the source of these slightly hoary touches, but he does remember precisely when Fosse ruined the show's ending—in his estimation—and why. In *Pippin*'s final moments, after the Leading Player has had the set torn down and the lights turned off and even gotten rid of the orchestra and Pippin and Catherine and Theo are shorn of all their showbiz accessories, the lovers were to engage in this brief question-and-answer session:

CATHERINE: Pippin ... do you feel that you've compromised?
PIPPIN: No.
CATHERINE: Do you feel like a coward?
PIPPIN: No.
CATHERINE: How do you feel? ...
PIPPIN: Trapped ... but happy ... which isn't too bad for the end of a musical comedy. Ta-da!

The audience would laugh after he said "Trapped," Rubinstein recalls, "and I would wait, and then say those two words: 'But happy.' And the audience would go, 'Ooooh'—like, *yes!* Because everybody feels trapped in their lives, to some degree, and when I would say those last words, the audience would feel relieved of all the cynicism they had just enjoyed so much. They would love it. It got huge laughs and applause in Washington and in New York."

About halfway through *Pippin*'s three weeks of preview performances at the Imperial, though, Fosse paid a visit to Rubinstein's dressing room before the performance. "Bob comes in and says, 'Hey, John? Cut 'but happy.' And I said to him, 'What? Are you fucking out of your mind?' And he told me he wasn't going to have the New York critics call him a goddamn sentimentalist. I argued with him. I said, 'No, the audience gets their unsentimental moment with "Trapped," but then we save them, and we save Pippin—without getting mushy. That's what the show is about; that's where it's leading us.' And he just said, 'Nah, it's bullshit.'"

Roughly two hours later, Rubinstein faced Clayburgh onstage and began speaking his final line. "When I said, 'Trapped,' the audience screamed with laughter; the New York audience loved that even more than the Washington audience. Then I waited till the laughter died down, and like always, I lifted up their hands"—Clayburgh's and Shane Nickerson's—"and I said, 'Which isn't too bad for the end of a musical comedy. Ta-da!' And the audience went"—Rubinstein makes a groaning sound. "Like someone had farted in their faces. And the curtain went down, and the applause was mild. When Bob came back to my dressing room after the show, I said, 'You see? It ruined the end.' And he said, 'Nah, I love it. We're keeping it.'"

Those two simple words—"but happy"—would figure heavily in Schwartz's eventual decision to pursue the right to go back to the script with Hirson and make changes of their own. "Taking out 'but happy' was one of the ways Bob took the heart out of the show, which I think became colder as a result," says Schwartz. But with opening night around the corner, Broadway audiences and critics would see the *Pippin* that had finally won Fosse's approval.

The director had, with Stuart Ostrow, arranged a party for the cast after the first preview, at a restaurant attached to the Edison Hotel on 46th Street. "We sat at circular tables," Cheryl Clark remembers. "I think Gene Foote was at mine, with our great Irene Ryan, who was hysterical; she said, 'Fuck the awards. Fuck the fame. Be in it for the money!' There was little Granny, saying this! We all loved her so much." There was a special performance the night before opening, Foote remembers, with several boldfaced names in attendance. "We scared Carol Channing to death! She was sitting in the fourth row, in the center, with these big glasses on. And there was a moment in the opening number called the 'walking cross,' where we talked to the audience, and Bob told me that on my third step he wanted me to throw my head back and start laughing hysterically, then go back to talking. And that scared her!"

When October 23 finally arrived, Rubinstein put whatever misgivings he had accumulated about Fosse's choices aside. Before heading to the theater, the young actor sat down with a piece of Barbizon-Plaza Hotel stationery and wrote to his director,

Dear Bob—

Two hours now before we open—and aside from a nasty case of shaky legs, all I can really feel is a true affection and gratitude to you for all you've offered and given during the past three months. You are so brilliant and sensitive, and observant, and caring, and incisive, you make an actor want to do anything in his power to realize your visions. You have, apart from allowing me to be one of the rare people whose dreams actually come true, shown me so much, opened my mind (not just as an actor) and heart, and I feel honored and happy to be part of your great show.

But even more, I feel terribly close to little Pippin, whom I gradually have come to believe to be not far from little Bob—and I feel in my heart that the three of us aren't too far apart in spirit, and somehow there's "glory in the air" for us, and we're leaping about there together.

Thank you, Bob.

Love always, John

There would also be notes and gifts from Fosse, though they arrived a bit late, Pamela Sousa recalls: "Bob felt so bad. I have a note he wrote me, where he basically said, I've been so busy that I didn't get you anything, but I'll get you something eventually. I think it was a couple of weeks later that we each got a bottle of Dom Perignon, in a case. Champagne in a case—that was new for me. And he wrote us the sweetest personal notes; the essence of mine was, 'I didn't know how extraordinary you are, and that's my fault, not yours.'" Candy Brown saved her note and the champagne bottle, which she still hasn't opened; on her own opening-night card to Fosse, she had written the word "love" more than twenty times, followed by, "hey . . . guess how I feel about you . . ." and yet a few more "love"s.

For Rubinstein, the opening show would be complicated by a last-minute technical decision. "It was a Thursday, and right before the curtain, Bob Fosse and Stuart Ostrow came into my dressing room to wish me luck and give me a hug. Bob said, 'Oh, by the way, tonight and tomorrow night"—the two nights when critics would attend—"we're going to add a bit more smoke to 'Magic to Do.' But don't worry, on Saturday night we'll go back to the regular amount. We just need it to look especially great for the critics." Rubinstein thanked them for the heads-up, but moments later, "when I took my first breath to sing 'Corner of the Sky,' I felt actual particles of whatever that smoke was made of"— dry ice, actually—"enter my throat and stick there. When I sang, my voice was noticeably hoarse and rough-sounding; I couldn't sustain the notes as I had always been able to, and my whole first song sounded like I was more or less unable to sing. It was a horrible moment I'll never forget. For all the critics, Pippin was being played by some kid who couldn't sing! My already serious qualms about my lack of a huge, solid singing voice were multiplied ten times. But I carried on, finished the song, and by the time we got to the next scene, the smoke had gone away, and the rest of the night was easier."

After the performance, while at least some cast members were anxiously waiting for the critics to weigh in, there was another "small gathering" at Sardi's, says Sousa, "because the producers didn't really have an abundance of cash." Sousa brought her parents, who had flown in from San Francisco. As Kathryn Doby's husband was in Vienna working on a film, she brought her mother. "She only spoke three or four words of English," Doby recalls. "It was her first time out of Hungary. In those days Hungary was still a Communist country, and it was very difficult to get permission to leave, even though her passport was only valid for that one trip. Being in New York on the opening night of a Broadway show was a really big deal. She met Bobby and almost the whole cast, and everybody was wonderful to her. She had the time of her life. She was talking about it for years."

Foote, not one to forget a juicy tidbit, recalls Fosse turning up with both Ann Reinking and Jennifer Nairn-Smith, "and they were both in men's suits." Doby, too, remembers matching pants suits: "I think they had derbies with them." Afterward, Jules Fisher hosted the company at his apartment. "I remember a loud, festive party," says Sousa. "At one point my dad saw Marlo Thomas and said he wanted to go up to her and say, 'Are you *that girl?*'"—a cheeky reference to her hit TV series of the same name. "I told him I would disown him. I was twenty years old!" Schwartz, notably, did not attend either party but rather celebrated with his wife and agent across town at Maxwell's Plum. Although the composer would later make it a habit to skip opening-night festivities, "It wasn't a strict policy yet. But because of the tensions between Stuart and Bob and me, I thought that it was better for me to observe it separately, for my sake and theirs."

When the verdicts began coming in, the *New York Times* set the tone. Clive Barnes summed up the musical itself as "a commonplace set to rock music" but had only kudos for its director: "Mr. Fosse has achieved complete continuity between his staging and his choreography, and his dances themselves have art and imagination. They swing with life." As many of his colleagues would, Barnes also applauded the design team, singling out Tony Walton for scenery that "manages an almost impossible combination of Holy Roman Empire and Fifth Avenue chic" and Patricia Zipprodt for "equal adroitness and elegance—her clowns look Italian and Fellini and her girls look French and naked." And while each of the principal actors received favorable mention—"The cast also lives up to Mr. Fosse rather than down to the material"—Barnes wrote, "It was, I felt, Mr. Vereen who really held the show together. Following his demonic performance last season as Judas in 'Jesus Christ Superstar,' Mr. Vereen here shows all the makings of a superstar himself."

Other notices followed suit, for the most part. "The chief glory of the occasion belongs to the Messrs. Fosse, Walton, and Fisher, and to Miss Zipprodt," wrote *The New Yorker*'s Brendan Gill, after pronouncing Vereen "brilliant"—and Rubinstein "unexpectedly vulnerable and touching"—but dismissing the "skimpy book" and "competent but not very interesting music." *The Villager*'s Donald J. Mayerson, similarly, called the score "pleasant but unremarkable" and quipped, "Once the plot is dispensed with, it's easy enough to get on with the show. And that involves the immense talents of Bob Fosse, who has staged the show with verve and style, borrowing not only from Fellini and the Italian theatre, but from Fosse's own rich background." Writing in the *New York Daily News*, Rex Reed agreed that "it is Bob Fosse who emerges as the master chef of this Fellini stew. Had he lived in Pippin's era, they probably would have knighted him."

There were outlets that gave Schwartz more credit: the *Wall Street Journal* identified his "fresh music and lyrics" among *Pippin*'s "exceptional" elements, while the *Daily News* found them "charming," and the *Christian Science Monitor* proclaimed that Schwartz "more than fulfills the promise he showed in 'Godspell.'" Rubinstein and other cast members received praise as well; *New York*'s John Simon was one of several reviewers who pointed to the pulchritude of the female Players, memorably observing, "One girl, Jennifer Nairn-Smith, could explain even the Vietnam War, if it were fought over her." The general consensus seemed to vindicate Fosse's choices, including his decision to beef up the role crafted for Vereen. *Life*'s own theater critic, Tom Prideaux, likened Rubinstein's Pippin to "a soft-core rock hero before the takeover of the electric guitar." After allowing that he found Eric Berry, Leland Palmer, and Irene Ryan more compelling, Prideaux began, "Then there is Ben Vereen, who is very appropriately billed as the Leading Player," and proceeded to gush over both the character and the performer:

> *A blend of Sportin' Life and Judas (whom he played in* Superstar*), he is a song-and-dance Lucifer, doubly wicked in* Pippin *because he wheedles for sympathy—and gets it—and because his magically ingratiating smile makes us forgive him, forgive ourselves, forgive the world for all its sins. As fine a dancer as he is a singer, Ben Vereen will doubtless win one of Broadway's annual prizes next spring.*

Schwartz's and Rubinstein's worst fears had been realized, with a show that was the toast of Broadway. For the composer and lyricist who had conceived the musical, the irony was especially cruel. "I had people come up to me and say things like, 'I hope that every night in your prayers you're thanking God for Bob Fosse,'" he recalls. "That's actually a direct quote from someone—I have a vivid memory of it."

Rubinstein dutifully began working on "being more present," as he puts it, but he was still peeved about that ending. Schwartz had given him, on opening night, a framed copy of the first page of sheet music for "Corner of the Sky," "and on it Stephen had written, 'To John—who also felt 'trapped,' but I hope ended up 'happy,' with deep admiration and thanks, not just for a show-saving performance, but for a morale-saving style. Your importance to me personally on this show can't be overstated. Thank you. Steve Schwartz.'" (Vereen received "Magic to Do," also framed and dedicated.) Rubinstein hung the gift in his dressing room, "which served as a sort of green room for the whole cast during the run, because it was the only dressing room on the stage floor of the Imperial Theatre."

One night, well into the run, Fosse would happen to spy the framed page and read what Schwartz had written. "So he angrily picked up my eyebrow pencil and wrote on the glass, 'How sweet! Bob F.' I felt a bit bad about it, but it was old news by then, so I didn't say or do anything about it. A few weeks later, Stuart Ostrow was also sitting in my dressing room during the show, and saw the same thing, including Bob's make-up-pencil comment. So he picked up the same pencil and wrote, next to Bob's message, 'Just send the cash back (Stu).'" I still have that framed song page, with Steve's very generous dedication, and the two sarcastic remarks by Bob and Stu."

For Schwartz—and no doubt Hirson, who had endured pans of his book knowing that Fosse was responsible for at least some its hokier aspects—there was surely some consolation in *Pippin*'s reception among fans, reflected in its box office performance. Although not an instant smash, the show, which had reduced its budget to roughly $500,000, would perform solidly enough to recoup its investment and earn an estimated $125,000 to boot by the next spring, as *Variety* reported in its April 4, 1973, edition. The article noted that the production had earned $401,851 in its first fourteen weeks on Broadway, then $125,144 between January 27 and February 24.

Tony Award nominations for the 1972–1973 season surely increased the show's visibility; *Pippin* earned eleven of them, including best musical, book of a musical, and original score. Although the production—or, more specifically, Ostrow, Hirson, and Schwartz—would lose in those categories, in each case to Sondheim's *A Little Night Music*, Vereen, Walton, and Fisher all took home trophies, and Fosse earned two, for direction and choreography. (Leland Palmer, Irene Ryan, and Patricia Zipprodt were the other also-rans; Zipprodt, rather surprisingly, also lost to a member of the *Night Music* team: the admittedly accomplished Florence Klotz, who would collect a total of six Tonys before her death in 2006.)

But *Pippin* would experience a real surge in ticket sales the next fall, thanks in part to a stroke of ingenuity on Ostrow's part, and Fosse's. The producer had the notion that a TV commercial might give sales a boost, particularly if it gave viewers a sense of the razzmatazz and sex that the

Life story had touted. At that point, television ads for Broadway shows had not featured live footage, but Ostrow and Fosse decided that the best way to sell their product was to let people see it dance. After some consideration, the Manson Trio, with its catchy refrain and its at once immaculate and erotic choreography—not to mention those titillating costumes on Candy Brown and Pamela Sousa, and the inclusion of star attraction Ben Vereen—was determined to be the proper showcase.

On the appointed day, Ostrow accompanied the dancers to a studio outside Manhattan. (Brown remembers it being in Astoria, Queens, while Vereen places it upstate in Purchase and Ostrow in Jersey City.) As Fosse had a commitment that day, another director was assigned who shot the whole dance from one vantage point, with the camera facing the performers as a live audience would. "It was terrible," says Ostrow, who in desperation called *Pippin*'s actual director to see if he could squeeze them in. "Then who comes around the corner but Bob Fosse," Sousa recalls. "Thank God. He really took over—he had this guy shooting it from every angle imaginable." Brown remembers, "Bob started saying, 'OK, put the camera up here on this ladder; now put it down on the floor; now put it behind me and make sure the lights go this way.'"

The result was a one-minute spot in which Vereen, Brown, and Sousa were seen performing a large chunk of the number from different vantage points, a spotlight on them and Tony Walton's fanciful *Pippin* logo behind them. Their chemistry was as palpable as their sex appeal. "When you perform a number like that for so long, you start to feel as one, to feel each other's energies and limits," says Sousa. "It's hard to find the right words for it, but you breathe and exhale together." The commercial would open and close with a male voice-over. "Here's a free minute from *Pippin*, Broadway's musical comedy sensation, directed by Bob Fosse," the voice actor said, then drily added, at the end, "You can see the other 119 minutes of *Pippin* live at the Imperial Theatre, without commercial interruption."

The response, Brown remembers, "was huge. Huge. Nothing like that had ever been done before." Placing commercial spots during popular prime-time series such as *Maude*, *Columbo*, and *Sanford and Son* had not been cheap, but Ostrow's venture swiftly paid off. "Apparently because of its intensive television advertising," *Variety* announced in January 1974, "*Pippin* has been more than holding its own against other established Broadway musicals and is continuing to earn substantial profit." Where other productions were only gradually recovering from the typical box office slump of the previous summer, the article noted, grosses for Pippin had "zoomed," with the show marking a total profit of $947,290, of which it retained a balance of $147,290. "On the basis of the customary split between the management and backers," *Variety* explained, "the latter received half of the $800,000 payoff, amounting to $400,000, or 80 % profit on their $500,000 investment."

The ad would also win a prestigious Clio Award and help ensure that seeing *Pippin* was de rigueur for any showbiz elite living in or visiting New York. "It was when celebrities started coming—that's when I knew we were the shit," says Brown. "Not only coming, but coming backstage. I still remember that Lena Horne had on this fabulous black velvet pantsuit. Margot Fonteyn's top had this square neckline, and her neck just looked like an expanse, so open, from all that ballet training. Phenomenal. And Gene Kelly was so generous and kind. I don't even remember what he said, specifically; I just remember standing there and beaming, thinking, 'Gene Kelly said that—to us!'"

Success reinforced the bonds between cast members and those in the crew. The ensemble's dressing room was located below stage level, "in the basement," as Will McMillan, the then-ten-year-old standby for Theo, recalls; it served as another communal space. "It was kind of like cubicles in an office—one side for the men, one side for the women, but not walled off. It took me a while, but I came to realize that all the gay men were in one area on one side, and then the two straight guys—Roger, the swing dancer, and John, who carried the torch—hung out together. The women were on the other side, and the hair and makeup people would rush in there and put a new wig on or touch up makeup. And the stage hands and the hair people and the makeup people and some of the musicians had an ongoing game of nickel-and-dime-and-quarter poker."

In the female dressing area, Clark would read Ann Landers's syndicated advice column out loud as the others put their makeup on, "and we would all be laughing hysterically," Clark remembers. And smoking,

McMillan adds: "The women were all heavy smokers. During the show, they would only be able to have two puffs before going back onstage, and I would grab the cigarette butts out of the ash tray—Pamela Sousa left beautiful red lipstick marks on hers. I spent a fair amount of time under the stage, and at the very end, when they have that little bit of pyrotechnics, that's when I figured it was safe to light up one of these only-slightly-smoked cigarettes, because there was other smoke to cover my smoke. I'm sure the stage manager would have been utterly horrified to know that there was this ten-year-old practicing smoking, but there was never an inferno, luckily."

Before one evening performance, Gene Foote arrived to find Irene Ryan seated at the stage door entrance, waiting for him. "She said, 'I understand there's a vase of flowers here for you.' I said, what? And the doorman said, 'Yes, it's true, flowers just came for you.' A man who was a florist—he owned a shop on the Upper East Side—had seen the show, and he sent me an arrangement as big as a bean bag. Irene was just beside herself; she could not believe that a man had gotten those flowers for me!"

Neither Foote nor his cast mates knew at this point that Ryan would be the first to leave their family, tragically. McMillan remembers that he and Lucie Lancaster, Ryan's standby, had to remain in the theater throughout each performance—this was before labor laws prohibited child actors from working that many hours—while other standbys could simply call in and see if they were needed; since rehearsals, Ryan had apparently been having trouble remembering her lines. "The cast would gather offstage and listen carefully over the intercom to see if she would remember, or what she would remember," McMillan says. Fosse sometimes grew impatient, according to Ostrow, who in his memoir recalled being summoned to Ryan's hotel room one afternoon about five months into the run; the actress asked if she could be replaced. "I was furious, thinking Fosse had finally gotten under her skin." The producer was mistaken: "She told me she had secretly suffered a stroke during our rehearsals last September and didn't tell a soul for fear she would be taken out of the show. 'I just want to be in a big hit Broadway musical before I die,' she said. We had a good cry and she made me promise not to tell the company until her final performance."

Soon afterward, Ryan suffered an apparent relapse and had to return to California, where she was hospitalized; a brain tumor was diagnosed, according to numerous reports. She died on April 26, 1973, some six weeks after her final performance, at the age of seventy. Fosse wrote an appreciation for the *Times*, published on May 6, extolling Ryan's generosity and concern for others, her love of applause, and her sometimes salty sense of humor. One actor, Fosse noted, "told me of a time when the newest of the sensational "How To" sex manuals was being passed around. After reading it, Irene announced, 'My goodness, look at what I've been missing all these years!'"

Lancaster assumed the role but was soon replaced by stage and film veteran Dorothy Stickney, making her musical theater debut on June 11, just days shy of her seventy-seventh birthday. That date also marked Betty Buckley's first performance, replacing Jill Clayburgh as Catherine, a role that Buckley would play for nearly three years. Schwartz was elated to finally have an accomplished singer in the role: "When Betty took over, that whole section of the show just came alive. I feel like she was responsible for at least an extra year for us." By then already a fan of Schwartz's from having seen *Godspell*, Buckley would also find working with Fosse revelatory. "One day, Bob said to me, 'Betty, you're a very facile performer; it comes naturally to you,'" she remembers. "Then he said, 'I just want to tell you this: When you're feeling great, know that it's wrong, because in this role you need to be looking at the most awkward, vulnerable part of yourself.' I thought that was brilliant. I still think of him as one of my great teachers."

Buckley's experience with her fellow performers was, she admits, more of a mixed bag. It was as if the tight-knit family that Fosse had encouraged to play a cult-like troupe—or certain members of the family, anyway—were wary of a new recruit. "The company could be a bit of a clique—a weird clique, an odd fraternity of persons. I loved some of them very, very much, but there were others who made me feel like I just couldn't be in that clique, because I hadn't been there from the beginning." Michael Rupert, who would replace Rubinstein as Pippin in November 1974—and remain with the production, except for a break in September and October 1976, through its final performance—also felt isolated at first from the camaraderie that original cast members clearly enjoyed. "My character is kind of the outsider in the play, and I was the outsider as this actor from Los Angeles. And I had the only dressing room on stage level, which made me feel even more alone. I really thought for a while, maybe I just need to ask Stu Ostrow if he could release me from my contract. I started to get depressed, to be honest."

Rupert began seeing a therapist, who helped him conceive a clever solution. "We decided, why don't I move to the chorus's dressing room, in the basement? It was five or six months into the run at this point, and I had gotten to know the ensemble a little better, and I mentioned it to a couple of them; they were like, 'That's really weird, but OK, why not?' So I ended up taking all my stuff into the boys' ensemble room, right next to the girls'—so that for the first time since joining the show, I was really part of the company. And my loneliness and depression started to go away. I started to go out with people after the show more, to hang out with them, and it ended up being a pretty good experience."

Vereen had also left the show by then; he first departed in February 1974 to shoot the screen musical *Funny Lady* but returned in May to fulfill his two-year contract, and was there for roughly the first month of Rupert's run. He was then replaced by his original standby, Northern J. Calloway, fondly remembered for his nearly two-decade tenure as David on *Sesame Street*. Other multitalented performers who would step into Vereen's shoes included future *Dreamgirls* star Ben Harney and Samuel E. Wright, long before the latter voiced Sebastian in the animated Disney smash *The Little Mermaid* or played Mufasa in the original Broadway cast of *The Lion King*. Priscilla Lopez was the first replacement for Fastrada, between January and August 1974, prior to her introducing the character of Diana Morales and the song "What I Did for Love" in *A Chorus Line*. Those who took over ensemble roles included several performers who would collaborate memorably with Fosse in the years that followed, from the statuesque Sandahl Bergman, later to lead the famously naughty "Take Off with Us" in *All That Jazz*—and flaunt her assets in *Conan the Barbarian*—and Chet Walker, with whom Bergman appeared in *Dancin'*.

Fosse would revisit the production periodically, as directors do. After catching a performance in June 1974, he was moved to write a letter to the cast, whom he addressed as "Dear Phenoms." "I've had a couple long running shows previously and I can't remember one, at this point in the run, that was in nearly as good shape as you are—and you should feel proud." After giving a few specific notes, Fosse concluded, "I love you and I'm proud of you because somehow with all of the repetition you must deal with, your personal problems, your tiredness, you know that each audience comes to this show new—and you send them out of there with them really having seen a show."

As the Broadway production of *Pippin* thrived, Ostrow cast his ambition across the Atlantic. The producer "awarded" the London premiere of *Pippin*, as he would write in his memoir, to the Australian-born British impresario Robert Stigwood, who had managed the bands Cream and the Bee Gees before seguing into musical theater with West End productions of *Hair* and *Oh! Calcutta!* and the original Broadway stagings of Andrew Lloyd Webber and Tim Rice's *Jesus Christ Superstar*, *Evita*, and *Joseph and the Amazing Technicolor Dreamcoat*. (Stigwood's numerous film credits would also include adaptations of *Superstar* and *Evita*, in addition to *Grease* and *Saturday Night Fever*; he brought a stage adaptation of the latter hit to the West End and Broadway.) Stigwood's presentation of *Pippin* opened October 30 at Her Majesty's Theatre, with Manfred Mann singer Paul Jones in the title role, Calloway as the Leading Player, and future dame Patricia Hodge as Catherine.

It was, certainly compared to its Broadway predecessor, an abject flop—opening to unenthused notices and closing after only eighty-five performances. "People in England just didn't get it," Ostrow says. Perhaps, as Schwartz posits, "There weren't as many people trying to find their corners of the sky, so to speak, when the class system was stronger, and individual quests were less prevalent. That's one theory, anyway." *Pippin*'s luck would prove better in Vienna, where Doby was enlisted to direct a production in German in early 1974. "We got the sets and costumes from London, so we saved a ton of money," she remembers, but adds, "The script had been translated by an elderly gentleman who never saw the show." Luckily, Doby's German husband and fellow Fosse collaborator, Wolfgang Glattes, was able to go through it with her, "and he made some changes, changing expressions to show you were talking about young people, basically, though he never took credit for it. The show ran the whole season. I think it went into two seasons, as part of the repertory, so it was an audience success. And the reviews mentioned that things happened in the show that had never happened in Vienna before."

Around the same time the Austrian production was taking shape, a different version of *Pippin* was being prepared in Melbourne, Australia, at another Her Majesty's Theatre. It would open on February 23, 1974, starring Down Under pop stars Johnny Farnham (later a member of the Little River Band) and Colleen Hewett, who had acted in the Australian cast of *Godspell* and recorded a chart-topping version of "Day by Day." Directed by Sammy Bayes, who had recently helmed a well-received *Godspell*, this *Pippin* was produced by Kenn Brodziak, a New Zealand–bred concert and theatrical promoter whose résumé rivaled Stigwood's—he had worked with everyone from Marlene Dietrich to the Beatles—and who had been selected over Ostrow's protestations in a dispute that would, in a historic move, lead to the publication of a revised edition of the musical.

While the Dramatists Guild provides authors the right to license a show, most Broadway contracts preassign producers the right to present in certain foreign territories, and it is, as Schwartz admits, "rare for authors to make substantive changes from the final Broadway version, or at least to do so in contravention of the wishes of the producers." But the conflict over "Trapped, but happy" had proven the final straw for Schwartz, who recalls that he and Hirson had wanted to make other restorations and revisions to *Pippin*, and by the spring of 1973, Ostrow had become aware that the creators wanted this new iteration produced in Australia. In a letter to Shirley Bernstein dated April 26, Ostrow's attorney, Alvin Deutsch, wrote the following:

Dear Shirley:
   We have been advised that it is Stephen Schwartz's intention to have Mr. Kenn Brodziak produce an Australian version of PIP-

*PIN, which differs from the Broadway production of the Play [sic].
I have previously advised you that Under Paragraph SIXTH (a)
(ii) of the Dramatists Guild Agreement dated November 22, 1971,
no additions, modifications or alterations in the manuscript of the
Play, as contracted for production may be made without the consent
of our client. This clause does not merely refer to productions produced
by the New York producer, since no such limitation appears in the
provisions of paragraph SIXTH. The sense of this clause is that no
producer should be obligated to risk or jeopardize his 40% interest in
the so-called subsidiary rights because of unauthorized changes from
the original production. This is particularly true of a Play which has
garnered five Tony Awards and is Broadway's major musical production, having earned the authors royalties to date of approximately
$150,000. To jeopardize a proven success with an altered production
is, at the very least, an unnecessary gamble.*

The letter went on to note that Stigwood had been willing to present either the original production of Pippin "or a production with such
changes as the authors may have wished" in Australia and added, significantly, "We have also been advised that Roger Hirson is taking no
position regarding this matter." Deutsch observed, "Our failure to receive
a copy of the Australian contract leads us to the inevitable conclusion
that an arrangement was reached to accept a lesser advance in return for
other conditions which would unilaterally serve the specific interests of
Stephen Schwartz," and concluded that if this were the case, "We will
have no alternative but to consider your formal discharge as agent for the
producer; and responsible for the return of any commissions which may
have previously been deducted by you."

If the threat to his agent and reference to "unauthorized changes"
Schwartz wished to make in his own work would have irked any artist,
he wasn't entirely unsympathetic to Ostrow's more pragmatic concerns,
or at least isn't in retrospect. "From Stuart's perspective, he had a responsibility to the fiduciary interests of his investors, and that's completely
valid," Schwartz says. The interests of *Pippin*'s cocreator, of course, lay in
preserving what he believed to be the quality and integrity of the show.

So when Ostrow "gave an indication" that he was willing to pursue legal action, as the producer now puts it, the matter quickly wound up in arbitration.

According to a brief filed on behalf of Ostrow, Schwartz commenced proceedings on May 18; Ostrow asserted counterclaims, and the case was brought to a hearing on September 7 and resolved about two months later, to Schwartz's benefit. "It was under the auspices of the Dramatists Guild, and there were three arbitrators," Schwartz recalls. Schwartz and Ostrow were each permitted to choose one, while the American Arbitration Association, to ensure some impartiality, appointed a third: Robert H. Montgomery. Bernstein told Schwartz that she "was very pleased, because she said that he was very smart and very fair, and that he represented writers. He was a good draw for us, so to speak."

Doby, Louise Quick, Phil Friedman, and Stanley Lebowsky were among the key members of the *Pippin* team called on to testify before the panel. "It put us in a very funny position," Doby remembers, "because we were working for both of these people"—Schwartz and Ostrow, and of course Fosse as well—"and we were put between them. I wish I could remember the exact questions; it was like, 'Was Stephen there for rehearsals?' 'Was he involved in putting the show on?' They even asked me stuff like, 'Do you think Mr. Fosse improved the show?' As if I was going to say, 'No, I don't like my director/choreographer's version of it.' That's not really fair. It was a shame we had to go through that."

On November 14, *Variety* reported that the arbitration panel had ruled two to one in favor of Schwartz. The Dramatists Guild, the national trade association representing playwrights, composers, lyricists, and librettists, had filed a brief on his behalf, whereas the League of New York Theatres and Producers had submitted an opinion backing Ostrow. The resulting contract gave Schwartz the right to eliminate changes that Fosse had made and make revisions of his own and also permitted him to both approve the script that would be used in Australia and choose its director and choreographer. The decision, the article observed, "not only appears to set a precedent in the matter of ownership of theatrical material, but many [*sic*] precipitate a decisive battle involving the legality of several major show business organizations." The report continued,

"Sparked partly by the 'Pippin' case, a move is under way for the Theatre League to demand the immediate start of negotiations with the Dramatists Guild for a new Minimum Basic Contract," the agreement that had overseen minimum terms for to playwrights, lyricists, and composers, including royalty payments, since 1926.

In fact, despite periodic updates, that contract had not undergone a major revision since 1961, and wouldn't until 1985. Moreover, as the *Variety* piece had also noted, the Guild's legal legitimacy remained in question as the result of a suit filed in the 1940s by a producer who claimed that terms of the Minimum Basic Contract, among other reasons, prevented him from making changes to a musical flop called *Stovepipe Hat*. "Authors were absolutely expanding their rights through the twentieth century Basic Contract structure, but the Guild and its agreement remained inherently fragile under the law," explains Brent Salter, the Stanford Center for Law and History Fellow at Stanford Law School and author of numerous articles and books on the history of the laws and practices of the performing arts. "It was unclear whether the dramatists could organize as a trade association of independent contractors under competition law. The Dramatists Guild was not a union of employees exempt from antitrust; that legal uncertainty has never been adequately resolved, and producers have used it over the last one hundred years to advance their bargaining position with the dramatists."

The Fosse-fied *Pippin* would be used for two national tours, and in the 1981 staging that aired, infamously, on Showtime the following year. Billed as *Pippin: His Life and Times*, the television event was filmed in Hamilton, Ontario, where Fosse had recruited a rather motley crew of stars to join Vereen as he reprised his Tony-winning role. Chita Rivera seemed a natural choice for Fastrada; though in her late forties, she was glamorous and fit—just five years past her star turn as Velma Kelly in *Chicago*, with more than ten to go before she would simmer in the title role in *Kiss of the Spider Woman*. More questionable, perhaps, were the selections of then–TV superhero William Katt (of *The Greatest American Hero* fame) for Pippin and über-ham Martha Raye for Berthe.

But casting ultimately proved less of an issue than direction—not Fosse's, as he was available to oversee only the last few days of rehearsal, but the technical direction of David Sheehan, an entertainment reporter, anchor, and host whose lengthy career would also encompass acting, writing, and producing. "I don't want to call him names, because he's dead, and that isn't nice," says Doby, whom Fosse had enlisted to check the performances and design and help in the editing process, of Sheehan, who passed in 2020. "But he was totally undisciplined. He would make a schedule and then sleep through it, because he would work for forty-eight hours and then sleep for twenty-four. At one point a taping I'd done over one day disappeared the next, because he had taped over it. Unreal."

Doby's central dilemma was that the performance came in at two hours and ten minutes, which was more than ten minutes longer than the format could accommodate—though Sheehan had apparently not warned Doby or Fosse of this in advance. "If he had told us, we could have cut the show during rehearsals," says Doby, who wasn't able to bring herself to watch the finished product—now readily available online—until a couple of years ago. "It was horrible. Chita, who was fabulous—he cut the beginning of her song completely. He did a cut in the middle of her dance. He took whole scenes out. When Bob had found out it needed to be under two hours, he did offer to help David make the cuts, but David didn't want the help. At one point he said, 'I'll show Bob Fosse how to edit a musical.'"

Fosse had sent a lengthy letter to Sheehan on September 18, 1981, elaborating on Doby's concerns and conveying his own. It began with this paragraph:

> Dear David:
>
> This is indeed a difficult letter to write because in all honesty I was distressed and disappointed in what I saw of the PIPPIN tape. It is difficult because what I believe are the mistakes are not consistent throughout. Frequently you make cuts in the middle of a movement or an idea which tends to weaken any impact that it might have. On the other hand you also frequently linger on a shot after its peak has been reached. Therefore you often catch actors at a distressing moment where they do not know what to do. This is bad for the actors and bad for the material.

This sense of controlled urgency was sustained as Fosse pointed out specific examples, at points expressing concern for individual performers whom he felt would not be represented to the best of their ability—and for Doby. (Doby did not perform in the show; aside from Vereen, Christopher Chadman and John Mineo were the only actors featured from the original Broadway cast.) "Most distressing to me was to see that you have not executed any of the notes that I sent to you with a copy to Kathryn," Fosse wrote. "I see no reason to continue this procedure unless these notes are executed or a reason supplied . . . why they can't work or are not a good idea."

Sheehan did send Fosse at least a couple of telegrams, one accounting for his "equivocation" and another assuring that Doby would have "everything she needs to work on your ideas for 'Pippin,' subject of course to the day-to-day fortunes and misfortunes that remain unpredictable until 'Pippin' is fully delivered and my creditability finally restored." But after seeing the finished tape, Fosse wrote another letter, this time officially distancing himself from the project. His tone was, predictably, sterner here—even the "Dear" and "Sincerely" were gone:

David:

Your actions towards Kathryn, my sole representative, and your exclusion of any corrections or changes made by her either alone or in conjunction with me in the final master, make it impossible for me to continue my further relationship with "Pippin." Your oft-repeated words of good intention are once again completely negated by your actions. I am saddened and dismayed by what I've seen on tape. In my opinion, you have maneuvered this into an impossible situation. What a shame.

Bob Fosse

For Fosse, it was not enough to make his displeasure known to Sheehan. After penning that last, terse message, he wrote a longer one, intended for each cast member and some who had been on the technical team of the "foolishly butchered," as he put it, presentation of the musical. "Please forgive the Xeroxed impersonal nature of this letter," he began, having left a space for every name. "I wish it could be on a more personal level, but because of time, I have decided to do it this way." Fosse then explained that he had only just viewed the master and was "extremely upset and frustrated by what I've seen and totally bewildered by the thinking by it," pointing out Doby's generosity and diligence in trying to resolve long-existing issues. The director and choreographer who had inspired such devotion in his dancers—who made them all feel special, as so many have said—added, "I truly feel that because of our working relationship and because many of you were drawn into the project because of loyalty or friendship or respect for me, and because of all the artistry and hard work you put into it, that I owe you an apology." Fosse signed off "Angrily," stressing how heavily this betrayal of their talents and faith weighed on him.

Schwartz, too, was and remains unhappy with the Sheehan cut, which even before the edits excluded any of the revisions he'd fought for. "I thought, well, now we'll have the worst of both worlds. It will be the version of the show I don't like as much, but not edited by Bob—who was such a brilliant film director! It still distresses me that the film is some people's only reference for what the show is." Fortunately, those who would seek *Pippin* out in the following decades were able to find no shortage of live productions in various cities and countries. A number of them were nurtured by Schwartz, who while always protective also encouraged his first Broadway baby to spread its wings under different guardians.

A few years before Fosse died, he and Schwartz met by chance in London. "My wife and I were there, and somebody took us to a casino," Schwartz recalls. "Bob happened to be there with Stuart—it was completely coincidental. Bob and I had a really pleasant conversation. The show had proven to be successful in stock and amateur by then, and all the tension between us seemed to be in the past." And Schwartz has come to recognize that having a visionary for a first director—even when that director's vision isn't always in sync with yours—is seldom a bad thing, in the short or long term.

CHAPTER TEN

The Motown Connection

THOSE WHO DIDN'T MANAGE TO SEE *PIPPIN* IN THE 1970S COULD AT least hear what some of the fuss was about on the original cast recording, which was different from any Broadway cast album before it in more than one respect—starting with the record company that released it. Stuart Ostrow had begun shopping the musical to investors at a fortuitous time, as one of the most prominent figures in American entertainment was looking to "diversify." That's the word Suzanne de Passe, then Berry Gordy Jr.'s creative assistant at Motown Records, uses to describe Gordy's strategy in the late 1960s and early 1970s, as television and the movies offered even more visibility to his biggest stars. Variety shows, even those with milquetoast hosts like Ed Sullivan and Dinah Shore, were one outlet. By 1972, Michael Jackson was singing the title song to *Ben*, a horror flick about a boy and his pet rat, on an album of the same name, while Diana Ross played Billie Holiday in *Lady Sings the Blues*.

Born and raised in Detroit, Gordy had entered the business as a songwriter, crafting tunes for the seminal R&B tenor Jackie Wilson. But when he received a royalty check for only three dollars and nineteen cents, he decided to strike out his own, using an $800 loan from his family's credit union to establish Tamla Records in 1959. The Motown label was later added and became the name of a parent company. It stemmed from "Motor City," a nickname for Gordy's birthplace—it felt like "Motor Town" to him—where his parents, like other Black men and women, had moved from the Jim Crow South to find better jobs and lives as the local auto industry flourished. (Gordy himself worked for the Ford Motor Company, doing stints in the foundry and on the assembly line at the Lincoln-Mercury plant before getting into the music business.) Gordy had discovered a poetic songwriter and fluttery-voiced tenor named Smokey Robinson, whose vocal group, the Miracles, was the first in a string of acts whose hits erased boundaries between pop and R&B—a roster that would expand as the Motown family grew to include other subsidiary labels.

These were the artists—backed by a collective of expert studio musicians who came to be known as the Funk Brothers—who moved, in every sense, a teenage Stephen Schwartz and fans of all races and backgrounds: the Supremes, Stevie Wonder, Marvin Gaye (and Tammi Terrell, Gaye's vocal partner in some of the most sumptuous pop duets ever recorded), Mary Wells, the Four Tops, the Marvelettes, Martha and the Vandellas, the Temptations, Gladys Knight and the Pips, and the Jackson 5, among others. With the departure of key Motown songwriting team Holland-Dozier-Holland in the late 1960s, producer/writer Norman Whitfield and lyricist Barrett Strong, who had recorded Motown's first R&B hit, "Money (That's What I Want)" (written by Gordy and Janie Bradford), brought Gordy's company into the era of psychedelic soul. Offices had been set up in New York and Los Angeles by then, and in 1972, the latter became its headquarters, putting Gordy in the perfect spot to parlay his top talent's star power into TV and film gigs.

Broadway, too, came calling. Gordy and Motown were no strangers to musical theater: "Growing up, listening to the radio, I heard a lot of great pop songs and standards by phenomenal composers and lyricists," Gordy says. "One of the first musicals I saw starred Diahann Carroll—*No Strings*," whose composer and lyricist was Richard Rodgers. "I admired his songs, and we later released an entire album of the Supremes singing his and Lorenz Hart's songs, most of them from Broadway musicals. At Motown, I wanted music for all people, and I believed these standards were to the key to taking our acts to the next level of show business, the top venues and nightclubs around the country, and the Supremes were the ones to open the door and lead the way." On 1965's *The Supremes at the Copa*, the vocal group can be heard at one of the most famous clubs, mixing their hits with classic show tunes; Gordy remembers how they "dazzled the crowd" with "Put on a Happy Face" from *Bye Bye Birdie*, "and I absolutely loved Diana's performance of Leonard Bernstein and Stephen Sondheim's 'Somewhere,' from *West Side Story*." *The Supremes Sing Rodgers & Hart* (1967) was followed the next year by *Diana Ross & the Supremes Sing and Perform "Funny Girl."*

De Passe, a New York City girl, had similarly eclectic tastes. She was roughly the same age as Stephen Schwartz, and the performing arts had loomed large in her own upbringing. "I was taken to many Broadway shows and to City Center and the Apollo Theater the Met, to all manner of concerts, to everything from flamenco to ballet," she notes. "I saw a whole array of what the city had to offer, and as a result I had an interest in every kind of music. And when things of a creative nature were presented to Mr. Gordy's office, it often fell to me to be an evaluator, if you will." So when an invitation arrived in 1971 to a presentation for potential investors in a new Broadway musical, de Passe was dispatched to New York, where she found herself at a gathering at Ostrow's town house, watching Schwartz at the piano.

"Stephen played this score, like a one-man performance machine, and I remember being wildly impressed," she says. "I called Mr. Gordy to say I thought it was brilliant. By that point I had brought a couple of acts to his attention"—including a little family outfit called the Jackson 5—"so that gave me some credibility. I think he was always open to any project in any medium if it was creatively exciting." A meeting was arranged with Schwartz and Ostrow on the opposite coast, at the Beverly Hills Hotel. "I had put up a big piano in my suite, and I had Stephen play," Ostrow recalls. "And Berry Gordy thought he was in heaven. He said, 'How much do you need?' I told him 300,000 dollars, and he said, 'You got it.'" Thus, Gordy became *Pippin*'s largest single investor and secured the rights to publish the score and release the original cast album, the record company's first. (Its second would be a recording of an all-Black revival of *Guys and Dolls*, staged at the Broadway Theater in 1976; the third would not arrive until more than forty years later, when Gordy coproduced and wrote the book for the jukebox homage *Motown the Musical*.)

If it seemed like an ideal marriage given the role Motown had played in Schwartz's musical enrichment, it was also an unusual one.

Certainly, Black musicians and jazz in general had informed musical theater since its earliest days, and composers and writers of color had made their mark even before 1921's *Shuffle Along*, the hit revue that combined Eubie Blake's music and Noble Sissle's lyrics with a book by the vaudeville-based comedy duo of F. E. Miller and Aubrey Lyles. Duke Ellington, Langston Hughes, and Ossie Davis would lend their gifts to Broadway in the decades that followed, and by the 1970s, when Davis adapted his play *Purlie Victorious* into a musical, *Purlie*, so would other all-Black creative teams. In addition to Melvin van Peebles's *Ain't Supposed to Die a Natural Death*, there was *Don't Bother Me, I Can't Cope*, conceived and directed by Vinnette Carroll with a book, music, and lyrics by Micki Grant—a multi-hyphenate who, like van Peebles, also performed, and was one of the songwriters who later collaborated with Schwartz on *Working*—and *Your Arms Too Short to Box with God*, scored by gospel artist Alex Bradford with additional music and lyrics by Grant. The period between 1975 and 1979 also brought *Eubie!*, *Bubbling Brown Sugar*, the Fats Waller tribute *Ain't Misbehavin'*, and, of course, *The Wiz*, with music and lyrics by Charlie Smalls. And orchestrators and arrangers such as Luther Henderson, whose Broadway career began with the original production of Rodgers and Hammerstein's *Flower Drum Song*, and Harold Wheeler, whose credits have ranged from *Promises, Promises* to *Ain't Too Proud*, emerged as prolific contributors.

But where the business of musicals and theater overall was concerned, little progress had been made. Producers and investors were, like their counterparts in film and television, virtually all white, and would remain predominantly so for decades. "I think Broadway has been, is, and always will be an exclusionary place," de Passe says simply. "There are anomalies, and we were one." (Ashton Springer, who produced or served as general manager for eleven productions between 1971 and 1981, was another, as was Ken Harper, who produced *The Wiz* in 1975.) Longtime press agent Irene Gandy, the recipient of a 2021 Tony Honors Award for Excellence in Theater, believes that social factors continue to reinforce this lack of diversity. "Producers will take anybody's money, and there are a lot of Black millionaires," notes Gandy, who began her career as an apprentice for the Negro Ensemble Company and later served as a producer for Broadway productions such as *The Gershwins' Porgy and Bess* (helmed by Diane Paulus) and *Lady Day at Emerson's Bar & Grill*. "But most investors are white because they're already at the table, so they know you can just put $25,000 in, or get ten of your friends to put $10,000 in. Berry Gordy was in a place where he knew that you didn't have to put all the money in yourself, that there can be a place for you. Change only happens with communication."

Another prominent Black industry veteran, Stephen C. Byrd, who independently and as Alia Jones Harvey's partner in Front Row Productions has produced several of the most high-profile Broadway projects in this century—from starry revivals of *Cat on a Hot Tin Roof*, *A Streetcar Named Desire*, *The Trip to Bountiful*, and *The Iceman Cometh* to new works as varied as the drama *American Son* and the musical *Ain't Too Proud: The Life and Times of the Temptations*—has been "advocating for BIPOC people for sixteen years. In every office that Alia and I went into, there was no one. We'd ask why not, and they'd say, 'We're looking.' It took George Floyd," the Black man murdered by police officer Derek Chauvin in May 2020—and the consequent surge of the Black Lives Matter movement and increased focus on social injustice—"to make a momentous change, and we'll see how long that can be sustained. With all the various diversity classes and courses, it's still like Noah's Ark, with one Black person in every office, whether it's public relations, general managers, across the board. Certainly, the Shuberts"—an organization of theater owners and producers founded by three siblings in the nineteenth century—"have been at the vanguard, and more theater owners are stepping up to the plate now." (Charlotte St. Martin, president of the Broadway League, the industry's national trade organization, cites initiatives such as a change in the bylaws of the League's Board of Governors, so that 20 percent of board members are now people of color, twice as many as before December 2021.) But Byrd is "still skeptical to some degree about whether it's cosmetic, where it's going to go."

Where Gordy's pivotal role in *Pippin* is concerned, Byrd, like Gandy, emphasizes the unique position the record company chief enjoyed as an entertainment tycoon as well as the superior business acumen he had cultivated in that role. "When Berry got involved, his name was golden, and he knew how to leverage his success with Motown. *Pippin* resonated with him musically, but he was astute enough to elevate his investment by getting the rights to the cast album. That mitigated his risk."

When it came time to record that album, Gordy recognized that Schwartz's driving, pop-savvy tunes would be natural vehicles for his leading talent. Deke Richards and Sherlie Matthews were producers and songwriters who worked with top Motown acts, and Matthews was also a backup vocalist who would work with dozens of R&B, jazz, and rock artists. They coproduced a recording of "Corner of the Sky" for the Jackson 5, which Marlon Jackson still considers "one of my favorite Jackson 5 songs. 'I've got to be where my spirit can run free/Got to find my corner of the sky' is my favorite lyric." Michael Jackson, then fourteen years old and still in possession of the mightiest boy soprano ever to land on vinyl (though it had deepened somewhat since early hits like "I Want You Back" and "ABC"), recorded a chiming, gently psychedelic "Morning Glow," also with Matthews and Richards, while the post–Diana Ross Supremes twinkled wistfully through "I Guess I'll Miss the Man," produced by Bob Gaudio, keyboardist and songwriter for Frankie Valli and the Four Seasons, who were then newly signed to the Motown label MoWest. (Ross herself would cover "Corner" in 1973 in a Las Vegas performance featured the following year on her album *Live at Caesars Palace*. Introducing *Pippin* as "one of the biggest Broadway shows out today," she described the musical as "the story of Emperor Charlemagne's son, who could never, ever find happiness. He tried everything. He tried war, he tried religion, and he even tried a little sex. But it didn't work. Too bad for him.")

The connection between *Pippin* and the Four Seasons does not end there. Bob Crewe, who cowrote the bulk of that group's hits with Gaudio, produced a single version of "No Time at All," not included on the album, recorded by another recent Motown acquisition: Irene "Granny" Ryan, whom Gordy had known from *The Beverly Hillbillies*. "I just loved her as the feisty Granny on that TV show," Gordy said, "and we signed the seventy-year-old actress and promoted her as 'Motown's newest teen sensation'"—though Ryan's recording career would of course be cut short by her death in 1973. De Passe recalls, "We all just really loved her in the show. I remember going to meet with her in her hotel, this place on 58th

Street between Fifth and Sixth. I can't remember the name, but a lot of Broadway performers from out of town stayed there at the time. She was lovely." (Another seasoned performer would include his own version of the song on a 1976 recording for United Artists: Bing Crosby changed a lyric here and there for his wistful reading.)

The *Pippin* company played its more extensive part in recording the score separately and in a single day, more or less. As de Passe recalls, union rules required the performers to record the cast album on a Sunday, as this was before matinees were held then. "There were other sessions to finish the album," she notes. "Ben Vereen may have come in to overdub some stuff, and then the mixing process was lengthy, I believe." Where Schwartz had produced the cast recording for *Godspell* himself, drawing on his time in the studio at RCA Records, he now had a coproducer with far more experience. At thirty-eight, the former child violin prodigy Phil Ramone had first established himself as an engineer, working with a wide array of jazz and R&B acts. By 1972, he was also becoming a leading producer, having collaborated with, among others, Quincy Jones, Harry Belafonte, Louis Armstrong, Burt Bacharach, and Peter, Paul and Mary, and on film soundtracks and another Broadway cast recording, for Bacharach's *Promises, Promises*. By the time of his death in 2013, Ramone, busy until the end, had built a résumé as eclectic and star-studded as that of any producer or engineer in popular music. "It was obvious that Phil was the right guy to do this album, with this music," says de Passe.

"Phil was brilliant, and an insane perfectionist," says Schwartz. "I remember we did fifty-four mixes of 'Morning Glow.' The forty-eighth mix is what's on the album. In those days you couldn't freeze the mix and just change one thing; if there was one tiny thing wrong, you had to do the entire mix again. Now you mix on a computer and if you want to change something, you can just nudge it and run it off again. We had to use all these faders and operate them manually, and Phil only had two hands and I only had two hands, and we had an assistant engineer, so there were just six hands, moving all the faders as the song played. It took forever. I wore hard contact lenses back then, and I would be in the studio for so long that by the time I went home and took them out, it felt like I had needles in my eyes—they had completely dried up."

Although Ralph Burns is credited as orchestrator on the album, Schwartz was able, in his producer role, to make his own tweaks. "The overall intention was to get more of a pop sound than we had in the orchestrations for the show. In those days, people who listened to pop music generally didn't listen to show music. I was trying to bridge the gap a bit"—as he had done in recording *Godspell*, but with more added layers to cut through in this case. "To achieve this, we had to put more emphasis on the rhythm instruments. So the number of times the brass played was substantially reduced throughout; the woodwinds less so, but still eliminated in some spots. Only the strings were pretty much kept unchanged." It was decided that a few tracks, starting with "Magic to Do," would end with fade-outs of the sort more frequently used on pop recordings. "The structure of several numbers was changed, particularly in the intros and the endings. While this is not unusual in transferring a show to a recording, in the case of *Pippin*, it was far more extensive than normal, at least in my experience."

Some songs were affected more than others. A vocal intro for "Morning Glow" was cut—"the one change I regret having made," Schwartz says—and what had been a brass part was played on piano. The brass was also substantially reduced on "Extraordinary," and for "Corner of the Sky," a piano intro was added, "and the track was recorded with pretty much rhythm instruments only." A new guitar part was created for "I Guess I'll Miss the Man," and piano added in spots; "Simple Joys" was restructured to open with the chorus, and many orchestral parts were eliminated, "to make the song more guitar-driven and pop in feel." For the finale, the "Magic shows and miracles" sequence was restored in its entirety, and the track arranged to end with a fade-out; "War Is a Science," conversely, was recorded without those interjections—"Skidoo!" "Doodah"—that had interrupted the song's rhythmic flow and irritated its composer.

Ramone also brought in a trio of "ringers," studio vocalists with strong, soulful voices to add heft to the ensemble singing—since *Pippin*'s Players had not been cast for their prowess in this arena—and support individual principals. The succession of "ooohs" at the beginning and in the fade-out of "Magic to Do" were thus added for the album, and the backing vocals for "Kind of Woman" were replaced by a different part, sung by the ringers—all of them, conveniently, women—with a gently swinging feel that made the song seem even more Bacharach-esque. Sweetening was provided in various other spots—in "Magic," for example, on the lyric, "Romance, sex presented pastorally," sung by Ann Reinking and Candy Brown in the show. Brown remembers that when she heard the album for the first time, "I was a little surprised, but then not really—nor disappointed. I don't remember speaking to Ann about it; if we did, we probably laughed."

The supplementary singers also backed John Rubinstein's vocal during the chorus of "On the Right Track." And Schwartz applied some tricks he had learned at RCA: "I think I was among the first to double backup vocals on a cast album; I did it for *Godspell*, and I do it to this day. 'Doubling' means the backup singers sing their parts once, and then you change the configuration, change where they're standing at the microphones, and they sing them again. Four people doubled actually sound bigger than eight people; the vocals phase against each other a bit, and you get that thicker sound. Those group vocals I loved on records by Crosby, Stills, and Nash, or the Mamas and the Papas—they used doubling to get that sound."

As was not uncommon practice, none of the three studio vocalists were listed in the album credits; neither was Cheryl Clark, who is still rather sore about it. Although a swing, as opposed to a regular cast member who was expected to sing these songs onstage at each performance, Clark insists, "The strong soprano on that album is my voice, and I haven't gotten credit for it. They said it was an oversight, and I did get paid, but my heart is still broken, because I loved singing on that album. I loved singing 'Glory,' and I loved singing 'Morning Glow'—that's my high voice coming through on those songs." (Clark has aired her grievance to Schwartz, who says, "I feel really bad if Cheryl was left out. I didn't always know what I was doing in those days; as a producer I should have been on top of the credits.")

Linda Posner, who as Leland Palmer got to record a solo track, also has regrets—not about anything that was excluded, but rather about what turned up on the album. The amount of time captured on a single vinyl disc was then limited; as Schwartz explains, "You had to do this thing called compression in order to avoid the record skipping, so you only had so many minutes. With *Follies*, for instance, they had to actually cut songs, because they didn't want to record a double album. I wanted to get all the songs from *Pippin* on the album, so we thought we could maybe speed up 'Spread a Little Sunshine'"—Fastrada's one song—"and save a little time. We had tried doing that with a few songs, and I think that was the one where it was least noticeable. The pitch was obviously raised a bit, but as I told Leland, I thought she sounded good. She knows her voice better than I do, of course, and she thought she sounded like Alvin the Chipmunk."

Posner uses different references in retrospect: "I ended up sounding like Molly Picon, Hermione Gingold, and ZaSu Pitts"—respectively, a Yiddish theater actress who transitioned to American film and television roles in middle age, a British character actress known for her nasal drawl, and a silent film star who served as the model for Olive Oyl before getting into talkies. "I was so upset. I know why Stephen did it—because the song was really more memorable when you saw it done, with this sexy, marvelous dance—but it took me a long time to get over it. I thought, this is my first album, and this is how people will think I sing." Indeed, while it's clear from the recording that Posner has vocal chops—pretty tone, a solid musical-theater vibrato, and a fluid rhythmic sensibility—the chipmunk analogy is not entirely unfounded.

Rubinstein had other qualms. "When we performed the show at the Imperial, there were, I believe, three microphones on the downstage edge of the stage floor. Otherwise there was no amplification for the voices, so we sang out at full volume in order to be heard over the orchestra. When we got to the recording studio, I was politely asked to sing not in the full-throated way that I, along with everyone else, sang in the show, but rather in a soft, breathy way that was trendy on pop records in those days. . . . So our cast album reflects a sort of stylistic departure from the more energetic traditional Broadway musical recordings that we all had grown up with. I still wince a little when I hear my slightly bland, whispery renditions of those lovely songs that I felt sounded much better when sung out with gusto and passion."

Where sales and radio were concerned, the cast album did not fare as well as its predecessor. While *Godspell*'s recording had reached No. 34 on the Billboard 200 and topped that trade magazine's Cast Albums chart, *Pippin*'s peaked at No. 129 and No. 10, respectively, on those charts. And the latter album would not produce a hit akin to "Day by Day," even with pop stars on board, though the Jackson 5's "Corner of the Sky" did make it to No. 9 on the R&B singles chart and No. 28 on the Hot 100. To no one's surprise, surely, "teen sensation" Ryan's single of "No Time at All" failed to make a mark on those charts, or any others.

In the community that cared the most, of course, none of this mattered. As Fosse biographer Kevin Winkler wrote in *Broadway World* in 2013, marking the arrival of Paulus's new production on Broadway, *Pippin*'s original cast recording was, in its time, the "one album [that] appeared among everyone's stack of LPs, and appealed to butch crew members, arty costume designers, self-serious actors, chorus dancers, male, female, gay, straight, confused, or closeted." And as those LPs were gradually replaced by eight-track and cassette tapes, then CDs, and eventually digital technology, the songs were passed from teachers to students and parents to children and between friends and siblings—many of them musical theater diehards, but not all. Jeanine Tesori's sister happened to see the production while visiting New York and brought the album home. The young Tesori—who would go on to compose the scores for such shows as *Far from Home* and *Caroline, or Change*—was listening to pop and classical music, "but then I heard the organ holding that E, as that great groove starts to play"—the intro to "Magic to Do." "That pop sensibility was like an invitation. It was my introduction to musical theater, through rhythm."

That mix of muscle and grace and theatricality—actually, very much in line with other artists whom Motown championed—would continue to distinguish Schwartz's scores from those of his more heavy-handed, rock-influenced peers in the years to come. It would also filter down to future generations of musical theater artists, and to pop musicians who fell in love with musical theater and in some cases began to write scores themselves—not just peers like Elton John and Paul Simon, who had absorbed at least some of the same prerock influences as Schwartz had, but also younger singer/songwriters, such as Stew, Duncan Sheik, Sara Bareilles, and Anaís Mitchell. "If we were smart, we would have signed Stephen," de Passe muses today. "Had we signed him, I don't think we ever would have let him go."

CHAPTER ELEVEN

The Theo Ending: A Boy's Afterlife and Other Post-Fosse Developments

IN THE YEARS SINCE *PIPPIN* FIRST BOMBED IN LONDON AND BLOOMED IN Vienna and Australia, the musical has flourished around the world. Since the 1990s alone, Music Theatre International has also licensed the show for professional and amateur productions in Argentina, Belgium, Bermuda, Brazil, China, the Dominican Republic, Egypt, France, Germany, Greece, Hong Kong, India, Indonesia, Israel, Italy, Japan, Mexico, the Netherlands, the Philippines, Poland, Qatar, South Africa, Sweden, Thailand, the U.S. Virgin Islands, Venezuela, and Zambia. A number of these presentations have been at international schools—a logical development, as *Pippin*'s buoyant score and tale of youthful yearning have made it a perennial favorite at schools and camps, where saucier aspects of the dialogue and choreography can be brushed over or watered down (if teachers and counselors even take a stab at Fosse's steps, that is).

Adam Feldman, theater critic and editor at *Time Out New York* and longtime president of the New York Drama Critics' Circle, saw one such staging as a nine-year-old at summer camp. "They did an unauthorized, forty-five-minute version, and I was enchanted by it," says Feldman. Decades later, he remains a big fan of the musical and is obviously more aware of the dynamics that shaped it, and that have made it enduringly appealing to older audiences and professional artists. "I think the material was deeply underrated in its initial reception. It's a wonderful score, full of beautiful songs and clever lyrics. But at the time, Stephen Schwartz was this kid just out of college, and more emphasis was starting to be placed on auteurist director-choreographers. You had Jerome Robbins, and even more so, perhaps, you had Bob Fosse, whose style is still so recognizable, even to people who haven't been able to see one of his actual productions. You know exactly whom you're imitating when you imitate Bob Fosse."

Not that Fosse, who hated to repeat himself in his own work, was necessarily encouraging imitation. "The Fosse imprint on the show is the dominance of *a* directorial style, *a* version of attractive and dangerous show-business glamour and power, of this magnetism that attracts and repels you simultaneously," says Feldman. "It doesn't have to be Bob Fosse's specific version of that. What Fosse did was create a space to be filled with directorial vision. If you evacuate his particular vision entirely, that space is still there, and it rewards being filled by an ambitious, auteurist director of any stripe. He made *Pippin* a really good canvas for directors to paint on."

Notwithstanding the poor performance of the first London run, *Pippin* would find an especially eager and influential interpreter in that city. The choreographer and director Mitch Sebastian had begun his career performing in and serving as dance captain for various West End productions in the 1980s and 1990s and had met Schwartz while serving as assistant to fledgling choreographer Matthew Bourne—later to win numerous prestigious awards on both sides of the Atlantic as well as a knighthood for his contributions to dance—for the 1991 world premiere in London of *Children of Eden*, a musical based on the Book of Genesis that teamed Schwartz with British playwright and director John Caird. The show was not a success—it has since been revised and adapted several times, like a number of musicals that Schwartz has continued to nurture—"but it was a great creative process," says Sebastian, and he was happy to cross paths with the composer again six years later, when Schwartz saw a production of *Romance, Romance* that marked Sebastian's debut as a West End choreographer.

That production had transferred from the Bridewell Theatre, a small venue off the West End built over a former Victorian swimming pool, where Sebastian had begun working regularly. "I was basically the in-house choreographer, churning out all kinds of things," he says. When asked what his next project should be, he thought immediately of *Pippin.* "In the U.K. it was a show that nobody had heard of, but I came to know it by watching that infamous video"—the television special that David Sheehan had edited. "I was very young when I saw it, and it appealed to me as a dancer, because of Fosse's amazing choreography, and also those amazing costumes by Patricia Zipprodt. I felt there was something magical there."

So it was that Sebastian received Schwartz's blessing to bring *Pippin* back to the United Kingdom in the spring of 1998. The production, which was to mark the rising choreographer's directorial debut, would be quite different from the one that locals had pretty much ignored fifteen years earlier. "I had this concept, and I thought, maybe I should just ask Stephen if I could play with it—because the Bridewell was like my playground at the time, my little factory," Sebastian recalls. "And he said, please, do whatever you'd like with it."

The first-time director "didn't build a set—we just had the tribe of Players under your feet, in the Victorian swim baths; we'd rebuilt the floor with this wooden board, and their hands were coming out along with smoke and lights. I wanted the horror of them being trapped inside, so that not only Pippin but everyone was trapped. Pippin entered from the audience, and I had all these wild conceits; as soon as the show started you heard this dial-up connection, like on the old computers, and the lines went down and this netting dropped, and in the netting were bits of dolls and things. I had too many ideas, and when you're young, you don't know how to edit yourself." Elements of techno and house music and hip-hop were incorporated into the orchestrations "to make the show a little more funky and sexy—more of what it already was. When Pippin was on his campaign to overthrow his father, we had the cast running around with cameras and live feed."

The most substantial twist, though, was in the casting of Theo and in that character's final moments onstage. Catherine's son became a young man, played by the now prominent stage and screen actor Michael Jibson, who had appeared a few years earlier as one of the street urchins in a Sam Mendes–helmed production of *Oliver!* Jibson was now seventeen—still tender enough that Sebastian felt protective when the gorgeous female cast members started disrobing during rehearsals on an unusually hot day, but not a boy anymore. And at the end of the musical, his character, rather than remaining beside his mother and Pippin, now began to follow the couple as they left the stage, only to turn back and begin to sing, a cappella, the chorus of "Corner of the Sky." After the second line—"Eagles belong where they can fly"—the orchestra, still at their seats, joined him, as the Players slowly reemerged, their leader reaching out as he had roughly two hours earlier. They had found a new victim, and Pippin's journey, the universal journey from innocence and indomitability to experience and compromise, would begin anew.

Schwartz dubbed it "the Theo ending," and he loved it. "Stephen happened to be going through London around the time of dress or tech rehearsal, and was able to watch a full run of the show and come in for a couple of notes sessions. And he said, 'You fixed it. You fixed the ending.'" For all the effort that had been put into restoring *Pippin*'s first last words after Fosse tweaked them, Schwartz thought that having Theo and the Players wrap the show reinforced the cycle that Pippin's story represented; it summed up something even more primal and bittersweet than "Trapped. But happy." Schwartz says, "I think Bob would have loved the new ending too—I'm sure he would have."

The Theo ending would be incorporated into subsequent productions, eventually making its way into Diane Paulus's Tony-winning revival and, as a result, the current version of the musical available for licensing through Music Theatre International. Like all revisions, it would have its detractors—among them the man who had first spoken what were originally *Pippin*'s final lines. When John Rubinstein's second wife, the dancer and actress Jane Lanier, was cast as Fastrada in a 2006 production of the musical at Seattle's 5th Avenue Theatre, Rubinstein took their two young sons to see their mom—the couple had amicably divorced by then—in the production. "They had never seen *Pippin*," he says, "and here was Theo, not eight or nine but sixteen—a man. I thought that was odd, this gangly teenager who was as tall as Pippin, complaining about a duck, but fine." (Not every director using the new ending would cast an older actor as Theo; Paulus used tween boys, for instance.)

"Then they got to the end," Rubinstein continues, "and I was waiting to hear my favorite lines in the show—but no. Catherine and Pippin and Theo step down off the stage and start to walk up the aisle to the back of the theater, and suddenly Theo lets go of Pippin's hand and runs back down the aisle and up the little steps, back on stage. Catherine and Pippin don't notice. Huh? Where are they going? To a Motel 6? Theo stands all alone and starts singing a cappella. I thought, what the hell? And the orchestra is still there"—in the original, they had left the stage during the Leading Player's final rant—"and they start playing again, and the curtains part—and here comes the Leading Player, looking evil, and all the Players come back on and surround Theo to take him back."

Rubinstein "almost had a heart attack. I'm sitting there with my two little boys, who are five and eight, and my mouth is hanging open. And they said, 'Dad? What's the matter, Dad?'" The following year, when Rubinstein was cast as the Wizard in the Los Angeles premiere of *Wicked*, he confronted Schwartz: "I said, 'What in God's name did you do to the end of *Pippin*—after all that you and I went through over "but happy"? All of our talks, the tears we shed over those two words being taken out, and how great it was that you and Roger were able to put them back in?' And Stephen said, 'But John, this is the way it always should have been. This is how life is: Each generation has to learn the same lesson. No matter what you tell them or show them, they make the same mistakes.' And I said, 'There are lots of plays about that! But you wrote about something else, about the disillusionments we face in life and the compromises we make—but you made it clear that those compromises can provide us with a sense of peace, and even of joy.'"

It would hardly be the last time that Schwartz granted considerable creative license to a director. "It's not as if *Pippin* was a show that needed to be solved," he says. With a few musicals, for which he and his collaborators have drafted substantially different iterations through the years—*Eden*; 1986's *Rags*, a tale of Jewish immigrants featuring Schwartz's lyrics and music by Charles Strouse; and 1977's *Working*, based on Studs Terkel's interviews with people across a range of vocations, which Schwartz has been keen to keep fresh—"it's been a case of trying to fix something that didn't quite work originally. With *Pippin*, it's been, well, how do we make this better?" And the composer has embraced the musical's fundamental malleability: "*My Fair Lady* is always *My Fair Lady*; you can't play around with it too much in terms of: who are these people; when and where is this taking place? *Wicked* is *Wicked*; you can change the set and costumes, but it doesn't lend itself to different interpretation in terms of big directorial ideas the way that *Pippin* or *Godspell* do."

Other takes on *Pippin* that have especially impressed and moved Schwartz include a 2009 Deaf West Theatre staging, presented in conjunction with Center Theatre Group at Los Angeles's Mark Taper Forum. Founded in 1991, Deaf West casts deaf and hearing actors in productions that incorporate American Sign Language; its acclaimed revivals of *Spring Awakening* and *Big River* have transferred to Broadway, and Schwartz still considers the latter "one of the most astonishing things I have ever seen." It turns out that *River*'s director and choreographer, Jeff Calhoun, was a mutual admirer, having seen the original *Pippin* as a teenager on his first trip to New York. "To my delight and surprise, Stephen worked very closely with us," recalls Calhoun, a protégé of Tommy Tune; the composer even contributed a new song to introduce Charles and Fastrada and Lewis titled "In the Bosom of the Family."

Although Schwartz ultimately decided that the song didn't work, he remains enormously fond of Calhoun's production, which used dual casting—having deaf and hearing actors double in principal roles—to underline Pippin's inner conflict. "The war within Pippin was so vividly theatricalized by having two actors play the role. My favorite part was at the end, when one half of Pippin—played by the speaking actor, Michael Arden—wanted to jump into the fire, and he fought bitterly against the other half—played by the deaf actor, Tyrone Giordano—until his voice vanished. I thought it was brilliant." Calhoun had introduced the conceit by presenting the Players as a troupe of magicians and having the Leading Player stage the illusion of sawing him in half. "Once I had stumbled on that," the director remembers, "the rest became about how I could work more magic into everything." In the opening, hands came up through the stage floor to pull the curtain open and reveal the Leading Player. "I wanted to empower the deaf community from the beginning,"

Calhoun notes, "by making arms and hands stars of the show." A giant hoopskirt was designed for Berthe so that when television and stage veteran Harriet Harris, whom Calhoun had cast in the role, sang, members of the ensemble could suddenly emerge from underneath it.

Several productions of *Pippin* have further emphasized the extent to which the Leading Player suggests a cult leader, sucking in and manipulating everyone else. For a 2000 revival at Millburn, New Jersey's, Paper Mill Playhouse, a leading national venue for musical theater, the choreographer Rob Ashford—who has since choreographed and/or directed such major Broadway productions as *Thoroughly Modern Millie* and *Frozen* and revivals of *How to Succeed in Business without Really Trying*, *Evita*, and *Cat on a Hot Tin Roof*—suggested that director Robert Johanson use some contemporary imagery. As a young dancer in 1986, Ashford had appeared in a tour of *Pippin* directed by Vereen, who also reprised his role as the Leading Player, with Kathryn Doby re-creating Fosse's choreography. "We wore the costumes from the original," Ashford remembers. "I had John Mineo's name in my costume, which was the biggest thrill. Fosse himself even came in for a few days and commented and gave some notes, which was a thrill beyond thrills."

For the Paper Mill production, which would include his own choreography, he wanted something different. "It was the time of a lot of fashion layouts—Gucci, Dolce & Gabbana, Tom Ford—where there would be a dozen gorgeous people in beautiful clothes, lying around a living room, all looking so gorgeous—and all looking so bored. Like, 'We're better than you.' Even the Versace ads were piles of people, intertwined, no one looking really engaged. The idea was that we should want to buy these clothes so that we could be like these people. I thought that's what the Leading Player and the Players could offer—they could be that photograph, and Pippin is any of us, looking in, as the Players say, come on in. 'Join us.' They would survive and thrive by absorbing people—taking their willingness and spitting them out at the end, like they're nothing."

In the production's opening number, Ashford remembers, "A big stretch limousine pulled up, and the door opened, and out came Jim Newman, who played the Leading Player, in black leather Gucci pants and a python shirt opened to the waist—very Tom Ford." (Fashion designer Gene Meyer had been hired to costume the scene.) "So he started seducing the audience, and then these Players started pouring out of the limo, one more gorgeous than the next, more extreme. It was this mixed world: Were they gay? Were they straight? Were they couples? It didn't matter—you just wanted to be in that limo. You wanted to be with Pippin."

Where his new choreography was concerned, Ashford tried to be guided by Fosse's "basic principles. For example, in the orgy scene following the Gisela ballet, "I didn't use the same steps as he did. But we did a section where each member of the ensemble had a body part that was featured, that was all Pippin could see through his eyes. They would be dancing around, like at a club, and Pippin would turn to look and one body part would be isolated. Fosse would isolate body parts, of course." Ashford recalls how, when Doby demonstrated the Gisela ballet for the Vereen production, "She taught the women to lead with their belly buttons when they walked , like a child with a secret. 'You're a little girl with a secret.' Something I learned from her is that every step has to mean something—it's not just for energy or atmosphere. That was a great thing to learn, that choreography can and should do that." Schwartz attended rehearsals, "and he wasn't precious about it in any way," Ashford notes. "He was really supportive about changing things up," even in how the score was presented: There were new orchestrations by David Siegel and dance arrangements by David Chase, one of Broadway's busiest music men since the mid-1990s. The associate musical director was a very young Alex Lacamoire, who would later work with Lin-Manuel Miranda on *Hamilton* and *In the Heights* and with Benj Pasek and Justin Paul on *Dear Evan Hansen*.

The following decade brought other notable revivals, a couple of them staged at other renowned regional theaters in the Northeast. In 2005, B. D. Wong was cast as the Leading Player in a production at the Bay Street Theatre in Sag Harbor, New York. Reviewing it in the *New York Times*, Anita Gates noted that the "anti-establishment, antiviolence and antiwar" musical played well two years into the war in Iraq but added, "Its attitude just doesn't seem so daring these days." Gates seemed more intrigued by a revival presented the following year by Goodspeed

Musicals in East Haddam, Connecticut, in which the actor playing Pippin, Joshua Park, was "glowingly, intensely young" and thus steered the audience's focus more to the character, as Schwartz had initially intended. Mickey Dolenz, a candidate for Pippin himself back in the day, played Charles—just as Rubinstein would on Broadway as a replacement in Diane Paulus's revival.

In the end, Schwartz says, "I feel like all of this was grist, if you will, for the production we did with Diane." But before that production could get under way, Schwartz had to focus on yet another concept Mitch Sebastian had developed for the show—this time with a potential screen adaptation in mind. No less prominent a figure at the time than Harvey Weinstein had secured the rights to *Pippin* around 2002 or 2003—when he was head of Miramax Films, and flush from the success of Rob Marshall's film version of *Chicago*—and taken the property along when he founded the Weinstein Company with his brother Bob three years later. Schwartz recalls, "He hadn't paid a lot of money to option the rights, though if he bought them, it was going to be a bigger payout. I said Roger and I wanted approval of two things: the director and the concept, which seemed reasonable to me; I didn't ask for approval of casting or the screenplay, for instance. But Harvey Weinstein, rather than give us that approval, bought out the rights; he paid the full amount. That was a nice payday for us, but a little annoying and, I thought, kind of funny."

Some time after that, Sebastian met with Schwartz in New York and made his new pitch: "I basically said that I could see *Pippin* as this online video game," Sebastian says. "The characters would all be players; you could just log in and have your avatar. And this young boy gets pulled into the game, with Pippin as his avatar, without realizing that it's a way of grooming teenagers to commit suicide—that's the secret agenda of the players. At the time, there was a lot of news about teens being groomed this way, spending their days and nights online without their parents knowing whom they were communicating with. It felt very filmic, and like a way to tell this allegorical tale anew to a new generation."

Schwartz was intrigued. So was Weinstein, says Sebastian, when the idea was brought to him—though, as the director remembers it, the movie mogul wanted to see a stage production using the concept first.

According to Sebastian, the artistic director of the esteemed off–West End theater the Menier Chocolate Factory, David Babani, was "very, very keen to have it—and so I got swept along. Stephen and I had talked about going to the University of Michigan, where they obviously have an amazing musical theater department, to workshop these ideas, and get young people who played these video games to give us, these two old fogeys, more information. I wish we had done that, in retrospect—something quieter."

Instead, Sebastian and Babani began forging ahead, at one point bringing Chet Walker on board as a consultant to ensure that Fosse's choreographic foundation was represented within Sebastian's framing of the story and dance numbers. Sebastian, Babani, and Schwartz did a presentation at one point at Weinstein's offices, which Sebastian remembers as "this big building that was like some Medici court in Venice. We had to wait in this huge room, and then it was, 'He's coming!' And, 'He's coming!' And, 'He'll be here in five minutes!'" After arriving, "Harvey said at one point—I'm going to get killed for saying this, but he said, 'Well, the book needs some work. Tom Stoppard's a very good friend of mine, you know.' I just remember thinking, you idiot—what on earth?"

In the end, Sebastian says, Weinstein pulled out of the production. He would later flirt with another plan for a *Pippin* film but lose the rights as the Weinstein Company was preparing to file for bankruptcy protection, after reports accusing him of sexual assault made headlines in 2017. The Chocolate Factory's *Pippin* proved a less high-profile debacle. "It was slaughtered by critics," Sebastian says. "It had needed more incubating, and we hadn't had the right venue; the Chocolate Factory is a small basement with a low ceiling. Having said that, we did some beautiful things, and I was proud of the work." Schwartz says, "The first twenty minutes or so of that production were amazing. When you entered the theater you walked past Pippin on his headset, playing this game on his computer in his little bedroom. Then when the audience was seated in the theater, there was a kind of flickering of the lights, and suddenly Pippin was in the middle of this video game, and you were in the middle of it with him. Unfortunately, the show fell apart from a conceptual point of view once Catherine became involved. All these internal logic questions arose:

Who is Catherine in the outside world, and is she playing the game? Are all of these other characters playing too? Do Catherine and Pippin meet in the real world? It was never really clear. Mitch's idea was enormously inventive, but in the time we had, we weren't able to make it consistent conceptually from beginning to end."

While this struggle was in process, Schwartz had been approached by Broadway power couple Barry and Fran Weissler, producers whose many credits dated back to the early 1980s and included Tony-winning revivals of *Gypsy*, *Fiddler on the Roof*, *Chicago*, *Annie Get Your Gun*, and *La Cage Aux Folles*. It seemed that *Pippin* was next on their wish list, meaning that a Broadway revival could finally be imminent. Schwartz told the Weisslers of his commitment to Sebastian and the Chocolate Factory: "I said, 'Look, if it works out then that will be that, but if it doesn't then I'm happy to come back to you.'" Sebastian's second *Pippin* opened in December 2011; by the following February, the director recalls wistfully, "The rights had gone straight from David Babani to Fran and Barry Weissler's pockets, and within twelve months it was on Broadway."

The first Broadway revival of *Pippin* actually began previews at the Music Box Theatre in March 2013 and opened there in April, though the production had begun performances late the previous year—that of *Pippin*'s fortieth anniversary—at the American Repertory Theater at Harvard University, where Paulus was a few years into her tenure as the Terrie and Bradley Bloom Artistic Director. She had also earned Tony nominations for productions of *The Gershwins' Porgy and Bess* and *Hair*; the latter had originated at the Public Theater and drawn particular praise for its buoyant, immersive approach, which sent actors into the aisles to share their flower power with audience members. If anyone could bring the era of Schwartz's youth and *Pippin*'s birth back, at least in spirit, it was surely this director. But Paulus's plans for this musical did not involve nostalgia in any capacity, and it would take a leap of faith on Schwartz's part—buoyed by trust in her talent—to bring them to fruition.

CHAPTER TWELVE

A Night at the Circus

IN THE SUMMER OR FALL OF 2009, DIANE PAULUS WAS IN LONDON, having lunch with Cameron Mackintosh, the knighted impresario whom the *New York Times* had referred to nearly twenty years earlier as "the most successful, influential and powerful theatrical producer in the world." No one played a more important role in the British conquest of Broadway in the late twentieth century than Mackintosh, whose commercial triumphs included *Cats, The Phantom of the Opera, Les Misérables,* and *Miss Saigon.* Now it was Paulus's star rising, and without the stigma of mega-musicals—seldom critical favorites, for all their commercial appeal—attached to it. Her production of *Hair* had earned the 2009 Tony Award for best revival of a musical, and she was in town to discuss plans to bring it to the West End. "I was thinking of what I wanted to do next," Paulus says, "and it didn't even take me a beat to decide." So when Mackintosh posed the question to her, she could answer without hesitating. "I said, 'Oh—*Pippin.*' And he looked at me and said, '*Pippin?*' Like, '*Really?*'"

By that point, Mackintosh, whose early credits had included presenting the world premiere of the revue *Side by Side by Sondheim* in London and arranging for its transfer to Broadway, had certainly demonstrated his appreciation for musical theater classics. Since the *Times* had trumpeted his omnipotence, he had helped the National Theatre bring a lovely and lacerating *Carousel*—helmed by Nicholas Hytner, who had also directed *Miss Saigon*—to Lincoln Center, and given Broadway a West End–based and similarly acclaimed (if less compelling) revival of *Oklahoma! Pippin* was younger and less widely revered than those Rodgers and Hammerstein gems, particularly in England, but Paulus was keen to make a case for it—and she had done her homework. "I grew up in New York City, and seeing Broadway shows was part of my childhood," says Paulus. She caught the original production of *Pippin* "multiple times, and it really marked me. As an eight-year-old, I didn't fully understand it, but that didn't matter; the theatricality of it was so powerful, so seductive. Then I grew up playing the cast album on repeat, like a lot of people. I knew all those songs. I played 'Corner of the Sky' on the piano at high school parties. I choreographed an original dance to the music from the Manson Trio, which I performed at my high school talent show. I sang 'With You' at my brother's wedding. So I had an instinctual understanding of the power and cultural significance of *Pippin*. But it wasn't until I got the script again and started reading it that I really understood—or began my journey of understanding, I should say—what *Pippin* is really about."

Paulus's theory was that the musical "had gotten a certain reputation, because the songs are so catchy and you can sing them at campfires, and it's done a lot at community theaters and at camps and high schools; there's a version you can license that's appropriate for kids. People had gotten to know it that way, as warm and fuzzy. But when I really looked at it, I saw something more intense—almost a medieval morality play. I came to understand that the show is a trial of the soul, a series of trials." The director also grasped something fundamental about the musical: that Roger Hirson and Stephen Schwartz—and Bob Fosse—weren't offering a prescription for living. Or dying. "I didn't want people to see the ending as saying that the right answer would have been to jump in the fire, or saying that the right answer was that family matters—Pippin leaving with Catherine and Theo to make a home with a white picket fence. No. The whole point was that Pippin had a choice—and that at that moment he listened, for the first time, to himself."

Paulus knew that Pippin's conflict would be especially resonant for performers, whose job it is to be extraordinary and who are known to make personal and professional sacrifices and take risks in that pursuit. That's particularly true for a breed of artist not generally associated with musical theater, whose milieu Paulus happened to be studying as her ideas for *Pippin* were percolating. The director had been enlisted to develop a show for Cirque du Soleil; called *Amaluna* and inspired by *The Tempest*, it would premiere in Quebec in the spring of 2012. By then, Paulus had signed on to helm *Pippin* for Barry and Fran Weissler, and she had become a fan of the 7 Fingers—also known as Les 7 Doigts de la Main, a Montreal-based collective founded by a septet of circus artists who for a decade had been merging acrobatics and theater with dance, music, and storytelling across media platforms. Barry Weissler was a fan as well; as Gypsy Snider, one of the group's founding artistic directors, recalls, he encouraged Paulus to set up a meeting and a workshop.

Snider had been born into a circus family, and though a fan of Fosse's work, particularly *Cabaret*—"The art of cabaret and circus are very similar in ways, so I felt connected to it," she explains—she was less familiar with *Pippin*. But the script moved her to tears. "I had just gone through one of the most difficult experiences of my life, where I'd survived advanced-stage colon cancer while I was separating from my husband, and we have two children. So for a period the arts took a back seat in my life, and by the time I read the part where Pippin sings 'Extraordinary,' I was just so deeply moved. I think that scene speaks to a moment every artist deals with, recognizing the incredible choices you have to make when you decide to dedicate your life and your soul to art. And you have to quadruple those stakes when you're talking about the circus, because of what you put your body through. I know that dancers can feel this too—the stress and abuse to your body can be so extreme. Pippin feels he has to risk it all, and the circus is death-defying—but also life-affirming."

Schwartz admits he was initially reticent about the concept. "Over the years, many people had talked about the idea of setting *Pippin* in a circus, and when Diane mentioned it, I pictured a circus like Barnum would have put on, and that seemed clichéd. I thought it wouldn't be dark enough. But I went along because I held Diane in such high regard, and once I saw what her vision was, I wound up really loving it." For Paulus, "It was like we were connecting to the DNA of the original, drawing on elements of circus that were part of Fosse's vision, and then pushing them further. That led to the idea of the Leading Player standing outside the circus tent, like a carnival barker, saying, 'Join us . . . we've got magic to do.' Come inside my tent—I dare you." The director was also drawn to the sheer theatricality of *Pippin*: "You have these different, almost Brechtian moments, looking at war, sex, love, the family, the home. Pippin kills his father and then his father comes back to life—I loved that." Paulus restored the musical's intermission, ending Act One after "Morning Glow," then letting Pippin relinquish the crown and bringing Charles back to life after the audience had its break in a scene called "Politics."

According to Chet Walker, whom Paulus recruited fresh from the Menier Chocolate Factory production, the initial plan was to have circus elements dominate the choreography. When Paulus made it clear that she wanted to also pay homage to Fosse, though, he advised that they proceed with caution. "I said that we couldn't just recreate bits of pieces of the original production. It needs to be of the same theme as Fosse's, but not his. I did want to keep the commedia; in 1973 we were a troupe, and we would be a troupe now—just a different troupe, an acrobatic troupe, a circus troupe. Circuses throughout history have traveled around from place to place."

The one routine that Walker wanted to keep exactly as Fosse had left it was the Manson Trio, "because it worked with our concept (for the revival)." And with the United States mired in Iraq for a decade when Paulus's production began performances on Broadway, and in Afghanistan for longer, the resonance of *Pippin*'s most patently antiwar number had not subsided. "During the original and the revival, there were major wars happening in the world," Walker says, "and I think the Manson Trio is a representation of how some can just dance through or around a war, acting as an observer." If the draft was no longer in progress in 2013, that only drove home the point that the socially and economically privileged were, as usual, in a better position to simply dance and observe.

Because so much would be demanded of the performers, the audition process was tricky and extensive. Snider notes, "Between Diane and Chet and Stephen and Nadia and me"—Nadia DiGiallonardo had worked with Paulus on *Hair* and was the musical supervisor and arranger—"we wanted to have the most well-rounded people in all their domains. We wanted dancers who could really get the Fosse in the choreography and were also incredible vocally, and we wanted circus performers who had experience in movement and character as well as musicality. Sometimes it meant I had to convince everyone to take these circus people from France who were sending us videos. It could be very tedious, but it was really rewarding."

The principals, of course, would be played by theater pros. Married Broadway veterans Terrence Mann, whose many credits ranged from *Cats* and *Les Misérables* to *The Rocky Horror Show*, and Charlotte d'Amboise, who had done numerous stints as Roxie Hart in the hit revival of *Chicago* and originated the part of Cassie in a 2006 production of *A Chorus Line*, were cast as Charles and Fastrada. Beloved actress and comedienne Andrea Martin was chosen to play Berthe, while the young British actor Matthew James Thomas, who had been appearing onstage and on television since childhood, was selected for Pippin. For Catherine, Paulus chose a member of her *Hair* cast, Rachel Bay Jones, whose wide-eyed, cherubic wholesomeness belied the fact that she was nearly twenty years older than her leading man.

Jones had been reluctant when Paulus asked her to audition for the role of Catherine. "I was forty-one at the time, and Matthew was in his early twenties. I was a little embarrassed. I actually turned it down." Then Jones considered that this character she had regarded as an ingénue was actually a performer in a troupe, "and that it could be that the actress who plays Catherine has been playing the part for too long. That was my way in: I imagined that the Players had been doing this for a long time, and that my character had been playing a young mother with a small boy since she was the appropriate age. And she's fucking sick of it—sick of playing the same part, sick of being used as a tool by the Leading Player. She wants to be seen for who she is, and this young man playing Pippin, tonight, sees her that way."

The part of the Leading Player was, as usual, especially tough to cast. It eventually went to another *Hair* alumna: a sinewy, siren-voiced triple threat named Patina Miller, whom Snider describes as "one of the fiercest human beings I've ever met—and I've met some fierce women." The notion of a woman in the role wasn't entirely new, as Schwartz points out: "There had been high school productions, and a concert once where there were five or six Leading Players and some were men and some were women. But our decision was very carefully determined; when we were auditioning, we saw men, we saw women, we saw actors of color—all different possibilities." After it was resolved that no man playing the role on Broadway could escape the ghost of Ben Vereen's performance, the list was narrowed down. "There was some concern, particularly on Roger's and my part, that having a woman as the Leading Player might distort the relationship when Catherine came into it—because it would be a little bit like two women fighting over Pippin. But I came to feel that it was actually better. We were able to add some put-downs; the Leading Player now says to Catherine, 'You're almost too old for this role,' for instance. If a man were to say that to the actress playing Catherine it would seem unpleasant, even abusive. I've come to really like the idea of having a woman as the Leading Player."

Miller, for her part, saw the relationship between the Leading Player and Pippin and Catherine as a love triangle, but with a twist: "To me, the Leading Player has both female and masculine energy. She's on this journey with Pippin and she decides which she should switch on at what time. With 'On the Right Track,' at the beginning I made it feminine and slinky, but by the middle there's a harder, more masculine feel to the dancing." Snider notes, "Women in the circus, the women I was raised by, are tough. I remember my mom breaking her foot and going to the hospital to get a cast put on, and four days later we were in the next town and she was using pliers to cut the cast off, because she had to keep working. Patina has that rigor. I won't lie—she scared me. She's so sweet and funny, but I did not want to disappoint her, and to have an actor push me like that was so exciting."

Part of Paulus's process was to have all the actors devise backstories for each of their characters and then prepare presentations for the company—each explaining, as Walker puts it, "where do I come from, why am I here, and what do I have to offer this circus." For Martin, "This was the most wonderful exercise that really informed my internal creation of Berthe. I remember playing music by Nino Rota"—an Italian composer who, fittingly, worked with Fellini and later scored *The Godfather* films for Francis Ford Coppola—"as the soundtrack of my story: a woman giving birth to a child, and longing for the man she loved, who had disappeared.

The woman I created in the exercise was sensual, and tough, but she had a broken heart. She had been a member of the circus, a clown, but now, without that identity, she was alone, a blank slate. But holding her child, she realizes she cannot give up; she has to live for her sake and her baby's. She has a new identity: mother." Martin has used the exercise in every production she's been involved with since.

After seeing Martin's presentation, Snider knew she had to create something special for Berthe's showstopper, "No Time at All." "I was looking at this character of a grandmother"—like Berthe, Martin was in her mid-sixties—"but being played by this super gung-ho, strong woman, and I knew that she had to be active and in control. I think normally someone would have put her in an apparatus where she could just be passive, doing pretty poses. But Andrea had to do something spectacular. After the first workshop, we didn't have an idea for her—I pretty much knew where everyone else was going to go acrobatically and choreo-graphically, but with her I didn't. Then I came home, and I had this vision of her doing a pas de deux with a beautiful young man"—in keeping with the lyric, "It's hard to believe I'm being led astray by a man who calls me 'Granny.'" Snider wound up inserting an interlude in which Martin—still svelte and remarkably fit after doing circus training in New York and Los Angeles—found herself dangling, swinging, and eventually singing from a trapeze, a buff male acrobat supporting her. "This incredibly funny woman had come up with this beautiful, tragically positive character who somehow was able to find the beauty in life's challenges—and that's where the comedy was."

Jones, in contrast, "was constantly coming up to me and asking about clowns, and their place in the ecosystem of the circus," Snider says. "The clown is always there to remind us all of our humanity, and to make us live in the moment. My father was a clown, and he knew that the tragic moments were where we really had to laugh, and Rachel got that. She did almost none of the other circus stuff, but she really pushed me to create that space in the show." Thomas, who had recently made his Broadway debut as an alternate for the title character in *Spider Man: Turn Off the Dark*—a gig that required him to literally fly over a theater audience, suspended by wires—arrived at rehearsals eager to get more physical and was readily obliged. As he recalls, "Screaming out a high C at the end of 'Extraordinary' whilst jumping off a pole and being thrown by an acrobat—that's a whole different landscape."

Snider muses, "Matthew always felt like the acrobats were doing all the 'cool' stuff in the show—whereas we were all like, 'Matthew James Thomas is the coolest guy ever; he can open his mouth and we all melt.' He was really hooking into why Pippin wanted to run away with the circus, and these acrobats were his peers but also street competition, playful competition. That's very much an energy I'm used to dealing with from the circus world. He was fearless, always so ready to live this whole show on the edge, and yet it never compromised him vocally."

Thomas says that creating a backstory for his character was a no-brainer: "I *was* Pippin. Diane and I discussed this, and I realized I've been fighting this story my entire life. There's the lack of perspective you have with all the facts, and then you come into a show where you're constantly tested about the things that make sense to you, things that are completely fantastical and also real: What does life mean? Why am I here? What is my purpose? As a coming-of-age story, *Pippin* seems to get abnormally close to answering those questions—and in its non-answers, it's unlike a lot of musical theater material in that it poses a very present and open question at the end." During rehearsals, Thomas expressed his own queries and opinions. "Diane and I both had strong ideas. What I love about her is that she's willing to get a bit bloody. There were a lot of people who were willing to get in the mud and play around"—including Schwartz. "Stephen is very wise. He would stand at the back monitoring and observing, then bring very positive and authentic thoughts to the process. It wasn't like, Stephen Schwartz, the boss, says this; the relationship was very collaborative."

Members of Paulus's music team describe similar experiences. Orchestrator Larry Hochman went back the farthest with *Pippin*, having briefly filled in for the original production's pianist back in 1974, when he was a senior at the Manhattan School of Music. Hochman had since worked in numerous productions of Schwartz's musicals, from *Godspell* and *The Magic Show* to the cult classic *The Baker's Wife*—one of those long-gestating projects that Schwartz has seen through different incarnations since the 1970s—while building a career that has earned him nine Tony nominations for orchestrations; he was a winner in 2011 for *The Book of Mormon*. "I've been able to appreciate how broad Stephen's range is," says Hochman, pointing to *Baker's Wife*'s lush, lyrical score—a precursor to *Wicked*'s in its mix of theatrical ballads and production numbers and soaring anthems—and to Schwartz's 2009 opera *Séance on a Wet Afternoon*, based on the novel and film of the same name. "With *Godspell* and *Pippin*, he chose to use more of his pop side. There's a groove to his music, a pop and rock flair that he has from the period, but there's always something else, something extra. Take 'Magic to Do'; if you heard the first four bars on the piano, you wouldn't know what else is coming. It really does have its own magic."

One of Hochman's ideas was actually to craft a new intro for that opening number, which had originally started—as anyone with a recording of the original cast album knows—with one note held for few beats on the electric keyboard, followed by those groovy piano chords. Hochman phoned musical supervisor DiGiallonardo, "and I said, 'Nadia, I've got this crazy idea: Imagine if the orchestra was tuning up at the beginning, but it's coordinated and ends on this note, and then the rest of the orchestra fades out and it becomes this intro.' So I wrote this thing that on paper looks like the sort of avant-garde mess that was trendy in the forties or fifties. It fooled the audience into thinking the orchestra was just tuning up—but then the show started." DiGiallonardo recalls, "As soon as the audience heard those piano chords, they went wild." (As with a couple of the Leading Player's other songs, traditionally sung by a tenor, DiGiallarmo had to shift keys to accommodate a female belter—though here and elsewhere she was able to use modulation to dramatic effect, "because Patina Miller's range was huge—as was Matthew James Thomas's.")

For the next, even more famous number, "Corner of the Sky," DiGiallonardo notes, "Larry brought acoustic guitar in, which I loved—while of course still having the piano. You couldn't lose that iconic 'Corner of the Sky' piano. That's what was so exciting: How do you take these songs that are some of the greatest hits of Broadway, and give people what they want to hear—but also make it feel like they're hearing it for the first time, as if Stephen Schwartz just wrote it? We spoke to Stephen about that—what did he feel attached to, and what did he feel he could let go of? And he was just so open. He let me go to town. There were two minutes of circus music at the top of Act Two. There was trapeze music for 'No Time at All,' and something we called 'The Carnage Capers' for the huge war sequence, and a lot of new underscoring. It was all pulled from the score, so it was all familiar, but I think we made it sound very fresh."

Charlie Alterman, who served as musical director and conductor in addition to sharing keyboard duties with Sonny Paladino, notes that Hochman had advised them all "not to obsess over updating the arrangements and orchestrations just for the sake of updating them. He said we would all have our sensibilities grounded in how music is made now anyway, which I think was a very astute point, and it guided us." Alterman had also worked on the 2011 Broadway revival of *Godspell* and notes, "What I admired about Stephen with both shows is that he was excited about what new takes we wanted to put on things. There were times he was blown away and invigorated, and other times he would say, 'I don't think that's it,' but he was always respectful—and he was always right. He gave us the confidence to play creatively, and he had great taste about what to use and what to dial back."

Among other things, Schwartz was impressed with this musical team's ingenuity in working with, in at least one key sense, only half the resources their Broadway predecessors had enjoyed. Hochman notes that there were twenty-four musicians in the original production's orchestra and twelve in theirs—a reflection of the related trends of shrinking budgets (for orchestras, at least) and advancing technology. "The budget specified that I would have a much smaller band than the original," Hochman notes, "but with the synthesizers I was able to make it sound a little bigger, though I had to rely on starker, less layered sounds." The orchestrator would have liked, he admits, "a couple more brass, a couple more woodwinds. . . . There are very few people who can play flute and clarinet and oboe really well, though I had one. I did not have a French horn, and I really wish I had. And yet I would say the major differences between Ralph Burns's [orchestrations] and mine were not because of the size of the orchestra, but because of new choices. The times they do sound similar, it was because I did some synthesizer tricks in order to get a fuller sound."

For Schwartz, "One of Larry's great strengths is that he can get more bang for the buck"—particularly with strings. "You don't get a huge string section on Broadway. I guess Richard Rodgers did, but now you're lucky if you get four of them. Larry has the ability to write for strings in a way that it sounds like a big string section." In 2000, Hochman had orchestrated the Broadway premiere of the musical *Jane Eyre*, which Schwartz's son, Scott, codirected, using two violinists; for *Pippin*, Hochman had one musician playing both violin and viola—plus a cellist and bassist, as *Jane Eyre* also had. That the new *Pippin*'s brass section was also tiny—one trumpet and one trombone—was less of an issue for Schwartz, who had always found Ralph Burns's orchestrations too brassy anyway.

Of course, when reviews for this *Pippin*'s premiere at A.R.T. began popping up just days into 2013, the more obvious amendments and additions—the circus elements, the new cast members, and Paulus's vision—got the most attention, and it was generally positive. "Anyone who's seen this production knows how magical theater can be," wrote Jeffrey Gantz in the *Boston Globe*. *The Arts Fuse* was rather less effusive, though the site's founder, veteran New England–based critic Bill Marx, clearly hadn't been a huge fan of the musical; he wrote that Paulus was "generally an efficient mover and shaker, propelling the production along with gusto so you don't have a chance to think too hard about disappearing characters, vanishing plot threads, and nonsense sentiments." Audiences in Cambridge were, at least by Paulus's testimony, far more engaged. "I would see people in their eighties crying. For them it was, 'I didn't run away with the circus—I made another choice in life.'" Younger viewers clung to their children at the end, when the Leading Player tried to entice them into the fire. "To me, that was the power of the show: Would you give your soul, give everything, to this circus troupe? Or if not, would you regret it?"

When the production opened on Broadway in April, a few prominent critics were underwhelmed or, rather, overwhelmed, suggesting that Paulus had tried to out-razzle-dazzle Fosse with her own style-over-substance formula. In a review titled "Candide Goes to Vegas," the *Wall*

Street Journal's Terry Teachout, for instance, wrote that Miller's "in-your-face performance sets the tone for Ms. Paulus's relentlessly aggressive staging, which is big, noisy and mostly humorless." The *Times*'s Ben Brantley and *New York*'s Jesse Green noted that Paulus faced a daunting task in reinvigorating a show that was, both reviewers agreed, noted more for Fosse's staging than for its book or story—though they also acknowledged the power of its score, which Green praised for its "rhapsodic pop melodies." Brantley was less satisfied overall, writing, "Ms. Paulus's 'Pippin' is often fun (with an exclamation point), but it's almost never stirring in the way her Tony-winning revival of 'Hair' was." (Notably, all three adored Andrea Martin's full-blooded performance in the show, as did everyone else.)

But such ambivalent and mixed notices were outnumbered by raves—one of them written by yours truly, while I was on staff at *USA Today*. I couldn't judge the revival against Fosse's original, having not seen it. But I was struck by the "soulful spectacle" of Paulus's staging, as I wrote, and how the cast and orchestrations did justice to a score I had cherished since childhood. (I was also one of seven hundred fans who turned up a few weeks later to sing the chorus of "No Time at All" for a new cast recording; it was an assignment, but one I relished.) Other notices were even more ecstatic. The *Chicago Tribune*'s Chris Jones called the revival "far and away the best musical production of the current Broadway season and a 'Pippin' that will make you afraid of ever seeing it again thereafter, lest the sheer joy of what transpires of the Music Box Theatre is compromised." In *Time Out New York*, Adam Feldman deemed it simply "the greatest show of the Broadway season . . . a thrilling evening of art and craftiness spiked with ambivalence about the nature of enthrallment."

Joe Dziemianowicz, in his review for the *New York Daily News*, enthused that this *Pippin* offered "everything you could dream of in a musical—including Stephen Schwartz's terrifically tuneful songs—and a few things you couldn't even imagine." The review drew special attention to veteran scenic designer Scott Pask's "bright blue canopy" of a set, a backdrop for fire effects and circus illusions. "The minute the drapes opened," Dziemianowicz says now, "I felt immediately transported. I thought the fact that *Pippin* is not really a story elegantly told made it a good match for this rough-hewn world of the circus. It wasn't polished marble; it was a circus tent, with juggling and knife-throwing and grandmothers hanging upside down, and probably some messes, and I thought that kind of cradled the story. Pippin is on a search, so why should he be polished?"

In terms of box office longevity, Paulus's *Pippin* wasn't the sensation that, say, the still-flourishing 1996 revival of *Chicago* has proven to be, though the former production enjoyed a very respectable seven hundred and nine performances before closing in January 2015. Paulus successfully launched a national tour—and has since overseen international productions, most recently in Australia—while she, Miller, Martin, and the revival itself all received Tony Awards. Among actors from the original *Pippin*, opinions about the new interpretation were mixed. "I loved it," says Betty Buckley, "because it retained so much of Fosse's style even with the additional circus aspect, which was fun. And Rachel Bay Jones—man, oh, man, she was just delicious. I kept saying to myself, my God, why didn't I think of that?" Gene Foote, in contrast, found Paulus's work "almost insulting. It looked like *America's Got Talent* meets Cirque du Soleil." Kathryn Doby says, "I think the circus element could have been fine, but there was too much of it. I found it distracting."

Doby notes that Fosse had also considered casting a female Leading Player at one point, as a replacement: "Debbie Allen was dying to do that part, and she was an incredible dancer, a good singer, a wonderful performer. It was an interesting thought, and Bob saw her three or four times, and her auditions were absolutely phenomenal. But he decided against it, because he thought it would add a totally different dynamic—that the whole camaraderie between the Leading Player and Pippin would be gone if one of them was female."

At that point, even as timelessly hip an artist as Fosse could not get past that bit of what now seems like provincial logic—and he surely could not have envisioned a time when identifying characters as male or female wasn't the only option. But just as human nature and history's bitter and better patterns would keep *Pippin*'s themes relevant, progress would open up new possibilities for the show, and the restless imaginations of young people—the musical's original creative source as well as its focus—would play a principal role.

More Magic Shows and Miracles

IN THE SUMMER OF 2021, THEATERS ACROSS THE GLOBE WERE GRADU-
ally starting to reopen after having been shuttered for more than a year by
the COVID-19 pandemic, and Stephen Schwartz took the opportunity
to check out a new production of *Pippin* in London. The city's long-
strained relationship with the musical was on the upswing: An open-air,
socially distanced production featuring only six performers had been
staged in September 2020, and was so well received by critics and audiences that three extensions were added. When a return engagement was
scheduled the following year at the Charing Cross Theatre, more dates
were initially scheduled, but the run was still extended twice.

For Schwartz, though, the most striking aspect of Dexter's production was how "Pippin-centric" it was. "When you came into the theater,
the first thing you saw was Pippin sitting onstage, writing in a journal.
Then he kind of summoned the Leading Player and then the troupe came
in, which is the reverse of what usually happens, and it was very clear
from 'Magic to Do' that this was all literally taking place inside Pippin's

Directed by West End veteran Steven Dexter, this *Pippin* was set
in 1967—when a teenage Schwartz had begun working on *Pippin,
Pippin*—with the Players decked out in brightly colored hippie garb.
Although the cast size was increased to eight at the Charing Cross, with
each actor playing a single principal role—in the previous staging, one
performer had doubled as Berthe and Fastrada and another as Theo and
Lewis—there were still no additional ensemble members, making it even
more apparent that these characters were themselves actors playing parts.

head. As the others were talking to the audience, welcoming them to the show, Pippin was also talking, saying things like, 'Do you know who these people are?' And Ryan Anderson, the actor playing this Pippin, was a very good dancer, so he was more front and center in numbers like 'Glory' and 'With You' and, particularly, 'On the Right Track.' In a way, it was closer to what Roger and I had envisioned before Bob Fosse came into it. I've come to embrace Bob's concept, so it's not as if I thought, 'Finally, someone's doing my show.' But on the other hand, it was reassuring to see that Roger and I weren't crazy."

Some members of Dexter's cast appeared, at least in photos, so young that they would have not seemed out of place in one of the high school or college productions of *Pippin* that remain so popular. This tale of a young person seeking a spectacular life but then choosing a less glamorous path can have, as Diane Paulus discovered, a particular poignance for older audience members, and not just in evoking the road not taken. Critic Peter Filichia was in his twenties when he first saw the musical, and while he had loved the score, the story, especially the ending, frustrated him: "I thought, here's a guy who wanted to be extraordinary, and he settled for being a husband and stepfather. But then some years later, a community theater here in Manhattan did a production. By then my oldest and dearest friend had become a surrogate father; a woman he'd worked with had become pregnant and the guy abandoned her. She and my friend didn't become romantically involved, but he started to pick the child up from school, and to this day, thirty-eight years later, he's like his father. So when I saw *Pippin* that next time, it impressed me that there is value in making a woman and a child happy—that's an excellent way to spend your life."

But *Pippin* also retains a special resonance for the young. As Paulus notes, "It questions the trials and meanings of life, which young people are trying to understand," while capturing the extreme highs and lows associated with that time in life—on the one hand, the excitement of discovery and great expectations and, on the other, the devastation that comes with first experiencing disappointment and failure. Benj Pasek, who is still in his thirties, remembers vividly. "Who isn't Pippin?" Pasek asks, rhetorically. "Who doesn't feel like they're searching for identity and meaning? It doesn't matter what age you are. The line that fucking kills me is, 'If I'm never tied to anything/I'll never be free'"—Pippin's epiphany in "Magic Shows and Miracles," during the finale. "That big message, that you find meaning in your connection to other people, and to yourself. That it's not waiting somewhere across the world; it's within you. Every year of your life, you need to hear that."

When Chet Walker protégé Kyle Pleasant directed and choreographed a 2020 production for Manhattan's Professional Performing Arts School—the alma mater of stars such as Claire Danes and Alicia Keys, where Pleasant is on the theater faculty—he and his performers, all of high school age, "got into the different journeys in the show and how they worked into Pippin's journey. That opened up a beautiful dialogue for the kids, about who they wanted to be and what they hoped to achieve, but also about where they had struggled." The subject of mental illness arose: "What are the consequences if you can't find your place? What does it mean, this choice that Pippin has to make? Does he jump into the abyss, make the ultimate sacrifice just to be remembered in a certain way? That opened up a conversation about suicide, and what that can look like for young people."

Pleasant was keen to make his *Pippin*—which could stage only one performance before the COVID closure—address other contemporary concerns. "I started to think about what the struggles were like out on the street at that moment. I toyed with the idea of making Pippin female, and looking at what it would be like as a woman fighting to find a place in a universe where she doesn't necessarily see herself all the time. I would have loved to go down that path, and I actually called back quite a few female actors for the role. Being a public school, we did not have the money we needed to transpose all the orchestrations to accommodate that, sadly—but it opened things up to having a person of color play Pippin, also trying to fit into that universe."

A Latino student, Diego Lucano Jiménez-Pons (stage name Diego Lucano), was cast in the part, and with new orchestrations available from the Paulus production in keys that accommodated Patina Miller's range, Pleasant was able to assign Leonay Shepherd, another young Black woman, the role of Leading Player. As some other directors have done,

Pleasant had his leading man sit in the audience initially. "We all knew who Diego was, of course, but the idea was that normally, no one would have known that this would be our Pippin—that he would get pulled out of that chair and sucked into this universe. So the questions were, why did this person come to the show this night? What did he need? That was part of the framework. And then, who is the Leading Player to Pippin? Because everyone in the company had been Pippin, at some point; they were all called to this universe in some way, and none of them left. Why does Pippin leave, and why have the others stayed? The kids were able to see all those different layers."

The young director and playwright Elisabeth Frankel, who in addition to developing her own projects is an assistant to the two-time Pulitzer Prize winner Lynn Nottage, became intimately acquainted with *Pippin* at twelve years old, while playing Berthe in a youth production. Not two decades later, she is working on her own staging, in which the title character actually is female—with Schwartz's blessing. "I've always thought of *Pippin* as a woman's story," says Frankel. "I think the fear of domesticity and commitment is so much more potent and interesting in women, because once you're a mother, you can never *not* be a mother. I assume I'll have kids, but there is the pressure of, if I settle down and marry and have kids, will that be my life—rather than being an artist, or a businesswoman, or a teacher? I'm ambitious, but I also want to be happy, and I can't think of a piece of art that nails that dichotomy more than *Pippin*."

Frankel has been holding Zoom meetings with Schwartz and David Hirson while working on *Pippin: Her Life and Times*, as she's calling her new interpretation, in which she'll incorporate aspects of both the original libretto and the version used in Paulus's revival. "I'm hoping people will see the core of the story: someone who tries something and fails, tries something and fails—which is so resonant of what life feels like." The actors will also serve as musicians—not members of a traveling troupe but rather participants in the musical concert that Pippin has come to see as her life. Orchestrations will be "in the feminist, folk style of artists who were pioneers around the time Stephen wrote it, like Joni Mitchell and Joan Baez."

Schwartz has been "very supportive and involved," Frankel notes, "particularly when it comes to shifting certain narrative choices, such as the role of the Leading Player." Like Dexter and others, she has come to see that character as a voice inside Pippin's head, but apparently a more nurturing one. "Who is the voice that wants the best for us, that sometimes criticizes us, that follows us wherever we go, and we always want their approval and are ashamed when we disappoint them? It's our mother. So our Leading Player will be a fabulous, warm, maternal, middle-aged woman, who will likely look like the actress playing Pippin. She'll be more grounded in the narrative of the show." Frankel envisions Theo as Thea, a young girl who will at some point embark on her own journey. In contrast, "Charles is definitely still a man, and there will be this very intense father-daughter relationship."

For the *Pippin* he directed at Five Towns College in 2022, Will Detlefsen was similarly "aware of historical tropes that can feel ignorant, that I'm interested in breaking." Detlefsen cast a Black woman as Theo, who became Thea, and a transgender man as Lewis. Among the actors he selected for principal roles, only two, those chosen for Charles and Fastrada, were white; Black actors were also cast as Pippin, the Leading Player, and Berthe, and Asians cast as Catherine and Lewis.

Schwartz remains eager to see other fresh takes on *Pippin*, and not just onstage. With the movie rights having been restored to him—he managed to reacquire them before the Weinstein Company held its bankruptcy auction, just as Lin-Manuel Miranda and Quiara Alegría Hudes did with *In the Heights*—the composer has become newly hopeful that the musical will, at last, be captured properly on-screen. "I always saw it as a natural film, because of the fantastical element and the Fellini-esque troupe," Schwartz maintains, "but people have had difficulties with the episodic nature of the storytelling." According to a 2018 article in *Deadline*, there were other factors; sources told the entertainment industry news site that Rob Marshall, who had directed *Chicago* for Harvey and Bob Weinstein's Miramax Films and a screen adaptation of the musical *Nine* for the Weinstein Company, had wanted to direct *Pippin* as well, but that working with Harvey on *Nine* had been "so stressful" that he wasn't keen to make another movie with the mogul. With Weinstein out of the picture, *Deadline* reporter Mike Fleming Jr. wrote, he'd heard that Marshall was interested again.

While Schwartz doesn't dangle any names, he has been speaking with a film director about *Pippin*, even with a hotly anticipated movie version of *Wicked* in the works. "The timing is better now, because now we know more about how to make *Pippin* really work," he says. "A film version would obviously have to be very different, but we're working from something that I think is more inherently sound"—the updated book, with the new ending that Schwartz is, again, certain would have pleased the show's original director.

Of course, the prospect of what Fosse himself would have done with a screen adaptation of *Pippin*—had the stars aligned so that he lived a bit longer, or had he and Schwartz somehow managed to put their differences aside and team up again—is one that will likely haunt anyone who caught that first stage production between 1972 and 1977. But as so many have pointed out, part of Fosse's gift—and Schwartz's and Roger Hirson's—is that the musical remains so open to new exploration, not only directorially or dramaturgically but also in terms of how it is orchestrated, sung, danced, and absorbed by seekers of all kinds, and with all kinds of experience. As a mysterious troupe leader first told audiences fifty years ago, the possibilities are there for us, anytime we want them—right inside our heads.

Acknowledgments

I was introduced to *Pippin* through an eight-track cassette of the original Broadway cast recording around the time I was seven or eight. I was already obsessed with musical theater by then, having been exposed—by a mother who had sung professionally, and an Austrian-born father who places Richard Rodgers above Mozart on his list of favorite composers—to the cream of the crop; by the time my parents started taking me to shows, I had memorized every song in the first three: revivals of *West Side Story*, *My Fair Lady*, and *Oklahoma!* But *Pippin* held a unique place in that we played the album in the family car, which was otherwise reserved for the cream of pop, from the Beatles' "Red" and "Blue" collections to the *Saturday Night Fever* soundtrack. It's not entirely an exaggeration, in fact, to say that I might never have become consumed enough with pop music to want to write about it had Stephen Schwartz not provided me with a gateway drug.

When I realized that the golden anniversary of *Pippin*'s premiere was approaching, I reached out to Stephen—whom I had interviewed a few times and always found gracious and eloquent—and asked if he might be interested in commemorating the occasion with a book. Librettist Roger O. Hirson had recently died, and with Bob Fosse, whose creative vision was just as integral to that first production, long gone, I knew that this project would be impossible without Stephen's generosity and candor—and he provided both in abundance. For months, we spoke pretty much every week on FaceTime as the COVID pandemic dragged on, at one point meeting in his New York apartment (masked, of course) so that he could go over old book drafts and pages of sheet music, which I was then allowed to take home for further reference. When he had trouble remembering conversations or events from five or six decades ago, he was quick to recommend other possible sources, and he didn't try to avoid potentially unflattering details, particularly those related to his less-than-harmonious relationship with Fosse. A "warts and all" account—his words—was our mutual goal. Stephen's assistant, Michael Cole, was also of great help, as was biographer Carol de Giere, whose *Defying Gravity: The Creative Career of Stephen Schwartz from Godspell to Wicked* was an invaluable resource, and who shared with me reams of her impeccable research to boot.

The cooperation of original cast members of *Pippin* was equally crucial, not only in providing me with a better sense of Fosse as an artist and a person but also in establishing how their own blazing talents and distinct personalities contributed to the production. Getting to know "The Pips," as a couple of these seemingly ageless individuals referred to themselves collectively, was a privilege I will always cherish. Following our initial conversations, I struck up regular e-mail and/or phone corre-spondences with John Rubinstein, Kathryn Doby, Candy Brown, Pamela Sousa, Gene Foote, and Cheryl Clark, who answered my relentless questions with great patience and wit—I hope to read their books one day—and volunteered their own insights. They also provided material from their archives, from rehearsal notes to personal memorabilia. Ben Vereen, whom I reached through his manager, Pamela Cooper, invited me to text him with any queries and delivered the sweetest responses, with emojis to match. Jennifer Nairn-Smith sent adorable pet pictures, Linda Posner inspired me with her eclectic personal journey, and Rich-ard Korthaze made me laugh out loud without saying anything snarky. I can only hope to be a fraction as vital as these folks are when I reach my seventies and eighties.

I could say the same for the behind-the-scenes players who spoke with me, among them producer Stuart Ostrow (still going strong in his tenth decade), lighting designer Jules Fisher, and sound designer Abe Jacob. Set designer Tony Walton—who left us, sadly, as I was completing final edits—not only granted a delightful interview but also offered access to his exquisite sketchings for the musical and to photos of the end prod-uct. His widow, Genevieve Leroy-Walton, and associate director Amanda Kate Joshi also have my deepest gratitude.

A number of other people who played key roles in the original *Pippin* had passed on before I started writing, but some special people were there to shed light on their work and lives. Roger Hirson's son, David, and Bob Fosse's daughter, Nicole, were kind enough to answer a few questions; I am also indebted to Mary Callahan, project manager at the Verdon Fosse Legacy LLC, who connected me not only to Nicole but also to several of the aforementioned cast members and other dancers. Milo Zonka, costume designer Patricia Zipprodt's nephew, granted permission to use her art. I contacted Ann Reinking's publicist, Lee Gross, shortly before Reinking's untimely death; Lee then referred me to William Whitener, a longtime friend and colleague of Reinking who confirmed what others had told me: that she was as lovely a person as she was a brilliant talent.

I'm grateful to the other remarkable dancers and choreographers who shared their memories of and thoughts about Fosse—Graciela Daniele, Linda Haberman, Jerry Mitchell, Chita Rivera, Bebe Neuwirth, Graciela Daniele, Casey Nicholaw, and Chet Walker, as well as dancer-turned-curator-turned-author Kevin Winkler, whose *Big Deal* was among the Fosse biographies I consulted—and to the renowned composers and lyricists who spoke about Stephen, including John Kander, Jeanine Tesori, Lynn Ahrens, Stephen Flaherty, Benj Pasek, and Justin Paul. (Getting a quote from Marlon Jackson was an unexpected bonus, for which I thank his manager, Steve Hart.) The representatives who put me in touch with these illustrious figures included Marie Bshara, Dennis Crowley, Merle Frimark, Heath Schwartz, and Michael Strassheim. Merle also connected me with Abe Jacob and original *Godspell* producer Edgar Lansbury, and Heath got me in touch with producer Barry Weissler and the talented performers and creative stars who brought *Pippin* back to Broadway in 2013—Diane Paulus, Charlie Alterman, Nadia DiGiallonardo, Larry Hochman, Rachel Bay Jones, Andrea Martin, Patina Miller, Gypsy Snider, and Matthew James Thomas—as well as the revered photographer Joan Marcus.

Directors of other noted productions of the musical—Rob Ashford, Jeff Calhoun, and Mitch Sebastian—helped me flesh out *Pippin*'s legacy, as did Will Detlefsen, Elisabeth Frankel, and Kyle Pleasant. (Eduardo Jimenez Pons, whose son Diego Lucano starred in Pleasant's high school production, and Gary Vorwald also provided great art.) Betty Buckley (and her assistant, Cathy Brighenti), Dean Pitchford, and Michael Rupert afforded me the perspective of key replacement players in the original staging, while Peggy Gordon, Robin Lamont, Stephen Nathan, Gilmer McCormick Reinhardt, Stephen Reinhardt, David Spangler, and the fabulous Paul Shaffer expanded on Stephen Schwartz's aptitude and ambitions as an even younger man.

As I thought it crucial to acknowledge the impact of Motown Records on this young composer and the role that the company played in getting *Pippin* on Broadway, I owe great thanks to Berry Gordy Jr. for his input and to his executive assistant, Brenda Boyce. Stephen Byrd, whom I reached through Aaron Meier, and Irene Gandy—long a favorite colleague, whom I reconnected with through Jeffrey Richards—shared the wisdom and savvy they've acquired as longtime theater industry insiders, as did the Broadway League's Charlotte St. Martin. Dr. Paul Allen Sommerfield at the Library of Congress and Jeremy Megraw at the Billy Rose Division of the New York Library for the Performing Arts were integral in facilitating my own research—I hounded Jeremy for months about old articles and photos, and he always responded with astonishing speed and good cheer—as were Richard Patterson, Drew Cohen, and Bert Fink at Music Theatre International. Dr. Helmut Reimitz of Princeton University and Dr. Brent Salter of Stanford Law School were equally accommodating, and the smart, piquant observations of my friends and comrades Joe Dziemianowicz, Adam Feldman, and Peter Filichia hopefully made me look a little wiser in my own wheelhouse.

This project would never have gotten off the ground without the gentle persistence of Sarah Lazin, who over decades has been more of a friend than an agent, and not just because of my lack of productivity. Sarah's colleague Catharine Strong became a razor-sharp partner and warm presence in my life after John Cerullo bravely offered me a contract with Applause Books. Chris Chappell was a magnificent editor, as articulate and insightful as he was patient and kind, and Barbara Claire, Laurel Myers, and Ashleigh Cooke at Applause gamely fielded all my stupid questions about the mechanics of publishing. I could not have asked for a happier experience on my first full-length book.

Finally, I must give thanks to the three mammals who spent the most time with me during this process. My husband, Aaron Zazueta—who as a social anthropologist publishes on more trivial matters, such as climate change, systemic poverty, and biodiversity—was unflagging in his encouragement. Our daughter, Lara, kept me posted on all the current Broadway dish while I immersed myself in the 1970s, and never complained when I couldn't cook dinner. (That's an inside joke.) We adopted our fourth family member, a gorgeous mutt named Nellie, from a shelter in Little Rock, Arkansas, and thus named her after *South Pacific*'s cockeyed optimist, which turned out to be perfect. A more steadfast, affectionate writing companion was never born. My days are brighter than morning air because I share my days with all of you.

SELECTED BIBLIOGRAPHY

Appy, Christian G. *American Reckoning: The Vietnam War and Our National Identity.* New York: Penguin Books, 2015.

Beddow, Margery. *Bob Fosse's Broadway.* Portsmouth, NH: Heinemann, 1996.

Benjaminson, Peter. *The Story of Motown.* Los Angeles: Rare Bird Books, 2018 (Grove Press, 1979).

Berson, Misha. "Composer Looks Back on 'Pippin.'" *Seattle Times,* May 4, 2006.

Crosby, John. "Crosby's Column: Enter Hero, Exit Neurotic." *New York Herald Tribune,* May 27, 1962.

de Giere, Carol. *Defying Gravity: The Creative Career of Stephen Schwartz from Godspell to Wicked.* Milwaukee, WI: Applause Theatre & Cinema Books, 2018.

Gaines, Caseen. *Footnotes: The Black Artists Who Rewrote the Rules of the Great White Way.* Naperville, IL: Sourcebooks, 2021.

Gottfried, Martin. *All His Jazz: The Life and Death of Bob Fosse.* Boston, MA: Da Capo Press, 1998, 2003.

Grant, Mark N. *The Rise and Fall of the Broadway Musical.* Boston: Northeastern University Press, 2004.

Grubb, Kevin Boyd. *Razzle Dazzle: The Life and Work of Bob Fosse.* New York: St. Martin's Press, 1989.

Guarino, Lindsay, and Wendy Oliver, eds. *Jazz Dance: A History of the Roots and Branches.* Gainesville: University Press of Florida, 2015.

Johnson, Laurie. "Fosse Discusses Creation of 'Pippin.'" *New York Times,* November 7, 1972.

Loney, Glenn. "The Many Facets of Bob Fosse." *After Dark,* June 1972.

Ostrow, Stuart. *A Producer's Broadway Journey.* Westport, CT: Praeger Publishers, 1999.

———. *Present at the Creation, Leaping in the Dark, and Going against the Grain: 1776, Pippin, M. Butterfly, La Bête and Other Broadway Adventures.* New York: Applause Theatre & Cinema Books, 2006.

Parker, Jerry. "The Birth Pangs of a Broadway Hit." *Newsday,* September 10, 1972.

Phillips, McCandlish. "For Stage Tryouts, 4 Seconds of Hope." *New York Times,* February 9, 1972.

Rehfeld, Barry. "Fosse's Follies." *Rolling Stone,* January 19, 1984.

Reinking, Ann. "Auditioning for Fosse." *Dance Magazine,* January 3, 2007.

Schulman, Bruce. *The Seventies: The Great Shift in American Culture, Society, and Politics.* Boston, MA: Da Capo Press, 2002.

Schulman, Michael. "Ann Reinking on Her Life as Bob Fosse's Lover, Muse, and Friend." *The New Yorker*, May 28, 2019.

Shurtleff, Michael. *Audition*. New York: Bantam Books, 1980.

Sturvetant, Paul B. "Everyman Has His Daydreams: *Pippin*, A Shockingly Medieval Musical." *The Public Medievalist*, July 14, 2014.

Shenton, Mark. "Stephen Schwartz: "I Had No Idea How Cut-Throat Musical Theatre Was." *The Stage*, October 27, 2016.

Thorpe, Lewis, trans. *Einhard and Notkker the Stammerer: Two Lives of Charlemagne*. Harmondsworth: Penguin Books, 1969.

Wasson, Sam. *Fosse*. Boston: Mariner Books, 2014.

Wilson, Derek. *Charlemagne: A Biography*. New York: Vintage Books, 2007.

Winkler, Kevin. *Big Deal: Bob Fosse and Dance in the American Musical*. New York: Oxford University Press, 2018.

INDEX